LEISURE IN THE INDUSTRIAL REVOLUTION

Leisure in the Industrial Revolution

c. 1780-*c.* 1880

Hugh Cunningham

CROOM HELM LONDON

© 1980 Hugh Cunningham
Croom Helm Ltd, 2-10 St John's Road, London SW11

British Library Cataloguing in Publication Data

Cunningham, Hugh
    Leisure in the Industrial Revolution, *c*. 1780-*c*. 1880
    1. Leisure – Great Britain – history
    I. Title
    301.5'7'0941   GV75

    ISBN 0-85664-398-X
    ISBN 0-7099-0425-8 Pbk

Printed in Great Britain by
Biddles Ltd, Guildford, Surrey

CONTENTS

ACKNOWLEDGEMENTS

I first developed some of the ideas presented in this book in papers given at the University of Kent at Canterbury, the Institute of Historical Research in London, the University of Colorado at Denver, and the 1979 Conference of the Pacific Coast Branch of the British Studies Conference, and of the Mid-West Victorian Studies Association. My thanks to all those who commented so helpfully on those occasions. Over the years I have received much stimulus from students at the University of Kent who have taken the course, Leisure in the Industrial Revolution. Many others have assisted in various ways, in particular Louis James without whom I would not have developed the theme of Chapter 1, and my wife, Diane, who has helped me to clarify both argument and expression. Neither is in any way responsible for the outcome.

INTRODUCTION

Ten years ago it would have been almost impossible to have written a book of this kind. With a few honourable exceptions, the history of leisure had been ignored by historians. Some of the secondary works that did exist, most of them by amateur historians, were of a very high quality, but on such subjects as music-hall or the seaside there was a mass of repetitious and unverifiable writing, and on other subjects there was nothing. On some there is still nothing. But in the last decade the output of writing on the history of leisure has been enormous, and my first and modest intention was to attempt a balanced survey of it. But the more I studied the more unhappy I became about many of the ideas which have informed our understanding of the history of leisure since the later eighteenth century. As a result the book has taken on an argumentative and assertive tone — and I hope it has also become more interesting. It may help the reader to be aware at this stage of the kind of conclusions I have reached, and of the extent to which they differ from much current thinking on the history of leisure.

The writings of other historians had led me to expect that for popular leisure the first half-century or so of the Industrial Revolution, from about 1780 to 1840, would be a period of gloom during which the combined forces of evangelicalism, industrialism and urbanisation were brought to bear on the 'traditional', 'pre-industrial' recreations of the people; and that the result was a 'vacuum'. '[B]y the 1840s', writes R.J. Morris, 'only chapel and public house filled the gloomy gap between bearbaiting and the maypole on one hand and association football and the music hall on the other.'[1] In fact I have come to see this half-century as one of vigorous growth of popular leisure and of a commercialisation of it comparable to the commercialisation of leisure for the middle class in the eighteenth century which Professor Plumb has identified.[2] This conclusion, I have become aware, has made me a candidate for the unwelcome embrace of the optimist school of historians; I see it myself as a confirmation of the argument of E.P. Thompson that the people had some capacity to make their own culture.

This first conclusion made me suspicious of the structure of much thinking and writing about the impact of the Industrial Revolution on the culture of the people. Many historians of the nineteenth century write on the implicit assumption that society before the Industrial

Revolution may be satisfactorily described in some such terms as 'traditional', 'pre-industrial' or 'the old society', and that with the Industrial Revolution we move into a period of rapid 'modernisation'; there are, it is admitted, some 'pre-industrial survivals' but all of these are doomed to oblivion. This essentially whiggish habit of thinking is thoroughly disabling, and the outcome is a failure to examine difficult questions about the context of popular culture. Let me give an example. In his recent *Leisure and Society 1830-1950* James Walvin describes the ratting which was so popular in mid-nineteenth-century London, and concludes: 'Yet these were the years of the railways and the Great Exhibition — a reminder of the strong survival of pre-industrial recreations in a rapidly modernising society.' Earlier in the same paragraph Walvin describes the ratting as a 'revival', a word with very different implications than 'survival', and one which invites one to ask why ratting should have enjoyed such popularity at that particular time in the world's greatest centre of population; once that question is asked it is no longer possible to dismiss ratting as yet another, if rather horrific, 'pre-industrial survival'.[3] The ratting example may help to make a further point. The 'pre-industrial' is often equated with the 'rural'. 'Urbanisation' therefore becomes a major 'agent of change'. Yet here we have 'pre-industrial' ratting in a manifestly urban environment. The kind of thinking which envisages a shift from 'rural pre-industrial' to 'urban industrial and modern' society once again, in its abstractness, leads to an evasion of difficult questions; questions which I have attempted, at least, to pose in this book. Put simply I have been less impressed than many other historians by the explanatory power of the distinction between town and country for an understanding of the history of leisure.

Continuities, indeed, are as much the theme of this book as changes; continuities between town and country and continuities over time. And continuities not simply as survivals, but as something more positive. Much of the history of leisure has been written on the assumption that what is new starts from high up the social scale and is diffused downwards. Such was the thinking of Joseph Strutt in his *The Sports and Pastimes of the People of England* published in 1801, and it permeates R.D. Altick's *The Shows of London* published in 1978. On the contrary what has struck me has been the flow in both directions, and in particular the degree to which essentially popular forms of entertainment in the first half of the nineteenth century influenced high culture. And this popular entertainment, although it was in many respects innovative, derived much of its strength from the experience of the past, a process which we can see most clearly in the history of drama.

Another hypothesis which I derived from other historians, one which has been much employed in recent enquiries into the history of leisure, is that the key divisions in Victorian society were those within rather than those between classes, in essence those between the respectable and the rough. Middle-class reformers, it is argued, linked up with the respectable working-class elite to oppose the culture of the aristocracy and the poor who were, in Geoffrey Best's words, 'never closer together than at the prizefight, the cockpit, the rat-catching, the racetrack, and the demi-monde saloon and casino.' Leisure, for Best, helped to keep social relations 'relatively speaking, sweet'. For Brian Harrison this uniting of the respectable of different classes in leisure had even more important consequences: 'The social conscience of temperance reformers and others', he writes, 'helped to prevent the polarization of English society which Marx in the 1840s forecast.'[4] My own research has led me to different conclusions. Certainly throughout our period strong hopes were expressed that leisure might have this class-conciliatory function; hopes which were expressed first in the unrespectable world of the Fancy, and then, from about 1840, in respectable middle-class reforming circles; hopes which sometimes found institutional form. But there are, as we shall see, a number of reasons to suppose that these hopes were ill-founded and that the experience of leisure, like that of work, served to reinforce class distinctions.

Harrison's argument does alert us to the important fact that the history of leisure has a political dimension. The growth of interest in the history of leisure over the last decade has been closely connected with the emergence of social history as a self-conscious discipline. The history of leisure has seemed to be self-evidently social history. In the past its study was left almost exclusively to amateur historians as a colourful, even amusing, branch of history on which no serious historian would waste much time. The espousal of the subject in recent years by academic historians has only partially reversed that status, and for the very reason that the history of leisure has seemed to be part of the self-contained social history which has flourished in the last decade, but which has had remarkably little impact on the writing of political or economic history. As a subspecies of social history, the history of leisure remains little more than a previously neglected by-way of history which, however fascinating, does little more than footnote our understanding of the nineteenth century. In fact the history of leisure is as much political as social. A glance at my references will show that many of my sources are political: legislation, and parliamentary inquiries and debates. Decisions and arguments about leisure were decisions and arguments about power and about control, that is to say they were political. Leisure too, it is necessary to emphasise, is economic history: a history of production (the leisure industries) and of consumption (both of time and of goods).

By this stage critical readers will be crying out for a definition of leisure. And typically at this point the historian will turn to the sociologist for help. The attempt to define leisure does indeed absorb the attention of the sociologists of leisure, but alas not very fruitfully, at least from the point of view of the historian. The first question sociologists seem to ask is: what time can be considered as leisure time? Can all time not at work be considered as leisure, that is including sleep, household or family obligations, political activity, and, in a modern context, productive do-it-yourself activity? Or should one exclude some or all of these? Associated with this is a second question: is leisure necessarily something pleasurable? Or should it include non-work activities which are not enjoyed?[5] None of this is very helpful, and rather than engage in the debate, it is more interesting to ask why it should take place. The answer is that leisure is one of those peculiarly difficult words which over time has accumulated manifold and changing meanings; and however much we would wish, we cannot ignore the history of the word. For a historian at any rate it cannot be pinned down to a neat one-sentence definition, for it is precisely the change in its use that is significant.

At the beginning of our period most of the population were not thought to possess such a thing as leisure. They had, if they were lucky, 'sports and pastimes' which were organised, communal and hence more or less obligatory occasions. Leisure meant free non-obligated time, and for the mass of the people such time was illegitimate; it suggested idleness. As Charles Hall succinctly put it in 1805, 'leisure in a poor man is thought quite a different thing from what it is to a rich man, and goes by a different name. In the poor it is called idleness, the cause of all mischief.' Thus immediately, and most significantly, leisure is related to social structure. Leisure properly exists only for 'the leisured' who by 1840 if not earlier are being described as 'the leisured or leisure classes'.[6]

The phrase 'sports and pastimes' gradually acquired an antiquarian and Merrie England tone. Autobiographers recalled with varying degrees of nostalgia the 'sports', 'pastimes' or 'diversions' of their youth as though these were very definitely things in the past of the nation as well as of the writer. But it was not 'leisure' which replaced them, but most commonly either 'recreations' or 'amusements'. The former had a more positive connotation than the latter; 'recreation' should re-create you, normally for work, whereas 'amusements' were a more or less grudgingly acknowledged necessity. Middle-class observers wrote articles about 'Popular Amusements', while middle-class reformers tried to propagate 'rational recreations'. Towards the end of our period the word 'leisure' was beginning to be used to describe the non-work time or activities of the mass of the people, and such leisure came to be accepted as legitimate, even if it was still a 'problem' in the sense that the time was, from the point of view of authority or reformer, frequently mis-spent.

'Sports and pastimes', 'recreations', 'amusements', 'the problem of leisure' are linked together by one thread: the language is that of observer or reformer, not of participant. I suspect that outside these circles there has never been one word or phrase in common circulation to describe that time or those activities which we think of as 'leisure'. People talk about concrete, discrete activities — going to the pub, or the races, or the choir-practice, watching television, or playing football — not about 'leisure'. 'Leisure' is an abstraction from common experience, an abstraction which only those who stand aside from that experience, at least momentarily, can perceive. It is, necessarily, a highly ambiguous word. In using it in the title and body of this book my aim is to shed some light on that ambiguity and on the layers of meaning which have accrued round it.

Finally a word about the geographical and chronological scope of the book. It is about England, though where it seems helpful I have made references to the experience of leisure in other countries, in particular Wales, Scotland, France and the USA. And it is about England in the first century of industrialisation, roughly from 1780 to 1880. Two points need to be made about these dates. First, unlike some other historians, I cannot see any particular year or event as peculiarly vital in the history of leisure; hence I am reluctant to tie myself down to any very specific starting or ending dates. But, secondly, the century I have chosen to study does have a coherence. It starts with the beginning of the Industrial Revolution. Despite the continuity with, and impact of, the past — which it is one of my objects to stress — the Industrial Revolution affected leisure as much as it affected work, initiating changes as a consequence of which the meaning and experience of leisure were transformed. In 1780 no one could have predicted the shape of leisure a century ahead. In 1880, by contrast, the lines of development are clear. Since then the time and money available for leisure have increased, technology has changed the form of leisure activities, and there has been a growth of the leisure industries and of governmental provision of facilities. But there is nothing in the leisure of today which was not visible in 1880. Thus for England the century 1780 to 1880 stands out as crucial in setting terms to the meaning and experience of leisure in advanced capitalist society.

Notes

1. R.W. Malcolmson, *Popular Recreations in English Society, 1700-1850* (London, 1973), p. 170, for the idea of a 'vacuum'; R.J. Morris, *Class and Class Consciousness in The Industrial Revolution 1780-1850* (London, 1979), p. 53.

2. J.H. Plumb, *The Commercialisation of Leisure in Eighteenth-century England* (Reading, 1973).

3. J. Walvin, *Leisure and Society 1830-1950* (London, 1978), p. 36.

4. G. Best, *Mid-Victorian Britain 1851-1875* (London, 1971), p. 201; B. Harrison, *Drink and the Victorians* (London, 1971), p. 25. For criticism of the theory see P. Bailey, *Leisure and Class in Victorian England* (London, 1978), pp. 175-9, and ' "Will The Real Bill Banks Please Stand Up?" Towards A Role Analysis Of Mid-Victorian Working-Class Respectability', *Journal of Social History*, vol. 12 (1979), pp. 336-53.

5. S.R. Parker, *The Sociology of Leisure* (London, 1976), pp. 17-20.

6. Hall quoted in S. Pollard, 'Factory Discipline in the Industrial Revolution', *Economic History Review*, 2nd ser., vol. XVI (1963-4), p. 269 n.2; *Oxford English Dictionary*.

1 THE GROWTH OF LEISURE IN THE EARLY INDUSTRIAL REVOLUTION, c. 1780-c. 1840

Decline and decay are the themes which have impressed most historians who have examined the history of leisure in the early Industrial Revolution. Growth for 'the leisured' is admitted, but few doubt that there was a radical curtailment of leisure opportunities and leisure time for the mass of the people. That there is much truth in this traditional viewpoint I do not wish to deny: in the latter part of this chapter and in the following two I shall present some of the evidence in support of it. But first I wish to emphasise the opposite case, to argue that there was an increase in leisure opportunities not only for the leisured class but also for many of their social inferiors; and that it was this dual growth which provided the context and set the tone for the often bitter conflict about leisure which marks the period. The outcome of that conflict, I shall argue, was much less of an outright victory for those who attacked popular leisure than friends, enemies and historians of that campaign have made out.

Growth and conflict, as themes in the history of leisure, are not unique to the era of the Industrial Revolution. On the contrary the experience of leisure in the centuries before the Industrial Revolution was by no means unchanging. Conflict was perhaps the most marked characteristic. Thus if such a phenomenon as a 'traditional' world of leisure ever existed, which may be doubted, it was destroyed in the sixteenth century by the celebrated combination of capitalism and Puritanism. Popular drama, for example, disappeared in Elizabeth's reign, in Norwich and Worcester in the 1560s, in York, Wakefield, Chester and Chelmsford in the 1570s, in Coventry in about 1590. This was no mere falling away of some picturesque but outworn custom of the past. Rather, as Charles Pythian-Adams describes the process in Coventry, 'not only were specific customs and institutions brusquely changed or abolished, but a whole vigorous and variegated popular culture, the matrix of everyday life, was eroded and began to perish'. Similarly in rural areas the alehouse's role in the provision of recreation for the poor became increasingly central in the later sixteenth and early seventeenth centuries owing to the erosion of alternative facilities, and in particular of the communal festivities and sports which had flourished in many late-medieval parishes.[1]

The seventeenth century witnessed an on-going and fluctuating argument between the Puritans, anxious to do away with Whitales, maypoles, Plough Mondays and other expressions of pre-capitalist communal life, and those traditionalists, centred on the Court, who saw in such activities a buttress of the social order.[2] Much of the argument turned on the use of the Sabbath, and on no issue was the intertwining of the religious and economic arguments so apparent. As Christopher Hill has written, 'the fight for Sabbatarianism and against rural sports was an attempt to extend the concern for labour discipline from the South and East of England into the dark corners of the North and West'. The outcome after the Restoration was a victory for the Sabbatarians, and the English Sunday appeared in its characteristic garb.[3]

The opposite side of this coin was growth, exemplified in the contemporaneous emergence of a leisure class. The flocking of the gentry to London in the sixteenth and early seventeenth centuries, and the emergence of a clearly defined London season with its attendant entertainment facilities, was a clear indication of a broadening of the demand for leisure.[4] The same was true of the steady growth of the spas from the mid-sixteenth century, and the speeding up of that growth in the second half of the seventeenth century. In 1697 Misson wrote of Bath, 'Mille gens vont passer là quelques semaines, sans se soucier ni des Bains, ni des eaux à boire, mais seulement pour se divertir avec la bonne compagnie. On a Musique, Jeu, Promenade, Bals, & petite Foire perpétuelle.' Bath, it is clear, was a well-established leisure centre before the days of Beau Nash.[5]

In the later seventeenth century, aspects both of the London season and of the spas began to be imitated in provincial towns. Assembly rooms were built, bowling greens and walks laid out, and the town gentry (people with independent incomes but without land) began to impose their mark on provincial culture. Theatrical and musical life began to flourish. New and imposing theatres, blessed by royal patents, sprang up in the provinces in the decade 1755-65, but long before that the provincial theatre, indeed whole areas of provincial towns, were being appropriated for the exclusive use and display of the wealthy. The thrust for leisure-class exclusivity was undisguised. As the promoter of a new mid-eighteenth-century theatre in Bath put it, 'nothing can be more disagreeable, than for Persons of the first Quality, and those of the lowest Rank, to be seated in the same Bench together . . .' A new provincial urban culture for the wealthy began to flourish, and not only in major centres like Preston or Norwich, but even in a small town like

Loughborough which in the reign of George III could support an elaborate round of balls, assemblies, concerts, lectures, card parties and florists' feasts with a population of only 3,000. Based on the new wealth created by capitalism, a new and more numerous leisure class was emerging, and with it new institutions and new social arrangements.[6]

This leisure class was rural as well as urban. From the late seventeenth century, and particularly in the eighteenth century, the gentry created rural sports specifically for themselves. Although some of these sports, like horse-racing, allowed a degree of popular participation this was incidental and often resisted; the thrust of development was towards class-specific sports. Consider three of these sports: shooting, hunting and racing. Shooting began to acquire its modern class associations in the seventeenth century. In 1671 an Act had disqualified all except the landed classes from game hunting, and under another Act in 1692 it was further stipulated that 'inferior Tradesmen, Apprentices, and other dissolute Persons neglecting their Trades and Employments' should not 'presume to hunt, hawk, fish or fowl'. As Chester Kirby has argued, the country gentlemen thus broke the royal monopoly and at the same time secured themselves against competition from below. Technical transformations, in particular the introduction of shooting on the wing in the late seventeenth century, universally adopted by 1750, reinforced the existing trend to tighten up the game laws. The introduction of the battue in the early nineteenth century made game preservation even more important. The era of big bags and competitive shooting had arrived. Performances like those of John Mytton and a friend, who once killed a head of game every three minutes for five hours, began to be recorded and admired. Such exploits were possible only with strict game preservation, and the confinement of the sport to those who were socially qualified. In 1796 an attempt to remove the qualifications failed, the Prime Minister, William Pitt, defending exclusive amusements for 'the higher orders of the state'. He was prepared to admit, however, that 'the second class, to whom a participation of this right might properly be given, were the occupiers of land, but in a more limited degree, and only on their own grounds; lest by too liberal an indulgence in this amusement, they might be diverted from more serious and useful occupations.' There could be no clearer indication of the class-specific nature of this part of the gentry's leisure life. As F.M.L. Thompson concluded 'shooting emphasised the solidarity of aristocracy and gentry, sitting together as magistrates trying poaching offences, and standing together at the butts. It also stirred the resentment of farmers and labourers and was a notable hindrance to rural harmony.'[7]

Fox-hunting, too, was becoming a crucial part of the life of the rural leisure class by the end of the eighteenth century. In the seventeenth century and for much of the eighteenth century English country gentlemen probably regarded hunting the hare as the supreme test of skill. They began to hunt the formerly despised fox at the same time as aristocrats deserted the deer for the fox. Hugo Meynell as Master of the Quorn from 1753 to 1800 bred hounds which could provide fast runs, and by the 1780s fox-hunting was becoming fashionable and spreading rapidly. Commentators insisted on its social respectability. Peter Beckford, in the first treatise on the sport in 1781, declared: 'Fox-hunting is now become the amusement of gentlemen: nor need any gentleman be ashamed of it.' The *British Sportsman* in 1792 thought fox-hunting 'the only chace in England worthy of the taste or attention of a high bred sportsman'. By the 1790s the Prince of Wales was patronising the sport.[8]

Fox-hunting has frequently been defended precisely because it is not class specific, and by the 1820s the notion that it linked the classes together had become a commonplace. The grain of truth within it was that tenant farmers and professional men from the towns could and did participate in a way they could not in shooting. Occasionally there was a well-publicised example of someone from lower down the social scale enjoying the sport – the best example was the chimney sweep who hunted with the Duke of Beaufort in the 1830s. But this was exceptional. Fox-hunting was dominated by the aristocracy and country gentlemen. Farmers and to a lesser extent professional men hunted, but they knew that their place in the sport was a subordinate one, just as it was in economic and social terms. The best hunting was dependent on the aggregation of land; as Raymond Carr has rightly insisted, it is a sport which cannot be carried on in peasant communities.[9] Its development owed much to the enclosure movement, and socially, not surprisingly, it reflected the post-enclosure rural balance of power. There was only one way the poorer sections of the community could hope to participate, and that was as followers on foot. They were rarely welcome. Squire Osbaldeston, Master of the Quorn in the 1820s, had constant difficulties with

the stocking-makers and weavers, who used to assemble in crowds at the covert-side. It seemed impossible to keep them together in the right place in order to let the fox go away. At first we could not manage them at all; we tried persuasion and kind words, without any success. Then we tried force; but being totally unsupported by any of the Meltonians that method also failed. At last we had recourse to bribery; we used to give every village two sovereigns a year for drink, and this plan had a far better effect, though on occasions the people were still unruly.

On Sundays the stocking-makers organised their own form of hunting, invading the precious coverts with their terriers and curs.[10] It was of course illegal, a desecration of the Sabbath as well as an invasion of property rights. Hunting depended on the willingness of farmers to allow landlords but not labourers to do what they would with their land. It was necessarily a socially exclusive sport.

By 1833 the *Quarterly Review* was condemning shooting and fox-hunting which 'is every day becoming more and more a piece of exclusive luxury, instead of furnishing the lord, the squire, and the yeoman, with a common recreation, and promoting mutual goodwill among all the inhabitants of the rural districts'. In this it was, according to the *Quarterly Review*, to be distinguished from racing for 'the owner of race-horses cannot gratify his passion for the turf without affording delight to thousands upon thousands of the less fortunate of his countrymen'.[11] Perhaps so, but there had been attempts to prevent the less fortunate from attending. The Act of 1740 'to restrain and prevent the excessive Increase of Horse Races . . .' was passed, amongst other reasons, because 'the great Number of Horse Races for small Plates, Prizes, or Sums of Money, have contributed very much to the Encouragement of Idleness, to the Impoverishment of many of the meaner Sort of the Subjects of this Kingdom'. The Act hoped to achieve its end by insisting that every race should have prize money of at least £50; it was a clear attempt to make racing more exclusive. The Act also confined matches (as opposed to races) to two locations, Newmarket and Black Hambleton in Yorkshire, exclusive venues for the rich.[12] Whatever the intention of the Act, developments in racing in the second half of the century vastly increased the spectator appeal of the sport. The typical four-mile heat was replaced by the short dash for the new young thoroughbreds. The English classics, all for three-year-olds, became established: the St Leger in 1776, the Oaks in 1779, the Derby in 1780, the 2,000 Guineas in 1809, the 1,000 Guineas in 1814. Most racing at this time, however, was an annual event for a local community; in 1823 87 out of 95 race-courses had only one meeting a year. Although these annual events were undoubtedly the occasion for a local holiday, the gentry continued to regard the races almost as their property. The spectators were tolerated provided they kept in their place. If not, there might be a pitched battle — as there was between the irascible Osbaldeston's cavalry and the infantry of Northampton shoemakers. In general the gentry and their womenfolk obtained seclusion in the stands, which were first built in the 1770s.[13]

Both in rural and in urban society, therefore, there had developed a leisure class with pursuits which were more and more exclusive to themselves. It is only when bearing this in mind that one can understand the attack on popular leisure at the end of the eighteenth century. Popular forms of leisure had been on the defensive since early modern times. The novelty of the situation on the eve of the Industrial Revolution lay less in the increasing intensity of the attack than in the fact that the defenders had lost some of their more powerful allies. 'The abdication on the part of the governors', which Professor Perkin has identified in a general sense and ascribed to the fact 'that the English landowners, or many of them, had sold their souls to economic development long before the Industrial Revolution', is nowhere more apparent than in leisure. The withdrawal of patronage coincided with and was in part caused by the growth of sport and leisure activities specific to the new leisure class.[14]

The effects of emerging capitalism on leisure were not limited to the development of a new leisure class. 'In capitalist society . . .', wrote Marx, 'leisure time for a privileged class is produced by converting the whole lifetime of the masses into labour time.'[15] Such at least was the aim, though it was only very partially achieved. And once again it was not the Industrial Revolution of the later eighteenth century that marks a break in attitudes to labour; employers of that era merely repeated, parrot-fashion, ideas which had been forged in the seventeenth century. Both in mercantilist theory and in pre-industrial practice, labour was the most important factor in production. The wealth of a nation, it was thought, lay in a large and properly employed labouring population — but not necessarily in a prosperous one. This was partly because it was believed that a favourable balance of trade could be achieved only in a low wage economy, for otherwise exports would not be competitive. More importantly, however, observation taught the great body of commentators that workers had a high leisure preference; high wages, it was believed, led to absenteeism rather than to accumulation, and hence to a decline in production.[16] It is true that there were voices raised against this seemingly cruel belief that a country's wealth could be achieved only through the poverty of the mass of its citizens; from the late seventeenth century some writers were advocating high wages because of the stimulating effect this would have on consumption and thereby on the economy generally.[17] But in mercantilist eyes the chief responsibility for inducing economic activity through consumption lay with the rich, who were encouraged by economists to spend freely. It is true, too, that quite apart from the question of wages and consumption, there was a more sympathetic attitude to the poor developing around the middle of the eighteenth century together with the beliefs that men might react positively to incentives and, as Adam Smith claimed, that 'no society can surely be flourishing or happy, of which the far greater part of the members are poor and miserable'.[18] Increasingly insistent as these voices are, however, they seem to be outweighed by those who believed the 'doctrine of the utility of poverty', that necessity was the only spur to labour. Throughout the economy, in agriculture and in industry, in country and in town, observers bewailed the propensity to mis-spent idleness, which caused damage to the national economy and led to the demoralisation and eventual poverty of the workers themselves. 'Where the price of labour is highest and provisions are the cheapest', wrote Joseph Townsend in 1786, 'there the poor rates have been the most exorbitant.'[19]

The most obvious solution to the problem of leisure preference lay in raising prices or lowering wages. But so endemic was the disease that authority attacked the symptoms as much as the cause — that is to say, it sought to control the actual leisure pursuits of the poor, in particular the alehouse. The records of central government and of quarter sessions in the eighteenth century abound with attempts to extend the licensing laws, to put down fairs and wakes, and to prevent horse-racing, prize-fighting and other sports. Typical is the preamble to the Act of 1752 for licensing places of public entertainment:

And whereas the Multitude of Places of Entertainment for the lower Sort of People is another great Cause of Thefts and Robberies, as they are thereby tempted to spend their small Substance in riotous Pleasures, and in consequence are put on unlawful Methods of supplying their Wants, and renewing their Pleasures: In order therefore to prevent the said Temptation to Thefts and Robberies, and to correct as far as may be the Habit of Idleness, which is become too general over the whole Kingdom, and is productive of much Mischief and Inconvenience . . .[20]

These government attempts at control of leisure were supported from the late seventeenth century by voluntary societies dedicated to bringing prosecutions for offences against the moral laws. By the begin-

ning of the eighteenth century there were at least 20 such societies in
London and a minimum of 42 in the provinces. Their overall impact on
behaviour may have been slight, but they initiated a trend of concerted
voluntary moral reform, and helped to create a climate of opinion
wherein leisure in the poor was perceived to lead to economic ruin and
moral dissipation.[21] Moral reformers joined hands with economists and
government to condemn and try to prevent the propensity to idleness.
The resulting cluster of ruling-class clichés about the leisure habits of
the poor was inherited by industrialists and others in the later eighteenth century and formed a reservoir of prejudice which could be
drawn upon at will.

That prejudice was not without a basis in fact. The poor *did* have a
propensity towards idleness, and a strong preference for leisure over
work. And in the early decades of the Industrial Revolution the opportunity to indulge that preference was growing. There is no 'vacuum' in
the history of popular recreations. In the first place many 'traditional'
sports and customs survived much longer than one might suppose,
sometimes after their demise had been celebrated. Secondly, recreations
which were threatened in one form could evolve; in particular a number
of sports, previously dependent on the patronage of the rich, learned to
survive and even grow when that patronage was withdrawn. And
thirdly, and most important, new forms of recreation were being created and invented. The outcome was an efflorescence of popular leisure
in the later eighteenth and early nineteenth centuries, an understanding
of which begins to make intelligible the virulence of the campaign that
was mounted against it.

There is no doubt that many sports and customs were under attack,
but even the most public and brutalising of them survived prolonged
attempts to suppress them. Indeed the attempts at suppression must
sometimes have acted as a stimulus to greater indulgence. Such seems to
have been the case with the Stamford bull-running which continued
until 1840 despite or because of the efforts of the RSPCA, the metropolitan police, the dragoons and local constables.[22] In Staffordshire it
was only with the establishment of the County Police Force in 1843
that animal sports were dealt with effectively. In that same year, 1843,
the Manchester authorities formally prohibited dog and cock fighting,
bull and badger baiting, a sign surely that they still continued.[23] The
Morning Chronicle reporter in 1851 was told how

The working men of Birmingham and the manufacturing districts of
Staffordshire were notorious during the first twenty-five years of the

present century — and, indeed, to a much later period — for the brutality of their sports. On Saturday afternoons in the open air, during the whole of Sunday in public-house tap-rooms, and again on the Monday at their usual haunts in the outskirts of the town, dog-fights, cock-fights, bull-baitings, badger-baitings, and pugilistic encounters were the favourite amusements of the operative classes, and of some portion of their employers. Much of the ancient love for these and other demoralising exhibitions still exists among the uneducated portion of the workmen and small manufacturers.

The reporter was told that 'both bull-baits and cock-fights . . . are still indulged in on the sly, by workmen of the old school'.[24]

London, too, was a centre of animal sports which showed a remarkable ability to survive. In 1801 Joseph Strutt noted that the practice of dogs chasing ducks, frequent near London from about 1760-70, had of late 'gone out of fashion'. But, he warned, 'I cannot help thinking, that the deficiency at present, of places proper for the purpose, has done more towards the abolishment of this sport than any amendment in the nature and inclinations of the populace'. Strutt was right to be cautious. Twenty years later Mr Golden of the Regent's Canal Company was complaining about the

low characters who resort to the canal for the purpose of hunting Ducks, Cats etc. with Dogs, sometimes in gangs of three to five hundred, particularly on Sunday mornings, that the lockkeepers and other Officers employed thereon, are completely intimidated, frequently being obliged to shut themselves up in their Houses, to escape their threatened violence.

Far from declining, it was claimed in 1828, duck-hunting and dog-fighting seemed to be more common than they used to be.[25]

More serious than duck-hunting was the hunting of bullocks in the metropolis. The Rector of Bethnal Green, Reverend Joshua King, described in 1816 how

every Sunday morning, during the time of Divine Service, several hundred persons assemble in a field adjoining the church-yard, where they fight dogs, hunt ducks, gamble, enter into subscriptions to fee drovers for a bullock; I have seen them drive the animal through the most populous parts of the parish, force sticks pointed with iron, up the body, put peas into the ears, and infuriate the beast.

This bullock-running happened on Sunday, Monday and sometimes Tuesday, with 1,000 or 2,000 men and boys leaving their looms to join in the pursuit. In 1822 it was claimed that the swearing-in of some 200 special constables for three or four market days in succession had led to the near suppression of the sport. But this was too optimistic. In 1826 the Home Office ordered 20 dismounted Horse Patrol and 30 Foot Patrol to assemble 'to prevent a recurrence of the outrages which have been committed by Bullock Hunting'. This at last seems to have brought an end to the practice but only after the same display of force as was required to put down the Stamford bull run.[26]

In 1849, giving evidence before the Select Committee on Public Libraries, the popular lecturer George Dawson claimed that in the Birmingham area brutal sports 'have died out; they have not been put down; all these things have died out; there has been a change in the source and current of the thoughts of the people'. There were many who thought likewise. Francis Place, for example, thought that the eradication of bullock-running in London was a pointer to the improvement of the people; yet at the time he wrote this, bullock-running still continued. The evidence suggests rather that most brutal sports resisted suppression, that many had powers of revival, and that in so far as they ceased to exist it was because they had been 'put down'.[27] In Birmingham itself about 1830 the police and magistrates had tried to suppress cock-fighting by seizing 40 spectators and tying them together with ropes, two by two. The men were then 'marched in procession through the principal streets of the town as an example, and then brought before the magistrates'.[28] This kind of public humiliation suggests a clash of cultures in which the victory of one culture over another was achieved more by force than by subtle means of acculturation. And that a process of acculturation had not been achieved is indicated by the fact that although the more public animal sports had certainly disappeared by mid-century, privately in the back and upper rooms of pubs dog-fighting and ratting enjoyed a considerable vogue. The forms of brutality may have changed but not the essence.

The animal sports were the most notorious of the pastimes which were under attack. Their symbolic role for authority was probably greater than their actual one in the lives of the people. In particular localities they might be important, but none of them had a national organisation. Their survival, and the manner of it, however, suggests a popular attachment to such activities which urban life in itself did little to quash.

A second group of recreations was able to do more than simply resist suppression. In the face of attack, and in particular the withdrawal of patronage from above, they adapted and often grew. Fairs, for example, nationwide in incidence, public, visible and popular, were deplored by authority and reformers, and their demise was frequently predicted. In London in particular there was a concentrated attack on them in the 1820s, but some important fairs survived at this point to enjoy a new lease of life. Like bull-baiting, those fairs which did disappear had to be put down, they did not simply fade away. Commentators were so convinced that the fairs were in decline that they could not see what lay before their eyes. Francis Place, a frequent and slightly nostalgic visitor to Greenwich Fair in the later 1830s, saw decline all around him; yet this was precisely the time when the railway was allowing Greenwich Fair to revive. By 1849 Place had come to realise his mistake, adding to his manuscript: '1849 N.B. Since the construction of the Greenwich Railway and the use of Steam-Boats on the Thames the number of Holyday Visitors have greatly exceeded those of former times'. Steamboats had been in use since 1815, the railway since 1836. Other fairs also capitalised on the advantages offered by the railway, proving themselves to be an adaptable growth industry, not as commentators liked to believe, 'relics of a barbarous age'.[29]

Many sports, too, which were unquestionably anathema to reformers, adapted under the attack on popular leisure. It is true that horse-racing owed this very largely to the patronage of the rich, not that that patronage did anything to secure the sport from the accusation and the practice of corruption. But horse-racing was developing not only under the sheltered wing of patronage, but also, around London in particular, quite without its benefits. And it survived and grew. In the early nineteenth century there were races in Kentish Town, Bayswater and Sadler's Wells; as the century continued, meetings were held at Harrow, Kingsbury, West Drayton, Croydon, Lillie Bridge, Enfield, Bromley and Streatham. It was not until after the first enclosed courses had been opened that these meetings were controlled by Act of Parliament in 1879. Until then the opportunities to see horses race in the metropolis increased rather than decreased.[30]

Prize-fighting started off the century with the same kind of patronage as horse-racing enjoyed; indeed there was a close connection between the two sports in personnel and venue. In the early decades of the Industrial Revolution — from the mid-1780s to the mid-1820s — prize-fighting was at the height of its fame. Pierce Egan described how after the Humphries v. Mendoza fight in 1788

Boxing became fashionable — followed, patronized, and encouraged. Sparring Matches took place at the Theatres and Royal Circus — Schools were established for the promulgation of the art; and the *Science* of SELF-DEFENCE considered as a necessary requisite for all Englishmen. Among its numerous splendid patrons and supporters were to be seen His Royal Highness the Prince of Wales, Dukes of York and Clarence, Duke of Hamilton, Lord Barrymore, Alderman Coombe, etc.

Prize-fighting was quickly commandeered by its supporters to the service of the nation. As Egan inimitably put it, '. . . the manly art of Boxing, has infused that true heroic courage, blended with humanity, into the hearts of Britons, which have made them so renowned, terrific, and triumphant, in all parts of the world'. This emphasis on the patriotic and martial qualities imbued by prize-fighting did the sport no harm in the decades of war up to 1815, but thereafter it began to appear atavistic. The sport was still capable of attracting large crowds — upwards of 30,000 were said to have attended the fight between Tom Spring and John Langan at Worcester Race Course in 1824 — but suspicions that fights were fixed, associations with criminals, and a harsher attitude on the part of the law, led to a withdrawal of patronage.[31]

The speed and extent of that withdrawal, however, must not be exaggerated, nor must its consequences. Most historians of the sport leap from the Regency straight to the Sayers v. Heenan fight of 1860, and treat all that lies between as murkily corrupt, lightened only by the religious conversion of Bendigo. In fact the Sayers v. Heenan fight is only intelligible if there is a greater stress on continuity. Patronage continued. Present at the 1830 fight between Simon Byrne and Alexander Mackay, in which Mackay was killed, were two such noted patrons as Captain Barclay and Squire Osbaldeston, as was 'Gentleman' John Jackson. In the late 1830s Barclay and Jackson were present at exhibitions of prize-fighting at the National Baths, Westminster Road, along with 2,000 to 3,000 spectators.

There continued to be money in the sport. When Broome fought Hannan in 1841 the stakes were £1,000. And if monied and socially prestigious patronage was not forthcoming then the sport was nourished from below. Joseph Lawson recalled how in Pudsey in the 1820s 'not at feast time only, but on Saturday nights and on Mondays as well . . . men might often be seen fighting till almost exhausted, and sometimes even women might be seen helping to form the rings, and shouting encouraging words to the combatants'. It was on such foundations, together with speculative promotion by publicans – Nottingham was a major centre for this – that prize-fighting continued. And the spectators were loyal and keen. In the Warwickshire coalmines in the 1840s, it was reported, 'when there is such a matter of universal interest as a prize-fight most go to see it, and it is a day's play. Upon the average there may be five or six such occasions in the course of the summer'. Harrassed by the magistrates and the police, condemned by the respectable, prize-fighting remained a popular sport which, like the horseracing in the environs of London, may well prove to have been growing. The decline came after not before the Sayers v. Heenan fight.[32]

Wrestling, another sport which scarcely commended itself to reformers, also enjoyed something of a boom. There were traditionally two main centres for the sport, the north-west and the south-west. It continued here, though as with prize-fighting there was probably a shift from patronage by the gentry to that by publicans. When Cann fought Polkinhorne at Devonport in 1826 there were said to be about 20,000 spectators, and crowds of up to 10,000 are reported in the Lake District in the mid-nineteenth century. What was new about wrestling in the 1820s was the attempt to mount the sport in London. 'Wrestling', reported Pierce Egan in his *Book of Sports*, '. . . has recently become a complete "*Fancy* article" in the Sporting World; and also quite an established species of amusement during the last five years in various parts of the Metropolis'. The chief promoter in London was Thomas Rouse of the Eagle Tavern in the City Road, and here and elsewhere in the second half of the 1820s and beyond, there were frequent and well-supported bouts. Howitt reports 8,000 spectators watching Westmorland wrestling at Chalk Farm in 1837.[33]

Other sports which – at least when they were not patronised by the rich – were regarded with some suspicion by the respectable probably also grew. Cricket and pedestrianism, both patronised by publicans, both popular in appeal, certainly did not decline under the impact of criticism; and while there has been insufficient research to be able to state positively that they grew, their subsequent history makes it almost certain that this was the case. The professional touring cricket teams of the 1840s were possible only because the foundations of the game had been laid, preserved and expanded in previous decades. The 20,000 crowd, largely working men and their families, who watched the Nottingham v. Sussex cricket match at Nottingham in September 1835 were men to whom cricket was a familiar enjoyment. And it was a popular sport. As Howitt noted, 'there was all the appearance of a fair', and the higher classes, especially the ladies, were conspicuous by their absence.[34]

Horse-racing, prize-fighting, wrestling, cricket and pedestrianism were all sports which at different times and to different degrees enjoyed the patronage of the rich. But they were also able to flourish without patronage, promoted perhaps by a publican; as such, in their organisation and ethos, and in the social status of their participants, they were fundamentally popular. And, in varying degrees again, they gave offence to reformers and to the respectable world in general. Despite this, the evidence points to growth not decline.

If these forms of recreation were adapting successfully, others, some of them in effect invented during the early Industrial Revolution, were positively blossoming. This was an era of popular drama and spectacle, a fact long known to (and until recently deplored by) literary historians, who have noted the retreat from the theatre of wealthier patrons, the enlargement of old theatres and the building of new to accommodate the new lower-class audiences, and the emergence of melodrama and spectacle to pander to their taste. Now that literary historians are beginning to explore the positive aspects of this era of popular drama it may be appropriate to try to document its pervasiveness.[35]

The most obvious signs of this era of popular drama are to be found in London where the two patent theatres were enormously enlarged while at the same time trying to meet the challenge from newer rivals. It is estimated that average nightly attendance at Covent Garden and Drury Lane rose from about 1,000 at each in the mid-eighteenth century to about 1,500 in the 1790s. Covent Garden was reconstructed in 1782 to increase its seating capacity to 2,170, and then refurbished in 1792 after which it could seat over 3,000. The new Drury Lane of 1794 could seat 3,919.[36] At the same time the minor theatres were beginning to mount their opposition to the monopoly of regular drama claimed by the patent theatres. It was a long-drawn-out battle, final victory for the minors not coming until 1843, but from the very early nineteenth century they had made successful encroachments on the monopoly.[37] This late eighteenth- and early nineteenth-century increase in the availability of theatre for Londoners was associated with a decline in the social status of the audiences.

Research on this topic is notoriously difficult, but there are four types of evidence which point to a decline. The first, and perhaps least convincing, concerns prices which after rising slowly for a century began to decline, but not until about 1820.[38] Secondly, there are contemporary descriptions of audiences. Actors and proprietors giving evidence before the 1832 Select Committee to Inquire into the Laws

Affecting Dramatic Literature were almost unanimous in claiming that the Surrey and Coburg theatres on the south bank, and the Pavilion in the East End attracted audiences from their neighbourhoods. Possibly, as the proprietor of the Coburg claimed, there was variation according to the day of the week: 'On Monday nights I conceive we have the working classes generally, and in the middle of the week we have the better classes, the play-going public generally.' In these huge theatres — the Coburg held about 3,800 — the working class formed at the very least a substantial proportion of the audience.[39] The behaviour of audiences, and this is the third type of evidence, suggests that this was the case. Disorder in the theatre has a long history, and is by no means a monopoly of the working class, but the disorders of the early nineteenth century have a social and political content which suggest a popular audience. The most famous of course was the Old Price Riot at Covent Garden in 1809 when for 67 nights the audience demanded not only the old and cheaper prices, but also protested against the increase in the number of private boxes at the expense of the gallery. Here was a class warfare in the theatre, a war won by the gallery. One can sense a similar alertness to the politics of theatre in the Haymarket riot of 1805 when journeymen and master tailors protested against what they considered an insult to their profession in the play, *The Tailors.*[40]

The final type of evidence about the social composition of audiences lies in the drama that was performed. Melodrama dominated the English stage from the very early nineteenth century, historians dating its birth with the presentation of Thomas Holcroft's *A Tale of Mystery* at Covent Garden in 1802. Until recently it has been the habit of historians and critics of theatre to bewail the decline of English theatre in the first half of the nineteenth century; the word 'melodramatic' itself has been one of abuse. Now some of the merits of melodrama are beginning to be discovered: its changes of pace and mood, and its emotional intensity enhanced by music and stage settings. The athletic and stylised acting was suited both to the new big theatres and to the display of emotion which was at the heart of melodrama. Its appeal was by no means confined to the working class, but, as one of the closest students of melodrama has argued, it was most popular with it. Melodrama offered the working class

> thrills, escapism, ideal friendship and love, perfect human beings, their very own heroes and heroines, supreme individualism, an inexorable code of justice, ultimate happiness and rewards to the virtuous poor . . . Melodrama was anti-aristocrat, anti-employer, anti-

landlord, anti-landowner, and anti-wealth, often violently so.[41]

All of these developments, which one can perceive with greatest clarity in London, had their echoes in the provinces. In the last quarter of the eighteenth century there was an expansion of provincial theatre and a rise in its status. Not only did an increasing number of provincial theatres acquire a patent in the second half of the eighteenth century, but also, at a national level, an Act in 1788 gave Justices power to license theatrical representations in the provinces of plays which had been presented at the patent theatres. For the first time, as Sybil Rosenfeld has argued, all strollers had 'the chance of being able to exercise their calling legally . . .'[42] But just as provincial theatre seemed to be on the verge of a golden age, we begin to hear the first complaints about the presence of a rougher element in the audiences. No more than Covent Garden or Drury Lane were the theatres of the provinces to be a preserve of the respectable. In Sheffield, whose theatre had Mrs Siddons on its boards in 1789 and 1799 and Kean in 1818, the behaviour of the gallery as described by Joseph Mather must have made the respectable wonder whether they should patronise the performances:

> To ger reit into't gallera, whear we can rant an' rooar,
>   Throw flat-backs, stooans, an' sticks,
>   Red herrins, booans, an' bricks.
> If they dooant play Nanca's fanca, or onna tune we fix,
> We'll do the best at e'er we can to braik sum o' ther necks.[43]

The consequences of such behaviour were predictable: the respectable withdrew, the gallery was an insufficient financial basis for successful theatrical management, and from 1820 there was decline in the prosperity of provincial theatre,[44] but not necessarily in its prevalence. I know of no figures that would enable us to state whether or not the number and seating capacity of theatres in the provinces was rising or declining in the first half of the nineteenth century. But without question if we expand our horizon to take into account the travelling troupes who worked the fairs and races, the availability of theatre for popular audiences was on the increase.

In London the theatre of the fairs enjoyed considerable prestige at least until the mid-eighteenth century. Then it began to lose its middle-class patrons, and by the 1780s St Bartholomew's 'was now purely devoted to the entertainment of the populace and the diversions of children'. The process of decline, however, was halted, and from the late eighteenth century until the 1830s Richardson and other showmen infused new life into St Bartholomew's and other fairs with elaborate spectacles in melodrama and pantomime. Richardson, together with Gyngell and Scowton, travelled what might be called the southern circuit, starting with the London spring fairs. The route can be traced precisely from a sale notice for Richardson's theatre in 1826, and it is worth quoting to indicate the range of places which would have the opportunity to see drama in the great portable theatre:

Greenwich (twice), Brook Green, Stepney, Bow, Wandsworth, Ealing Green, Fairlop, Brentford, Staines, Chertsey, Ham Common, Kingston, Hounslow, Uxbridge, Iver, Reading, Henley, Great Marlow, Wickham, Oxford and the Forest Meeting, Ascot Heath Races, Cotton Hill, near Guildford, Windsor, Bristol, Portsmouth, Portsdown, Mornhill Fair near Winchester, Dover, Stroud near Chatham, Maidstone, Ashford, Dartford, Bromley, Mitcham, Charlton, Deptford, Cambridge, Sturbitch, Bury St Edmunds, Stowmarket in Suffolk, Ipswich, Harwich, Colchester, Tiptree Heath, Chelmsford, Newmarket, Prittlewell, Brentwood, Romford, Hoddesdon, Wandes Mill, Edmonton, Enfield, Waltham Abbey, North Hall, Harley Bush, Stebbing, Reckington Common, Lynn, Wisbech, Sandwich, Camberwell, Bartholomew, Peterborough, St Albans.

In the winter Richardson retired to Horsemonger Lane. He was the leading showman of the south, illiterate, shrewd, deliberately old-fashioned, standing, Thomas Frost recalled, 'on the steps of his portable theatre, clad in a loose drab coat and a long scarlet vest which looked as if it had been made in the reign of George II'. His investments paid dividends, and on his death in 1836 it was rumoured that he left between £20,000 and £40,000.[45]

If Richardson dominated the world of travelling theatre in the south, he had his rivals elsewhere. Little Jemmy Scott's Coronation Pavilion, seen by W.F. Wallett at Gainsborough Mart Fair, 'was the most magnificent show that travelled at that time, far surpassing Richardson in his glory'. 'Hurd's theatre was as famous in Gloucestershire', we learn from W.E. Adams, 'as Prince Miller's in Scotland or Billy Purvis's in Northumberland'. And Billy Purvis himself, specialising in pantomime, but producing also marionettes, *fantoccini* and melodrama, and engaging pugilists to give exhibitions, was well known throughout the north-east and southern Scotland from 1810 until mid-century.[46]

The initiative and versatility of these travelling showmen is perhaps best seen in the story of 'Old Wild's'. James Wild, born in 1771 and apprenticed to a ropemaker, became leader of Cleckheaton Old Band. When the Kite and Morris Circus visited he turned professional and joined the band. Marrying Mrs Kite, he inherited the circus on her death. Initially circus performers and in hard times mountebanks, the Wilds started theatrical performances in the mid-1820s, and travelled the feasts, fairs and races, staying occasionally three to four weeks or even three to four months in the same place. The performances ranged from plays to conjuring and Punch and Judy to circus. Wild's became well known, and when James Wild died in 1838 it 'was as much talked of then, all over the country, as was Sir Francis Crossley's demise six years ago'. Sam Wild, James's son, concentrated on theatre, and in the winter began to appear with his company of between 25 and 30 performers in temporary wooden theatres in Bradford. In the winter of 1850-1 he engaged the Riding School in Huddersfield for three months, in 1853-4 he appeared in the 'New Theatre Royal' at Bury, a temporary wooden building specially built for Wild, in 1856 in another temporary wooden theatre in Dewsbury. Throughout the 1850s he continued this life, travelling in the summer, and appearing in temporary buildings in the winter. It was a transition stage, and one from which Wild was not sufficiently adaptable to move on. He overspeculated in an equestrian amphitheatre, but failed ultimately because success now lay less in travelling than in permanent theatre. It was a lesson that Richardson's successors in the south were also learning.[47]

It would be wrong to suggest that popular entertainment escaped the effects of the attack on popular leisure. Nearly all the performers had their brushes with authority. James Wild spent three months in prison for performing illegally. Even the mighty Richardson clashed with the authorities at Greenwich Fair in the 1820s. In the 1840s Warminster Justices labelled the showmen as vagabonds.[48] Alongside these occupational hazards were the often bitter rivalry of fellow showmen and the occasional hostility of audiences. For the showman, failure and poverty were a more frequent outcome than success; life was hard and insecure. But whatever the fate of individual showmen there can be no doubt of the demand for entertainment, and the proliferation of it. These travelling showmen in the first half of the century brought drama, pantomime, puppet shows and circus to anyone who could find his or her way to fair or race-ground, or, in winter, to the flimsy wooden structures, graced with the name Theatre Royal, which the more enterprising among them erected in the larger towns. To have performed *Richard the Third* twenty times in seven hours, as Prince Miller claims to have done, is some testimony to the initiative of the performers and the demands of the audience.[49]

The travelling showmen, it will have become clear, were offering more to their clients than what contemporaries understood by the term 'legitimate drama'. Two forms of entertainment which they presented deserve further attention. Pantomime was not invented in the Industrial Revolution, but it attained a new form during it. This it owed very largely to the comic genius of Joseph Grimaldi who performed regularly at Covent Garden and Sadler's Wells from 1806 to 1822, as well as undertaking provincial tours. Pantomimes of the early nineteenth century were not simply Christmas entertainment for children. As David Mayer has noted, they 'were attended by adults of all social classes and by comparatively few children'. In London there were four seasons during the year: On Lord Mayor's Day, 9 November, and for some weeks following; from Boxing Day to mid-February; on Easter or Whit-monday; and in early July at the summer theatres. Under Grimaldi it was not so much the pantomime as the harlequinade that followed it which was the attraction. To witness this must have been like seeing a Rowlandson or Gillray cartoon in motion; to quote Mayer again, 'The comic racing and chasing, the satires, the grotesqueness, the gluttony, the disregard for law, the ludicrous violence of the Grimaldi harlequinades are all products of the Regency . . .' Pantomime was universal in its appeal, and could be seen in both Patent and Minor theatres and in the fairground booths. Francis Place, for example, visiting Greenwich Fair, was unwillingly fascinated by the Columbine in the Melodramatic Harlequinade at Richardson's booth.[50]

Secondly, circus was an invention of the late eighteenth century. There had been rope-dancers and vaulters at Sadler's Wells and Vauxhall Gardens from the late seventeenth century, but, leaving aside some minor pretenders, modern circus with its equestrian emphasis was founded by Philip Astley in the late 1760s. By the early nineteenth century, circus, and the hippodrama which was derived from it, had begun to make a major impact on the entertainment world, invading the boards of Covent Garden for the first time in 1811, and frequently thereafter, and made well known in the provinces by Astley's winter tours.

Soon there were rivals. By about 1830, according to Thomas Frost, 'the northern and midland counties were travelled . . . by Holloway's, Milton's, Wild's, and Bannister's; the eastern, southern, and western by Saunder's, Cooke's, Samwell's and Clarke's'. These were small affairs with rarely more than three or four horses, the first elephant appearing at a circus in 1828.[51] But big or small the visit of the circus was a memorable event in the life of any community; when the American lion tamer Van Amburgh visited Redruth in Cornwall in July 1842 he headed a procession of 40 horses and carriages, drove 8 horses in hand himself, and attracted a crowd of over 7,000. At the other end of the country in Hartlepool in 1843 there was a public holiday to watch Van Amburgh's entry.[52]

The flourishing state of circus in the early 1840s owed much not only to the founder of the art, Philip Astley, but also to the phenomenal Andrew Ducrow, now the subject of an excellent biography. Ducrow's life serves to make several points about the development and influence of circus. First, his success was no accident but, like that of Grimaldi, owed much to a rigorous training in childhood: Ducrow received what amounted to professional training in dance, rope-dancing and equestrianism. Secondly, his performances in England from 1823 onwards made circus respectable and influential. Before this Ducrow himself had appeared on the legitimate stage, for example, at the Theatres Royal at Bristol and Bath in 1814-16, but only with his triumphant debut at Covent Garden in 1823, after five and a half years on the Continent, did the influence of circus in the entertainment world become paramount. By 1828 the Royal Family was patronising Astley's. Ducrow, as W.T. Moncrieff wrote in 1851, found circus 'a mere ring for ground and lofty tumbling, for buffoonery and rough riding; and he made it a scene of picturesque, rational, and chivalric entertainment, full of dramatic and olympian attraction'. Without Ducrow it would have hardly been possible for Dickens to celebrate Astley's.

Thirdly, Ducrow's life gives pointers to the rapidity of the growth of circus. Much about this still remains obscure, not least because buildings may not always have lived up to the high-sounding names they were given. But even before Ducrow rose to fame there were permanent circus buildings in the provinces, in cities as diverse as Bath and Liverpool. Then in the 1830s Ducrow seems to have embarked on an ambitious provincial building programme, in Hull, Leeds, Bristol and certainly elsewhere. It was, for example, in Ducrow's Amphitheatre in Leicester, holding 3,000, that Thomas Cooper rallied the Chartists in 1841. And in Bristol James Ryan's 1826 Olympic Circus was rivalled by the National Olympic Arena built by Ducrow in 1832, itself followed by a new permanent building erected by Ryan in 1837 and by Price and Powell's New Circus Royal in the early 1840s. The details of much of this circus building — and Ducrow was certainly not the only entrepreneur at work — remain obscure, but the evidence points to rapid growth, heavy investment and a marked influence on other forms of entertainment.[53]

Closely linked to the circus was another novel form of entertainment, the travelling menagerie. Showmen had travelled the roads with one or two animals for centuries, but on nothing like the scale with which George Wombwell was to gain nationwide fame with his tours, which began in the first decade of the century and continued until his death in 1850. At one point Wombwell owned more than twenty lions and five elephants. The exterior of the menageries alone was enough to excite, as Thomas Frost recalled:

I never failed, in my boyhood, to visit Wombwell's, or Atkin's show, whichever visited Croydon Fair, and could never sufficiently admire the gorgeously-uniformed bandsmen, whose brazen instruments brayed and blared from noon till night on the exterior platform, and the immense pictures, suspended from lofty poles, of elephants and giraffes, lions and tigers, zebras, boa constrictors, and whatever else was most wonderful in the brute creation, or most susceptible of brilliant colouring.

So well known was Wombwell, so universal his presence, that the song, 'The Rigs of the Fair', specially adapted for use at any fair, contains the lines:

Wombwell's wild beast is come again
Where works of nature's art is seen;
Lions, tigers, panthers, apes and bears
Are all to be seen at − − Fair.[54]

Historians with an apparently insatiable compulsion to compartmentalise have seen these different forms of entertainment in isolation one from the other − there are histories of sport, of drama, of the pantomime, and of the circus. Yet what is most striking is the connections between these different forms of entertainment, connections so strong that one can speak of this world of entertainment as part of one close-knit popular culture. All these forms of entertainment were frankly commercial in nature, all aimed to attract spectators, all employed professionals. And beyond this there were personal and institutional connections: people like Billy Purvis, familiar with different forms of entertainment, and buildings which could play host to pantomime or circus, sport or drama. It was no accident that wrestling could be seen at the Eagle Tavern, soon to become the Grecian Saloon, and not simply coincidence that Pierce Egan was at home in both the theatre and the prize-ring, nor that so many of these forms of entertainment could be witnessed at the horse-race or fair. One man could straddle this whole world: for example, David Prince Miller was at various times publicist for Richardson, impersonator of a black giantess, prize-fighting sparrer, conjuror, equestrian, fortune-teller, employee of Wombwell, magician, manager of the Royal Adelphi Theatre, Glasgow, lessee of the Queen's Theatre, Manchester, and interviewer for Henry Mayhew.[55]

The different components of this culture were further drawn together by the political necessity of defending it. On the receiving end of a barrage of hostile comment and legal manoeuvrings, the culture retaliated in its own way: by puncturing the pretensions of politicians, and portraying them as showmen;[56] by fighting for a freer stage and an end to theatrical monopoly;[57] and, as we shall see, by elaborating at every opportunity on the claim that their culture promoted patriotism and class harmony and prevented effeminacy. On occasions there could be embarrassing conflicts within the culture, as when, to Pierce Egan's horror, prize-fighters allowed themselves to be brought in to try to control the Old Price riots at Covent Garden.[58] But more generally there was a consistent radical cutting edge to the culture, and it is again no accident that much of our information about it comes from two radicals, William Hone in the 1820s, and the Chartist Thomas Frost, recalling his youth in the 1870s; the latter indeed being one of the few people to perceive the unity of the culture.[59]

It is customary to think of this as a cultural world on the wane — yet another doomed survival from pre-industrial times. This is a serious misinterpretation, and for four reasons. First, it was not a *survival*: so much in this culture was new, an invention of the Industrial Revolution era. Secondly, the culture was as at home in the big city as in the village, and could move easily back and forth from one to the other; it was not a victim, as we too easily assume so many things to be, of 'urbanisation'. On the contrary many of the entrepreneurs of the culture flourished precisely because they were alert to the new opportunities open in the big towns. Thirdly, the culture had a remarkable and (to opponents) alarming ability to diffuse itself upwards. Time and again entertainers who had started in the humblest circumstances, touring the fairs and races, received the supreme accolade of a royal command performance; and did so while still working the traditional circuits. Wombwell gave no less than five performances before royalty at Windsor; Van Amburgh not only displayed his talents and his lions before royalty, but was also the subject of a famous painting by Landseer. Ducrow, as we have seen, won royal patronage for the circus, and it was while travelling in dire poverty with Richardson that the young Edmund Kean received a summons to recite at Windsor.[60]

In part this is simply to say that entertainment was a career open to talent. But it is more than this. Not only were individual performers rising to fame, but whole types of performance, popular in origin, were having a marked impact on high culture. The most obvious sign of this is in the appearance of animals on the legitimate stage. It was with an eye to profit but with a sense of betrayal of high culture that the managers of Covent Garden and Drury Lane admitted horses, lions and elephants to their stages. And having done it once it was hard to stop. As late as the 1850s when Charles Kean was supposedly inaugurating a revival of legitimate drama at the Princess's Theatre, he followed the example of William Cooke, who was equestrianising Shakespeare at Astley's, and once more brought horses on to the stage; an example which reminds us that influence did not flow in one direction alone, for since very early days circus proprietors had built stages alongside their rings, and had made popular that curious hybrid, hippodrama.[61]

But what I think one can assert is that there was an upsurge of influence from below which left the defenders of high culture in sorry straits: none more so than the painter Benjamin Haydon whose exhibition at the Egyptian Hall was ignored by a public who streamed to see the American Barnum's display of Tom Thumb in the very same building and at the same time, a conjunction of events which resulted in Haydon's suicide.[62]

This then is a culture diffusing itself upwards. And finally it is a culture which does not peter out into those sorry street showmen interviewed by Mayhew, but leads us directly to the music-hall. I shall have more to say about the continuities later, but for the moment one can nod in assent when Louis James comments that theatre programmes of the first half of the nineteenth century show 'the promiscuity of a music-hall bill', or when Ronald Pearsall writes of the saloon theatres that they were 'already music halls'. If leisure for the middle class became commercialised in the eighteenth century, as Plumb has argued, for the mass of the people it was being commercialised from the very early nineteenth century, and in a form which gave rise to a vigorous popular culture of entertainment.[63]

The term 'popular' to describe this culture is one which, unless carefully defined, might in the present context be described as evasive. By 'popular' I mean 'of the people', as opposed to the culture of those in positions of power and authority who, since early modern times, had developed their own high culture in isolation, so far as possible, from popular culture; and had been so successful in this that in the late eighteenth and early nineteenth century, under the impetus of romanticism, they had to rediscover popular culture. But the popular culture of the Industrial Revolution that I have described did not consist solely of the traditional customs which began to be so lovingly described by antiquarians.[64] It was, as we have seen, essentially an innovatory culture. And, in contrast to the culture of the leisure class, it was inclusive, welcoming into its ambit the huge human and occupational variety covered by the words 'labourers, artisans, shopkeepers and tradesmen'. From its petty capitalist base it reached up and down the social scale, and penetrated to remote hamlets and to the heart of big cities. It cannot by any stretch of the historical imagination be described as 'a working-class culture', but at the same time it was imbued with a sense of popular rights. Its politics were the politics of instant reaction to threats to what it perceived as its customary and legitimate independence.

As such, in the conditions of the early Industrial Revolution, it was necessarily radical. But it had no long-term goals for the people, no vision of improvement; and in its live-and-let-live hedonism it was opposed by other cultures, not only that of the leisure class but also two minority cultures which, like the popular culture, drew their impetus from the people. These were a secular radical and a religious culture, both of which had visions of a new destiny and role for the people, whom the former in particular now began to think of as 'the working class'. These two cultures opposed the popular culture not because they lacked class consciousness but precisely because of their growing sense of it. The popular culture, as they perceived it, had too many ties with paternalism and 'Old Corruption', too little sense of the dignity of the people. In proposing their programmes of political and religious reform they were recognising the coming of a society in which class was experienced much more directly and constantly than in the past; from within the people they were making a claim for the leadership of the people.

The secular radical culture had its origins in that movement towards rationality in the later eighteenth century which was more provincial than metropolitan. The tone was serious but not puritanical. In Birmingham while the middle classes enjoyed concerts, cards and dancing in the genteel surroundings of the Vauxhall Gardens or the Assembly Rooms of the Royal Hotel, the working people of the town formed themselves into clubs and cliques like the Birmingham Musical and Amicable Society, founded in 1762, devoted not only to mutual providence and benefit, but also to beer, song and sociable discussion.

They formed tavern and debating societies, read the new newspapers, patronised the theatre.[65] They were neither aggressively proletarian nor aggressively reformist, but they tilled the soil for a later generation of rationalists whose impact on popular recreation was to be more profound. As Robert Colls has written of this later generation, 'Those radicals who pushed for working-class "improvement" in all of its guises, Teetotalism, Owenism, Chartism, Trade Unionism, Benefit and educational clubs, socialism, secularism, they all had their own particular sincerities, but equally they all also had the destruction of the old popular culture as integral to their ends.' That popular culture, they believed, patronised as it was by the rich, was destructive of working-class self-esteem. As Cobbett, certainly no Puritan, put it in 1826, writing to the working classes of Preston:

> Other opportunities will offer for speaking to you of the family of Stanley, and of the *benefits* you are likely to derive from them; other occasions will offer for asking you whether you will again suffer yourselves to be cajoled by ten or a dozen of poor fowls being set a fighting, and three or four horses set a gallopping, by the family of Stanley; other occasions will offer for expressing a hope, that you are no longer to be thus *amused*, as the Romans were, after they became the slaves of haughty and insolent nobles, who, while they fed them like dogs on offal and garbage, instituted shows and games to amuse them . . .

This was a letter written in the aftermath of an election defeat. The destruction of the old sports, and of the ambience which surrounded them, was a necessary step on the road to working-class political power.[66]

Any contact between this tradition and the methodist and evangelical one was necessarily fraught with difficulty, as Zachariah Coleman found in *The Revolution in Tanner's Lane*.[67] But in their different ways they both worked to undermine the older popular culture; and unquestionably it was this second tradition, mainly in the form of

Methodism, which had the larger impact.

The Wesleys attacked and confronted the old popular culture from the moment they started open-air preaching in 1739. As Charles Wesley reported in 1744 from Cornwall, 'At the last revel, they had not men enough to make a worthy match all the Gwennap men being struck off the devil's list, and found wrestling against him not for him'. Starting as a minority culture, Methodism in the course of a century grew to become one which set the tone and standards for the community. It achieved this because at one and the same time it both confronted the older popular culture and retained links with it. Methodism's success owed not a little to its ability to impart excitement and in its blatant poaching, not least in its music, from secular traditions. The rowdy singing of psalms and music round the bed of the dying was inherited, less the drink, from popular culture. Open-air preaching was deliberate spectacle — processions through towns might rival those of the showmen. Methodism offered its adherents an alternative form of recreation, but one which retained the sense of community, of drama, and of participation that had been part of the old.[68] Consider this account of Methodist miners in Cornwall in the 1840s:

> They had given up the public-house — they had now something better to cheer them than dreams of smuggled spirits — they felt no need and had no thought of theatre or dancing room. All the relief, the refreshment, the congenial excitement of their underground life they found in the preaching-house or in the classroom. There they let themselves go; they shouted they wept, they groaned, they not seldom laughed aloud, with a laugh of intense excitement, a wonderful laugh.[69]

Precisely because it was more attuned to popular culture it seems likely that Methodism, in the communities where it took root, was more successful than the heavy hand of upper- and middle-class Evangelicalism in changing it.

Perhaps its greatest impact, and this was one it shared with the Anglican Evangelicals, was that on children. Although the Sunday Schools were Establishment in origin, it has been convincingly shown by T.W. Laqueur that many of the later ones were working-class in membership and in organisation. Unquestionably the Sunday Schools were one of the more successful spearheads in the attack on popular culture, directing their energies less to the abolition of the old than to the encouragement of the new as a counter-attraction. This is at its most obvious in the excursion movement of the 1840s, but the beginnings can be seen in the famous Manchester Whit Walks, started in 1802 in an attempt to lure children away from Kersal Green races. The working men and women who taught in the schools aimed to remake leisure for their communities so that it conformed to a culture of self-help and self-improvement. New patterns of leisure, it is suggested, were coming into being less because of enforcement from above than of persuasion from below.[70] The success of this remaking was much greater in relatively small communities where Methodism flourished than in the larger towns, but even there it provided a challenge, often an attractive one, to the older popular culture.

These three cultures we have been discussing – the popular, the secular radical and the religious – had three things in common: the social centre of each was located amongst the people as opposed to those with authority; they were all growing; and they were all leisure cultures, by which I mean that they were active in out-of-work hours. Further, each of these cultures had both patrons and persecutors amongst those with access to power. Some feared the Radicals, others the Methodists, others the popular culture. The debate within the working class about the tactics appropriate for the elevation of that class was mirrored by a debate amongst their social superiors about methods of control. William Windham, for example, in 1802 condemned the Methodists and linked them with the Jacobins as both equally desirous of destroying 'the old English character, by the abolition of all rural sports . . . Out of the whole number of the disaffected', he continued, 'he questioned if a single bull-baiter could be found, or if a single sportsman had distinguished himself in the Corresponding Society'.[71] The attack on the leisure of the people during the Industrial Revolution was aimed not only at the popular culture, but also at the other two – indeed most virulently at the radical secular culture. Nevertheless it was the popular culture, as the most visible and as the most preponderant numerically, which attracted the greatest degree of hostile attention.

The belief that the late eighteenth century witnesses a new and more intensive phase in the attack on popular leisure stems mainly from the flurry of activity surrounding the issue of the Royal Proclamation for the Encouragement of Piety and Virtue in 1787. The background to the Proclamation reveals the mixture of motives that went into its making. In 1786 an energetic West Riding JP, Reverend H. Zouch, was instrumental in persuading the Quarter Sessions to recommend that citizens form themselves into groups to enforce the law and protect property.

Impressed by the success of this, William Wilberforce set out to make the movement a national one and to change its emphasis towards enforcement of the moral laws. If his motives were Evangelical he did his best to conceal this. As he put it to Addington in August 1787, 'from the situation in which I now am, my appearing to the world in the light of a man over-religious might be prejudicial to interests of the first importance'. The Proclamation itself differed little from its many predecessors, and taken in conjunction with a covering letter from the Home Secretary which explicitly stressed the necessity of protecting property, it was hardly surprising that the campaign appeared as one concerned essentially with law and order.

There is no doubt that the Proclamation had its effects all over the country. Quarter Sessions issued resolutions in its favour, and the licensing of alehouses became much stricter.[72] It would be easy, however, to exaggerate its importance and to mistake its thrust. It simply brought to a head an on-going and continuous eighteenth-century concern about disorder and the threat to property. And although its impact was immediate, it is not clear that it was more than short-lived.

The Evangelical imprint was more clearly evident in the Society for giving Effect to His Majesty's Proclamation against Vice and Immorality, which, like the earlier Societies for the Reformation of Manners, from 1692-1738 and 1757-66, sought to bring prosecutions against offenders. This Society had faded into inactivity by the late 1790s, but was revived under a new name in 1802 as the Society for the Suppression of Vice, chiefly but not entirely Evangelical in membership. The Society set out to put an end to Sabbath-breaking, to suppress blasphemous and licentious books and prints, and to campaign against private theatricals, fairs, brothels, dram-shops, gaming-houses, illegal lotteries and fortunetellers. In its early days at least it followed the example of the previous societies in giving priority to the campaign for Sabbath observance. Of the 678 prosecutions which it brought in its first two years, 623 resulted in convictions for breaking the Sabbath laws. The Vice Society received much publicity, not least from its enemies, and that, together with the prominence of the people associated with it, has assured it so much attention from historians.[73] It seems doubtful whether it had much real impact on the leisure of the people.

The same is true of the Evangelical MPs in Parliament. In the period 1784-1832 there were never more than 50 Evangelical MPs at any one time in the House of Commons, nor could all of these be relied upon to follow the lead of Wilberforce. They did not initiate parliamentary attempts to reform the morals of the people, but played a merely supportive role. Even on their main platform, Sunday observance, the Evangelicals proposed no legislation between 1799 and the beginning of the campaign of Sir Andrew Agnew in 1833. Agnew was associated with a group of some eleven MPs centred round the militantly Protestant *Record* newspaper between 1825 and 1833. Until then the Evangelical MPs, with one notable exception, seemed reluctant to turn to legislation in order to improve the morals of the people.[74] The exception was Wilberforce, who in the 1790s wrote a note 'On the importance of legislative measures for promoting public morals'. In 1797, in *A Practical View of the Prevailing Religious System of Professed Christians in the Higher and Middle Classes in this Country contrasted with real Christianity*, he had attempted to sow the seeds of reform amongst those classes by persuasion. As for the lower classes there was a duty, he believed, for the legislature to 'guard with peculiar care the rights and comforts of the poor'. Whereas the rich could be left to suffer the consequences of their dissipation, the poor needed the threat of the law to save them from the temptation to vice.[75] It was a paternal doctrine, a pointer perhaps more to Wilberforce's social stance than to his religious stance. As a whole the Evangelicals made little attempt to influence leisure patterns by legislation in the first 50 years of the Industrial Revolution.

The real impact of the Anglican reform movement can be seen more at local than at national level. On the profits of enclosure many parsons rose to gentry status, became part of the leisure class, and aspired to the bench of magistrates. From the late eighteenth century an increasing proportion of JPs were clergymen, by 1832 about one-quarter of the total. In some counties they made up more than half the total, and they were nearly always the most active and regular members. The clerical Justices, according to Esther Moir, were the leaders 'in that crusade "for the Reformation of the Manners of the Lower Orders" which swept the county Benches between 1786 and 1800'. Moreover the clergy could take the initiative quite apart from any position they might have on the Bench. In 1788 'the Minister, Churchwardens, and Principal Inhabitants' of Pebmarsh took upon themselves to prohibit the customary Midsummer assemblage of booths and stalls in the parish and to direct the Constables to prevent any gathering of people 'called a fair'. And in 1825 the curate of Madeley in Shropshire put down bull-baiting by employing a posse of constables to search for stakes used in tying up the bull and to rip up the floors of colliers' cottages while they did so.[76]

But again we must avoid ascribing too much long-term importance to such actions. At Haworth in the early eighteenth century the villagers

> had been in the habit of playing at football on Sunday, using stones
> for this purpose, and giving and receiving challenges from other
> parishes. There were horse-races held on the moor just above the
> village, which were periodical sources of drunkenness and profligacy. Scarcely a wedding took place without the rough amusement
> of footraces, where the half-naked runners were a scandal to all
> decent strangers. The old custom of 'arvills', or funeral feasts, led to
> frequent pitched battles between the drunken mourners.

Reverend William Grimshaw, arriving as curate at Haworth in 1742,
started to put a stop to all this, horse-racing ending after Grimshaw's
prayers providentially coincided with torrents of rain. But after Grimshaw's time there was a return both of 'arvills' and of football on
Sundays with challenges to neighbouring parishes. Similarly in Miss
Mitford's village, Sunday evening cricket, halted by 'an unnatural coalition between a high-church curate and an evangelical farmer' was
resumed after some years under the patronage of a publican. The
Evangelical foothold was always precarious.[77]

The Anglican clergyman, therefore, whether or not he was an
Evangelical, was most likely to have more than incidental effect on the
leisure of the poor when he was also a magistrate. And he and his
fellow JPs depended for much of their impact on the police. By the
second quarter of the nineteenth century it was probably the police
who were having the major impact on the leisure of the people. Harrison
and Trinder emphasise the importance of the police in bringing about a
decline in violent recreation in Banbury. D. Philips stresses how 'from
its establishment, the Staffordshire County Force cracked down on the
popular and rowdy recreations of the Black County — the wakes and
fairs, the prize-fights, and the animal sports — bull-baiting, cock-fighting,
dog-fighting'. In London the police were heavily involved in attempts
to put down bull-running and fairs. The existence of a police force gave
new power to a reforming magistracy, and as in Leeds detailed instructions might be issued to police to enforce the laws about cruelty to
animals. The new police were a visible sign in every community of
authority's determination to control the leisure of the poor.[78]

Employers of course backed these efforts of the magistracy and the
police. Their presence was felt not at national level — in Parliament or
in the nationally-circulated periodicals and newspapers — but locally, in

a particular enterprise. As we have seen, employers inherited a stock set of attitudes towards the labourers' propensity to idleness and irregularity of work. Efficient use of labour demanded that they try to overcome this, to eradicate the celebration of St Monday, for example. To an extent the machine, where it existed, did their work for them. As Trinder writes of Shropshire, 'Both in the pits and ironworks discipline was imposed as much by the dangers of the tasks and the motive of self-preservation as by any action of the employers.' But to most employers this enforced discipline on the job needed to be supplemented by discipline in leisure. This posed more of a problem, for habits and customs were deep-rooted. Persuasion on its own rarely succeeded; Josiah Wedgwood confessed his failure in 1776: 'Our men have been at play 4 days this week, it being Burslem Wakes. I have rough'd & smoothed them over, & promised them a long Xmass, but I know it is all in vain, for Wakes must be observed though the World was to end with them'. Others, like the inhabitants of Walsall and Wolverhampton, revealed their frustration in a petition to Parliament:

That the Country for many Miles round them is become very populous, by reason of the Manufactories and very extensive Collieries, Iron Works, and Lime Works, established and carried on therein; and that such Manufactories, Collieries, Iron Works, and Lime Works, have of late Years greatly increased, and are daily and rapidly increasing, and many Miners, Artificers, Workmen, and Labourers, are constantly wanted or employed in the different Mines, Works and Manufactories; and that, for some Years past, the Practice of Bull-baiting hath prevailed amongst the lower Classes of Society in the Neighbourhood, in a very alarming Degree, to the great Prejudice of the Persons concerned therein, the Distress, and sometimes the Ruin, of their respective Families, and to the great Annoyance and Injury of the Public at large; and that such Practice is usually promoted and encouraged by Persons notorious for their Depravity; and Drunkenness, Idleness, Gaming, Swearing, and every other Species of Disorder and Riot, are the Consequences of it, and it is become highly offensive to all peaceable and well-disposed Persons.

Others still concentrated their attention on children. In Tiverton, Charles Wilkins's 'Association for the Promotion of Order' rounded up children and drove them to school on Sundays. All hands at Strutt's and Arkwright's under the age of twenty had to attend school for four hours on Saturday afternoons and on Sundays 'to keep them out of mischief'. Horrocks' employed a man 'for many years to see that the children do not loiter about the streets on Sundays'.[79]

No employer in the Industrial Revolution could ignore the problem of labour discipline. It was as much a problem in an increasingly capitalised agriculture as it was in the new industries. And although the employer often sounds frustrated and dispirited, there can be little doubt that the impact of new forms of work on leisure, experienced intimately in each and every community, was more profound than the pressure-group activity of Evangelicals or the fulminations of magistrates.

Evangelicals, magistrates, police, employers, they form an impressive alliance ranged against the leisure of the people. But it would be wrong to see it as a united ruling-class alliance; on the contrary there was a split within that class, which had profound importance for the future of leisure. Well into the nineteenth century there existed a politically mixed alliance in defence of the rights of the poor to enjoy themselves as they would, and in opposition to the withdrawal of patronage. Its finest spokesman on the Tory side was William Windham, Secretary for War 1794-1801. 'The common people', he said, 'may ask with justice, why abolish bull-baiting, and protect hunting and shooting? What appearance must we make, if we, who have every source of amusement open to us, and yet follow these cruel sports, become rigid censors of the sports of the poor, and abolish them on account of their cruelty, when they are not more cruel than our own?' It was a theme taken up in the Whig Sydney Smith's 1809 *Edinburgh Review* article directed against the Society for the Suppression of Vice:

> A man of ten thousand a year may worry a fox as much as he pleases, — may encourage the breed of a mischievous animal on purpose to worry it; and a poor labourer is carried before a magistrate for paying sixpence to see an exhibition of courage between a dog and a bear! Any cruelty may be practised to gorge the stomachs of the rich, — none to enliven the holidays of the poor.

The theme is stated and elaborated in all the parliamentary debates on cruelty to animals in the first half of the nineteenth century. Brougham, for instance, again on the Whig side, opposed a further bill to prohibit bull-baiting in 1823 'because it tended to draw a distinction between the lower and higher classes of his Majesty's subjects, with respect to amusements in which there was equal cruelty'.[80]

The argument was directed not only against gentry who indulged in the new sports while condemning the old. It was also aimed at those Evangelicals who were working for a general reform of the manners of the poor. As General Gascoyne, the horse-racing and staunchly Conservative MP for Liverpool put it in 1802, 'it was with regret he observed a disposition in many of the members to deprive the poor of their recreations, and force them to pass their time in chaunting at conventicles'. The rural sports, it was being claimed, bull-baiting amongst them, served a number of important purposes: they kept the poor content; they provided a harmonious meeting-place for different classes; they helped instil martial qualities and prevent effeminacy; and they were truly patriotic and British. The language in which these claims were made is often so inflated as to raise little more than a wry and condescending smile from the modern reader. If boxing were suppressed, wrote R.P. Knight in 1805, 'There will be an end of that sense of honour and spirit of gallantry, which distinguishes the common people of this country from that of all others; and which is not only the best guardian of their morals, but perhaps the only security now left either for our civil liberty or political independence'.[81] Surely no one in his senses could argue that the significance of boxing was that serious? On the contrary, it is my contention that they were serious, and that their arguments must be taken seriously. Not only was there a large body of literature in the first half of the nineteenth century which made these arguments and employed this kind of language; more important the language and the sentiments were appropriated in mid-century by those who had been most vigorously opposed to them in earlier years.

First came the argument that these sports were a harmonious meeting-place for different classes. At a prize-fight, wrote Pierce Egan, there was 'a union of all ranks', and 'A cockpit, like a race-course . . . is free for every person; and selection of company is entirely out of the question. The noble lord, and the *needy* commoner, are both at home . . .' There was even, Egan hoped, a common literature of sport, for his *Book of Sports* was to be 'a "BOOK for EVERY BODY;" in which, topics will be introduced to interest the DUKE and attract the *Commoner*, to please the Rich Man and afford amusement and information to the Poor One'. It is a theme that runs through D.P. Blaine's much reprinted *An Encyclopaedia of Rural Sports*. Cricket has 'a particular claim to patronage, for it is in every sense a game of the people generally, from the highest to the lowest; it excites no envy by its exclusiveness, as it equally enjoys the attention of the prince and the peasant'. As for spectator sports, cock-fighting was perhaps 'the only one, except racing, that unites the plebeian and aristocratic spectators so harmoniously in common pursuits'. And most important of all, 'Amongst a thousand other advantages belonging to fox hunting, the bringing together the different ranks of society is not the least'. Fox-hunting, in another writer's words, made the claim to 'link all classes together, from the Peer to the Peasant'.[82] In this literature there is a world peopled by princes, peers and peasants, somewhat odd language for industrial England, but one which, as we shall see, was remarkably evocative and persistent. Its very inflation suggests a certain lack of correspondence with reality. Not only is the modern student of fox-hunting hard put to find a peasant in the field; even these nineteenth-century writers could be full of contradictions. Pierce Egan, for example, can be found lamenting that at racket playing at the Eagle Tavern, City Road and at White Conduit House, 'the company is not sufficiently select . . .'[83] Many of these sports were becoming socially much more exclusive just as their class-conciliatory nature was being celebrated in print; and the resonance of that celebration, however awkwardly it fitted with reality, was to be considerable.

So too was the language used by these writers to stress the second way in which these sports were socially and politically significant. In an industrial and urban civilisation they were the great guard against effeminacy. In an early issue of Cobbett's *Annual Register*, with whose foundation Windham had been connected, there appeared an 'Advertisement' on the Peace. John Bull, it reads, should

keep himself in the habit of fighting, by the exercise of manly sports, such as singlesticks, boxing, and *bull-baiting*; as he will shortly be called upon to fight a more desperate battle than ever, compared with which all his former bouts will seem to have been mere play. Above all things he is earnestly entreated to avoid the *methodist conventicle, a place which is found woefully to debase all the nobler passions of the mind*.

With the coming of peace in 1815 the dangers of effeminacy seemed ever greater. Vigorous sports and pastimes might halt the decay of the race. If hunting was stopped, wrote Blaine, 'we should see nothing but an effeminate race'. The sport helped 'to counterbalance', to use the language of the *New Sporting Magazine*, 'in some degree, the proneness to effeminate degeneracy which a high state of civilization is so apt to produce'. Sports were, in a much used word, 'manly'.[84]

It was the combination of manliness and class conciliation which gave these sports their third significant characteristic, namely their fundamentally British character. Nothing is more pronounced in the literature of sport in the early nineteenth century than its strongly patriotic tone. Egan never tired of repeating that prize-fighting was 'wholly BRITISH', and addressed himself in the first volume of *Boxiana*

to those persons who feel that Englishmen are not automatons; and however necessary discipline may be for the precision and move-ment of great bodies, that it would ultimately be of non-effect, were it not animated by a native spirit, producing that love of country, which has been found principally to originate from, what the fastidi-ous term — *vulgar Sports*!

This, the language of wartime, continued into the years of peace. In 1827 *Blackwood's Magazine* urged the Lords and Commons to

recollect that cock-fighting has been part of the system under which the country has become the terror, and envy, and admiration of the world . . . One rash enactment may destroy, in a few years, that manly spirit which it often requires centuries to generate in a nation.

In similar vein, the *New Sporting Magazine*, in its first number in May 1831 claimed that

To talk of the decline of the sport [hunting] is to talk of the decline of the empire; it is coeval with the country itself, adopted by our ancestors, improved by their successors, and perfected by us . . . It is of no foreign growth, but the indigenous birth-right of the soil, and is fascinating alike to the peer and the peasant.

In the following year its older rival, *The Sporting Magazine*, also fearful of the future, said of field sports that 'with their decline we may expect the fall of that spirit of manly independence for which the English people are remarkable'.[85] Commentators delighted in claiming a truly national or British character for the sports they supported: to Blaine cock-fighting and racing 'are now national sports'; to Egan the 'manly and noble game of Cricket may be considered, without the fear of contradiction, one of the truly denominated BRITISH SPORTS'. At a time when there were many contenders for the title of patriot these writers and others pushed the claims of sport with unequalled vigour.[86] And their claims rested on the manliness and class conciliation which in their rhetoric they saw as inextricably part of the sports. It was because a sport united peer and peasant in a manly way that it could make a claim to being national. All three parts of the argument irked their opponents, and all three were in time to be appropriated.

The lines of battle can be detected. On the one side a body of thinking with strong Tory overtones, but not without appeal to anti-Evangelical Whigs and Radicals, lauding the virtues of a way of life which was under threat; a body of thinking which stressed the role that rural sports played in keeping society cohesive, loyal, patriotic, contented, with the lower orders linked by ties of patronage to the higher. As Windham put it, 'If a set of poor men, for vigorous recreation, prefer a game of cudgels, instead of interrupting them, it should be more our business to let them have fair play'. It was important to those who argued that rural sports should continue that the rich should participate as patrons. Opposed to this body of thinking were those who sought to impose some control over society in quite different ways: by legislation, by work discipline, and through the labours of voluntary organisations dedicated to the reformation of the manners of the poor. Windham's opponents on the bull-baiting issue were diverse in their religious and political beliefs; they included Wilberforce and other Evangelicals, but also Sheridan. And after 1802 it was the Whig and former Lord Chancellor, Lord Erskine, and the eccentric Irishman, Richard Martin, who took up the parliamentary fight against cruelty to animals.[87]

Few MPs voted with the single-minded confidence of Windham on the one side or Wilberforce on the other. Canning, who had perhaps with a touch of flippancy defended bull-baiting in 1800 as a 'most excellent' amusement which 'inspired courage, and produced a nobleness of sentiment and elevation of mind', abstained in the vote in 1802 because he had been convinced of the cruelty of the sport in Staffordshire, and because he had been informed of the importance which the magistrates attached to the matter.[88] Nor should the proponents of abolition be depicted as men who wished to do away with all the recreations of the poor. Sheridan himself had been involved in a scheme to revive rural sports. William Smith, the Liberal Whig Unitarian MP, close to but not of the Clapham Sect, argued that the belief that the poor were 'entitled to their own amusements . . . arose . . . from a contempt for the lower class of people . . . if they wished to make them rational beings, let them not educate them with one hand, and with the other turn them loose to sports like these'.[89] This was a positive argument which would bear fruit in numerous schemes for rational recreation. Traditions with a long history to run can be discerned in embryo in these debates on bull-baiting: the Tory/Radical evocation of Merry England on the one hand, and, on the other, the belief that leisure was a fit subject for reform and improvement.

Popular leisure has rarely been free from criticism, and in that sense there was nothing new about the attack on it in the early decades of the Industrial Revolution. What was new was not the attack but the context. In association with the growth of capitalism since the sixteenth century there had emerged both a leisure class and a new and generally unsympathetic attitude on the part of authority towards labour. As one outcome of these processes patronage had been withdrawn from sports and leisure occasions with plebeian participation. But at the same time, by the later eighteenth century, the growth of population and towns had opened up new opportunities for the entrepreneurs of popular entertainment. Mostly small-scale capitalists, they had a close rapport with their audiences, forming with them a popular culture which was growing rapidly and diffusing itself upwards.

This was the context for the attack which was mounted by a ruling class lacking in unity. Tory traditionalists, men inclined to a romanticisation of Merry England, and defenders of the freedom of the individual were joined in uneasy alliance against the attempt to use the law to put down popular entertainments. Faced with this opposition the nationally-known Evangelicals were cautious. Their contribution lay primarily in attempts to reform the Sabbath, and even on this issue they were disinclined to try to change the law until the 1830s. Indeed the attack as a whole, although it generated obviously national organisations – the Lord's Day Observance Society, the Society for the Prevention of Cruelty to Animals, the Vice Society, and so on – is best seen in a local context.[90] Nor is it one in which the outcome was obvious. The popular culture had a resourcefulness, an inventiveness, and a capacity to evolve which frequently left its enemies defeated. And in so far as there was a transformation of popular culture it seems likely that it owed less to upper- and middle-class reformers than it did to working-class attempts to create a self-made culture whether this had a radical and political emphasis or one which was primarily religious.

Notes

1. P. Burke, *Popular Culture in Early Modern Europe* (London, 1978), p. 219; C. Phythian-Adams, 'Ceremony and the Citizen: The Communal Year at Coventry

1450-1550', in P. Clark and P. Slack (eds.), *Crisis and Order in English Towns 1500-1700* (London, 1972), p. 57; K. Wrightson, 'Aspects of Social Differentiation in Rural England, *c.* 1580-1660', *Journal of Peasant Studies*, vol. 5 (1977), pp. 37-8, 43.

2. K. Thomas, *Religion and the Decline of Magic* (London, 1971), pp. 75-6; T.G. Barnes, 'County Politics and a Puritan Cause Célèbre: Somerset Churchales, 1633', *Transactions of the Royal Historical Society*, 5th ser., vol. IX (1959), pp. 103-22.

3. C. Hill, 'The Uses of Sabbatarianism', in *Society and Puritanism in Pre-revolutionary England* (London, 1964), pp. 145-218.

4. F.J. Fisher, 'The Development of London as a Centre of Conspicuous Consumption in the Sixteenth and Seventeenth Centuries', *Transactions of the Royal Historical Society*, 4th ser., vol. XXX (1948), pp. 37-50.

5. R. Lennard, 'The Watering-Places' in Lennard (ed.), *Englishmen at Rest and Play* (Oxford, 1931), pp. 1-78.

6. P. Borsay, 'The English Urban Renaissance: the Development of Provincial Urban Culture *c.* 1680-*c.* 1760', *Social History*, no. 5 (1977), pp. 581-602; A. Everitt, 'The English Urban Inn 1560-1760', in Everitt (ed.), *Perspectives in English Urban History* (London, 1973), pp. 91-137; P. Corfield, 'A Provincial Capital in the late Seventeenth Century: The Case of Norwich', in Clark and Slack, *Crisis and Order*, pp. 290-3; E.D. Mackerness, *A Social History of English Music* (London, 1964), pp. 112-16; S. Rosenfeld, *Strolling Players and Drama in the Provinces, 1660-1765* (New York, 1970), pp. 181 and passim.

7. C. Kirby, 'English Game Law Reform' in *Essays in Modern English History in honor of Wilbur Cortez Abbott* (New York and London, 1971), pp. 345-80; 4 W and M, c. 23; *Parliamentary History*, vol. XXXII (1796), p. 851; Nimrod, *Memoir of the Life of the Late John Mytton, Esq.* (2nd edn 1837, repr. London, 1903), p. 84; F.M.L. Thompson, *English Landed Society in the Nineteenth Century* (London, 1963), pp. 137-44.

8. D.C. Itzkowitz, *Peculiar Privilege: A Social History of English Fox-hunting 1753-1885* (Hassocks, 1977), p. 12; R. Carr, *English Fox Hunting* (London, 1976), pp. 25-46.

9. Itzkowitz, ibid., p. 24; Carr, ibid., pp. 46-9.

10. *Squire Osbaldeston: His Autobiography*, ed. E.D. Cuming (London, 1926), pp. 96-7.

11. *Quarterly Review*, vol. XLIX (1833), p. 449.

12. 13 Geo. II, c. 19; *Victoria County History, Yorkshire*, vol. II (London, 1912), pp. 507-10.

13. R. Longrigg, *The Turf* (London, 1975), pp. 35-6, 59; W. Vamplew, *The Turf* (London, 1976), p. 25; Osbaldeston, pp. 125-7; J.H. Plumb, *Commercialisation of Leisure*, p. 18.

14. H. Perkin, *The Origins of Modern English Society 1780-1880* (London, 1969), pp. 183-95; R.W. Malcolmson, *Popular Recreations*, chs 6-8.

15. K. Marx, *Capital*, Everyman edn (London, 1930), vol. II, p. 575.

16. D.C. Coleman, 'Labour in the English Economy of the Seventeenth Century', *Economic History Review*, 2nd ser., vol. VIII (1955-6), pp. 280-95; E.S. Furniss, *The Position of the Laborer in a System of Nationalism* (Boston and New York, 1920), pp. 117-37.

17. R.C. Wiles, 'The Theory of Wages in Later English Mercantilism', *Economic History Review*, 2nd ser., vol. XXI (1968), pp. 113-26.

18. C. Wilson, 'The Other Face of Mercantilism', *Transactions of the Royal Historical Society*, 5th ser., vol. IX (1959), pp. 81-101; A.W. Coats, 'Changing Attitudes to Labour in the mid-eighteenth Century', *Economic History Review*, 2nd ser., vol. IX (1958), pp. 35-51, 'Economic Thought and Poor Law Policy in

the Eighteenth Century', *Economic History Review*, 2nd ser., vol. XIII (1960-1), pp. 39-51, and 'The Relief of Poverty, Attitudes to Labour, and Economic Change in England, 1660-1782', *International Review of Social History*, vol. XXI (1976), pp. 98-115.

19. Furniss, *Position of the Laborer*, pp. 117-56, quoting Townsend p. 123.
20. S. and B. Webb, *The Parish and the County* (London, 1906), pp. 536-44; E.G. Dowdell, *A Hundred Years of Quarter Sessions: The Government of Middlesex from 1660 to 1760* (London, 1932), pp. 27-43; 25 Geo II, c. 36.
21. D.W.R. Bahlman, *The Moral Revolution of 1688* (New Haven, 1957); E.J. Bristow, *Vice and Vigilance* (Dublin, 1977), pp. 1-31; T.C. Curtis and W.A. Speck, 'The Societies for the Reformation of Manners: A Case Study in the Theory and Practice of Moral Reform', *Literature and History*, no. 3 (1976), pp. 45-64.
22. Malcolmson, *Popular Recreations*, pp. 126-35.
23. D. Philips, 'Riots & Public Order in the Black Country, 1835-1860' in R. Quinault and J. Stevenson, *Popular Protest and Public Order* (London, 1974), p. 167; R.D. Storch, 'The Policeman as Domestic Missionary: Urban Discipline and Popular Culture in Northern England, 1850-1880', *Journal of Social History*, vol. IX (1976), p. 483.
24. P.E. Razzell and R.W. Wainwright, *The Victorian Working Class* (London, 1973), pp. 313, 315.
25. J. Strutt, *The Sports and Pastimes of the People of England* (1st edn 1801, repr. London, 1830), pp. 284-5; H.O. 44/12, f.37; S.C. on the Police of the Metropolis, PP 1828 (533), vol. VI, p. 141.
26. S.C. on the State of the Police of the Metropolis, PP 1816 (510), vol. V, p. 151; S.C. on the Police of the Metropolis, PP 1822 (440), vol. IV, p. 148; H.O. 60/1.
27. S.C. on Public Libraries, PP 1849 (548), vol. XVII, q. 1276; M. Thale (ed.), *The Autobiography of Francis Place (1771-1854)* (London, 1972), pp. 68-70.
28. Razzell and Wainwright, *The Victorian Working Class*, p. 318.
29. H. Cunningham, 'The Metropolitan Fairs in the Nineteenth Century' in A.P. Donajgrodzki (ed.), *Social Control in Nineteenth Century Britain* (London, 1977), pp. 163-84; Place Papers, B.L. Add MS. 35144, ff. 173-234; J. Grant, *Sketches in London* (London, 1838), p. 320; S. Alexander, *St Giles's Fair, 1830-1914* (Ruskin College, Oxford, 1970).
30. Longrigg, *The Turf*, pp. 39-40; *Memoirs of Joseph Grimaldi* (London, 1968), p. 267; Vamplew, *The Turf: A Social and Economic History*, pp. 36, 99.
31. J. Ford, *Prizefighting: The Age of Regency Boximania* (Newton Abbot, 1971); P. Egan, *Boxiana* (1st edn 1812, repr. Leicester, 1971), pp. 3, 110.
32. *Manchester Guardian*, 12 June 1830; Osbaldeston, pp. 136, 205-6; D.P. Blaine, *An Encyclopaedia of Rural Sports* (London, 1840), pp. 1227-8; Poster on Broome/Hannan fight; J. Lawson, *Letters to the Young on Progress in Pudsey During the Last Sixty Years* (Stanninglen, 1887), p. 57; A. Lloyd, *The Great Prize Fight* (London, 1977), pp. 10-11; R.C. into the Employment and Condition of Children in Mines and Manufactories, PP 1842 (380), vol. XV, p. 123; *The Badminton Library of Sports and Pastimes: Fencing, Boxing, & Wrestling*, 2nd edn (London, 1890), pp. 142-3.
33. J. Rule, 'Methodism and Recreational Confrontation in West Cornwall' (Paper to Society for the Study of Labour History Conference, Brighton, 1975), pp. 9, 13; W. Rollinson, *Life and Tradition in the Lake District* (London, 1974), pp. 162-3; *Victoria County History, Cumberland*, vol. II (London, 1905), pp. 482-90; P. Egan, *Book of Sports* (London, 1847 edn), pp. 321-36; W. Howitt, *The Rural Life of England*, 2 vols. (London, 1838), vol. II, p. 280.
34. P. Bailey, *Leisure and Class*, pp. 132-4; R. Bowen, *Cricket* (London, 1970),

pp. 68-89; Howitt, *Rural Life of England*, vol. II, pp. 274-8.

35. For a good modern account, see M.R. Booth, 'The Social and Literary Context' in *The Revels History of Drama in English*, vol. VI (London, 1975).

36. J. Donohue, *Theatre in the Age of Kean* (Oxford, 1975), pp. 17-18.

37. W. Nicholson, *The Struggle for a Free Stage in London* (Boston and New York, 1906).

38. Booth, 'Social and Literary Context', pp. 9-10.

39. PP 1832 (679), vol. VII, qq. 1204, 1267-70, 1597, 2133, 2606-8.

40. Donohue, *Theatre in the Age of Kean*, pp. 52-5, 155; G. Raymond, *Memoirs of Robert William Elliston* (London, 1844), pp. 274-6.

41. Booth, 'Social and Literary Context', p. 33; this paragraph owes much to papers presented at the Conference on Popular Theatre and Film at the University of Kent, 1977.

42. Rosenfeld, *Strolling Players*, pp. 1-2; Nicholson, *Struggle for a Free Stage*, pp. 138-9; Raymond, *Memoirs of Robert William Elliston*, p. 340.

43. K. Barker, *The Theatre Royal, Bristol, 1766-1966* (London, 1974), p. 61; R.E. Leader, *Sheffield in the Eighteenth Century* (Sheffield, 1901), pp. 134-8.

44. R. Southern in *Revels History of Drama*, vol. VI, p. 83; S.C. on Dramatic Literature, Report p. 3, qq. 3758-3809, App. 13.

45. S. Rosenfeld, *The Theatre of the London Fairs in the 18th Century* (London, 1960), esp. pp. 9-70; T. Frost, *The Old Showmen and the Old London Fairs* (1st edn 1874, London, 1881), pp. 217-22, 317-20; A.B. Osborne, 'Bartholomew, Frost and Suburban Fairs . . .', Guildhall Library.

46. J. Luntley (ed.), *The Public Life of W.F. Wallett, the Queen's Jester* (London, 1870), p. 10; W.E. Adams, *Memoirs of a Social Atom* (New York, 1968), p. 92; D. Mayer, 'Billy Purvis, Travelling Showman', *Theatre Quarterly*, vol. I (1971), pp. 27-34.

47. [Sam Wild] , *The Original, Complete and only Authentic Story of 'Old Wild's'* (London, 1888).

48. Wild, ibid., p. 13; R. Longhurst, 'Greenwich Fair', *Transactions of the Greenwich and Lewisham Antiquarian Society*, vol. VII (1970), pp. 205-6; 'Lord' George Sanger, *Seventy Years a Showman* (London, 1926), pp. 178-81.

49. D.P. Miller, *The Life of a Showman* (London, n.d.), p. 107; cf. P. Egan, *The Life of an Actor* (1st edn 1825, repr. London, 1904), pp. 196, 199.

50. D. Mayer, *Harlequin in his Element: the English Pantomime, 1806-1836* (Cambridge, Mass., 1969); Place Papers, B.L. Add MS. 35144, ff. 202-3.

51. A.H. Saxon, *Enter Foot and Horse* (New Haven and London, 1968); T. Frost, *Circus Life and Circus Celebrities* (1st edn 1875, London, 1881), pp. 1-68.

52. J.G. Rule, 'The Labouring Miner in Cornwall *c.* 1740-1870' (unpublished Univ. of Warwick PhD Thesis, 1971), p. 318; R. Wood, *Victorian Delights* (London, 1967), p. 67.

53. A.H. Saxon, *The Life and Art of Andrew Ducrow and the Romantic Age of the English Circus* (Hamden, Conn., 1978); C. Dickens, *Sketches by Boz*, Scenes, ch. XI; *The Old Curiosity Shop* (Penguin edn 1972), pp. 375-9, 392-3; *The Life of Thomas Cooper Written by Himself* (4th edn, London, 1873), pp. 162-3; K. Barker, *Bristol at Play* (Bradford-on-Avon, 1976), pp. 26-7; Frost, *Circus Life*, p. 96; R.W. Procter, *Manchester in Holiday Dress* (London, 1866), pp. 42-50.

54. A.B. Osborne, 'Bartholomew, Frost and Suburban Fairs'; Frost, *Old Showmen*, p. 259; R. Palmer and J. Raven, *The Rigs of the Fair* (London, 1976), p. 12; cf. Cooper, *Life*, p. 17, and A. Bennett, *The Old Wives' Tale* (Everyman edn, 1935), Book I, ch. 4.

55. On Egan, J.C. Reid, *Bucks and Bruisers* (London, 1971); Miller, *Life of a Showman*.

56. J.M. Butwin, 'Seditious Laughter', *Radical History Review*, no. 18 (1978), pp. 17-34.

57. Nicholson, *Struggle for a Free Stage*; C. Barker, 'The Chartists, Theatre, Reform and Research', *Theatre Quarterly*, vol. I (1971), pp. 3-10, and his 'A Theatre for the People' in K. Richards and P. Thomson, *Essays on Nineteenth Century British Theatre* (London, 1971).

58. Egan, *Boxiana*, p. 333.

59. W. Hone, *The Every-Day Book*, 2 vols. (London, 1826, 1827); *Table Book* (London, 1827); *Year Book* (London, 1832); Frost, *Old Showmen, Circus Celebrities,* and *The Lives of the Conjurors* (London, 1876). On Frost, see B. Sharratt, 'Autobiography and Class Consciousness' (unpublished Univ. of Cambridge PhD Thesis, 1973).

60. E.H. Bostock, *Menageries, Circuses and Theatres* (New York, 1972), pp. 5-6; Egan, *Life of an Actor*, pp. 200-2.

61. Nicholson, *Struggle for a Free Stage*, pp. 240 ff; Saxon, *Foot and Horse*, pp. 89-93, 153-61, 168-70.

62. R.D. Altick, *The Shows of London* (Cambridge, Mass. and London, 1978), pp. 413-14.

63. L. James, *Print and the People 1819-1851* (London, 1976), p. 84; R. Pearsall, *Victorian Popular Music* (Newton Abbot, 1973), p. 28; Plumb, *Commercialisation of Leisure*.

64. Burke, *Popular Culture*, pp. 3-22, 270-86; R.M. Dorson, *The British Folklorists* (Chicago, 1968), pp. 1-43.

65. J.H. Plumb, 'Reason and Unreason in the Eighteenth Century: the English Experience' in *In the Light of History* (London, 1972), pp. 3-24; J. Money, 'Birmingham and the West Midlands 1760-1793: Politics and Regional Identity in the English Provinces in the late Eighteenth Century', *Midland History*, vol. I (1971), p. 16.

66. R. Colls, *The Collier's Rant* (London, 1977), p. 94; W. Cobbett, *The Poor Man's Friend* (London, 1829), Letter 1 para. 17.

67. M. Rutherford, *The Revolution in Tanner's Lane* (5th edn London, n.d.).

68. Rule, 'Methodism and Recreational Confrontation', p. 8 and passim; Colls, *Collier's Rant*, pp. 76-96.

69. Quoted in Rule, 'Labouring Miner', pp. 300-1.

70. T.W. Laqueur, *Religion and Respectability: Sunday Schools and Working-class Culture 1780-1850* (New Haven and London, 1976), esp. pp. 227-39.

71. *Parliamentary History*, vol. XXXVI, pp. 833-5.

72. S. and B. Webb, *The History of Liquor Licensing in England* (London, 1963), pp. 59-90 and App.; J. Pollock, *Wilberforce* (London, 1977), pp. 59-69; L. Radzinowicz, *A History of English Criminal Law*, vol. III (London, 1956), Part III and App. 3.

73. F.K. Brown, *Fathers of the Victorians* (London, 1961), pp. 428-44; Bristow, *Vice and Vigilance*, pp. 32-50; Radzinowicz, *English Criminal Law*, Part III and App. 4.

74. I. Bradley, 'The Politics of Godliness: Evangelicals in Parliament 1784-1832' (unpublished Univ. of Oxford D.Phil Thesis, 1974), esp. pp. 7-15, 115, 128, 253 ff.

75. R.I. and S. Wilberforce, *The Life of William Wilberforce*, vol. II (London, 1838), pp. 448-51.

76. W.R. Ward, *Religion and Society in England 1790-1850* (London, 1972), pp. 9-11; E. Moir, *The Justice of the Peace* (Harmondsworth, 1969), pp. 106-8; S. and B. Webb, *Parish and County*, p. 48, n. 2; B. Trinder, *The Industrial Revolution in Shropshire* (London and Chichester, 1973), p. 366; H.D. Miles,

Pugilistica, 3 vols. (London, n.d. [1880-1]), vol. III, pp. 142-3.

77. Mrs Gaskell, *The Life of Charlotte Bronte* (London, 1905), pp. 19-22; M.R. Mitford, *Our Village*, ed. E. Rhys (London, n.d.), p. 171.

78. B. Harrison and B. Trinder, 'Drink and Sobriety in an Early Victorian Country Town: Banbury 1830-1860', *English Historical Review Supplement*, no. 4 (1969), p. 47; Philips, 'Riots and Public Order', p. 167; Storch, 'Policeman as Domestic Missionary', p. 483.

79. Trinder, *Industrial Revolution in Shropshire*, p. 362; S. Pollard, 'Factory Discipline in the Industrial Revolution', *Economic History Review*, 2nd ser., vol. XVI (1963-4), esp. pp. 256, 268-9; *House of Commons Journals*, vol. 57 (1801-2), pp. 344, 364, 371, 380.

80. *Parliamentary History*, vol. XXXV, p. 207; *Edinburgh Review*, vol. XIII (1808-9), p. 340; *The Times*, 22 May 1823.

81. *Parliamentary History*, vol. XXXVI, p. 844; R.P. Knight, *An Analytical Inquiry into the Principles of Taste* (London, 1805), p. 325. On Knight see F.J. Messman, *Richard Payne Knight: The Twilight of Virtuosity* (The Hague, 1974).

82. Egan on prize-fight quoted in Ford, *Prizefighting*, p. 21; Egan, *Book of Sports*, pp. 2, 146; Blaine, *Encyclopaedia of Rural Sports*, pp. 134, 445, 1211; Itzkowitz, *Peculiar Privilege*, p. 24.

83. Egan, *Book of Sports*, p. 226.

84. *Cobbett's Annual Register*, vol. I, 19 June 1802; Blaine, *Encyclopaedia of Rural Sports*, p. 445; *New Sporting Magazine*, vol. III (1832), p. 55.

85. Egan, *Boxiana*, pp. iii-iv, 14; 'Gallus Gallinaceus', 'A Modest Commendation of Cockfighting', *Blackwood's Magazine*, vol. 22 (1827), p. 592; *New Sporting Magazine*, vol. I (1831), p. 52; *Sporting Magazine*, 2nd ser., vol. V (1832), p. 358.

86. Blaine, *Encyclopaedia of Rural Sports*, p. 1211; Egan, *Book of Sports*, p. 337; cf. G. Newman, 'Anti-French Propaganda and British Liberal Nationalism in the Early Nineteenth Century: Suggestions Toward a General Interpretation', *Victorian Studies*, vol. XVIII (1975), pp. 385-418.

87. *Parliamentary History*, vol. XXXV, p. 205; E.S. Turner, *All Heaven in a Rage* (London, 1964), pp. 110-37; S. Lynam, *Humanity Dick; a Biography of Richard Martin, MP, 1754-1834* (London, 1975).

88. *Parliamentary History*, vol. XXXV, pp. 211-12; *The Windham Papers*, 2 vols. (London, 1913), vol. II, pp. 188-90.

89. *Parliamentary History*, vol. XXXVI, p. 851; W. Sichel, *Sheridan*, 2 vols. (London, 1909), vol. I, p. 79; R.W. Davis, *Dissent in Politics 1780-1830: The Political Life of William Smith, MP* (London, 1971), p. 107.

90. B. Harrison, 'Religion and Recreation in Nineteenth-Century England', *Past & Present*, no. 38 (1967), pp. 98-125.

2 THE DEFENCE OF CUSTOM: WORK AND LEISURE IN THE EARLY INDUSTRIAL REVOLUTION

The most pressing reason for work in pre-industrial as in industrial economies has always been the necessity to procure food and shelter. Once the need for these was met — and the level was set by custom — workers in pre-industrial times had a strong preference for leisure, and would work further only in so far as it was necessary to procure funds to enjoy that leisure — and the forms of leisure were themselves customary. It is true, of course, that in all societies some forms of work are intrinsically satisfying, true too that where work itself is drudgery, a communal organisation of it may bring some compensation for its nature. But, except in primitive societies, people have always been aware of a separation between work and leisure, and have put a high value on leisure. Leisure itself, a harvest celebration for example, may have been inextricably bound up with work, but to pretend that participants were unaware when they were working and when they were not is sheer romanticism.[1]

In the eighteenth century, E.P. Thompson has argued,

> a substantial proportion of the labor force actually became *more* free from discipline in their daily work, more free to choose between employers and between work and leisure . . . than they had been before or than they were to be in the first decades of the discipline of the factory and of the clock.[2]

Such workers had a high preference for leisure, and for long periods of it. The year was punctuated by days of festivals and fairs, and the working week was irregular, work being concentrated in the latter part of the week so as to leave time and provide money for days rather than hours of leisure. Some of these days customarily had a particular value: Christmas or New Year, Easter or Whitsun, Wakes Week. Varying from one part of the country to another, such customary holidays were celebrated with a tenacity which the sternest employers could not break. At the eve of the Industrial Revolution workers in every trade and every region had a high preference for leisure as against work, and engrained notions of the customary annual and weekly pattern of work and leisure.

Custom did not necessarily have deep historical roots, though people keen to defend it might pretend that this was the case. In the relations between work and leisure, as in politics, actions might be defended by reference to some mythical past. What was thought to be customary might in fact be quite new. It was in the eighteenth century and not before that it became customary to think of a normal working day, a fair day's work, as ten hours, from 6 a.m. to 6 p.m., with two hours for meals. Recent though its introduction was, it provided an essential point of reference for those campaigning to prevent the increase of hours in the Industrial Revolution.[3]

The new breed of employers of the Industrial Revolution deplored all these customs — the irregular work patterns, the traditional holidays, the norm of only ten hours work, together with in many trades habits of drinking and 'larking' on the job. The rational pursuit of profit called for the elimination of such atavistic habits, yet the workers were recalcitrant. In nearly all cases employers had to settle for some form of compromise, had to submit in some degree to the force of custom. Just how much they had to submit was dependent on two circumstances. First, the extent of mechanisation in their trade, and second the degree of organisation amongst the labour force. Where steam was triumphant and labour weak, there custom could most easily be eroded.

The impact of the machine on work habits can be most clearly discerned in the cotton industry. Lacking a custom in their own industry to refer to, the operatives were unable to resist the imposition of between twelve and thirteen and a half actual hours of work per day as a norm. And although as late as 1800 spinners might be missing from the factory on Monday and Tuesday, it was not long before a regular working week was established. With very high rates of turnover of labour, organisation to defend known habits of working proved impossible, and the machine and the employers were able to impose their will.[4] Not, however, for very long. Years before middle-class philanthropists awoke to the need for effective factory reform, workers were agitating for a shorter day. The first short-time committee, consisting mainly of operative spinners, was formed in Manchester in 1814. As early as 1817 Robert Owen was suggesting eight hours a day as the ideal — and the notion of an eight-hour day was almost certainly derived from a mythical custom of the past; the belief that the good King Alfred had divided the day into three equal parts of which only one part, eight hours, should be for labour. By the early 1830s Doherty and the Owenite Society for National Regeneration had adopted the demand for a reduction of the working day to eight hours.[5] Ten hours work a day, however, was the more widespread demand, and the period 1820-50 sees its gradual achievement, the Ten Hours Act of 1847 being a symbolic return to a pre-industrial norm.

Despite the voluminous evidence embodied in the Parliamentary Papers and elsewhere it is very difficult to assess either the motives and aims of those who advocated shorter hours or the degree to which workers participated in the movement. What should we make, for example, of the demand of Pudsey reformers in 1836 for 'time for Rest and for play — yes, for play — for Fireside Improvement, Domestic Improvement, Literary Advancement by Evening Schools and, above all, for Religious Instruction for all Factory Workers'?[6] Does this express their own real wishes or what they think will appeal to a parliamentary committee? The bare text raises the question but cannot answer it. What is clear at a general level is that it was not only and perhaps not primarily a demand for leisure which motivated the workers in the short-time committees. Probably of primary importance, certainly in the 1820s and 1830s, was a desire to protect employment. Two ways of doing this were to reduce output per worker-day so as to ensure a more constant demand for labour, and to reduce or eliminate the work of children and women in the factories. But again it is difficult to say whether the concentration on the hours worked by women and children represented a real concern among the workers or was perceived as a necessary tactic in the fight to reduce the hours of all workers. Nor can we be sure just how important the reduction of hours was within a working-class movement which had many other grievances to voice, and which might reasonably be suspicious of a campaign which enjoyed so much middle-class participation. Certainly by the time the Ten Hours Act was passed, there was, as we shall see in a later chapter, good evidence of a positive demand for leisure amongst the cotton operatives. But equally, so traumatic had been the experience of the previous half-century that the achievement of ten hours was perceived not as a return to custom but as the opening of the door to a new way of life.

Many commentators, indeed, were convinced that the break with the past for the cotton operatives was so sharp that there had come into being a new breed of person for whom custom was meaningless. R. Guest, in a book published in 1823 and mainly designed to disprove the importance of Arkwright in the progress of the cotton industry, was one of the first to note how the operative workmen 'had their faculties sharpened and improved by constant communication', and that the amusements of the people have changed with their character. The Athletic exercises of Quoits, Wrestling, Foot-ball, Prison-bars and Shooting with the Long-bow, are become obsolete and almost forgotten; and it is to be regretted that the present pursuits and plea-sures of the labouring class are of a more effeminate cast — They are now Pigeon-fanciers, Canary-breeders and Tulip-growers.

In this, of course, there is an unrestrained tone of romantic nostalgia. The same is true of later commentators, for example P. Gaskell in *Artisans and Machinery* (1836) where the ruddy complexion and clean limbs of the domestic manufacturer of 'the days of quoit and cricket-playing — wakes — May-day revels — Christmas firesides, and a host of other memorabilia, now ranked as things that were' are contrasted with the high intelligence of the present artisan who seeks 'his amusement in the newspaper, the club, the political union, or the lecture-room; looking for his stimulus in the gin and beer shops; . . . he is debarred from all athletic sports, not having a moment's time to seek, or a bodily vigour capable of undertaking them; he has an active mind in a stunted and bloodless body'.[7]

In the next decade Engels follows in Gaskell's footsteps, and Samuel Bamford, setting out to give an account of 'the games, pastimes, and observances, which were prevalent amongst both the youthful and the more mature classes of the working population of my neighbourhood at the time I am writing about' (i.e. Middleton in the late eighteenth century) comments, 'most of the pastimes and diversions which I shall describe, are no longer practised, — some of them not even known, — by the youthful population of the manufacturing districts of the present day. Thus we are enabled distinctly to perceive the great change which, in a few years, has taken place in the tastes and habits of the working classes'.[8]

Such comments were written at a level of generality which could obscure the processes by which change had been brought about; descent to detail laid them bare — it was the mill and the work disci-pline that it imposed. Consider the case of hunting near Ashton. There, according to a report in 1849, the harriers used to be followed by

the Ashton weavers, armed with huge leaping-sticks, by the help of which they could take hedges and ditches as well as the boldest rider of the hunt . . . The mill system has, however, utterly extirpated every vestige of the ancient sporting spirit. The regularity of hours and discipline preserved seem, by rendering any such escapades out of the question, to have at length obliterated everything like a desire for, or idea of, them.

Earlier in the decade, in 1841, the principal of Messrs Pole and Stopford's Hat Manufactory at Denton, near Ashton-under-Lyne, had told the Children's Employment Commission how the hatters used to hunt two days a week, but that now the pack was nearly broken up; the reason was evident; 'We made a rule that we would not employ any person who wished to be off his two days. Now the men we employ are as regular as any set of men'.[9]

The picture seems clear. Custom had died. The factory system had produced a new breed of men who were physically weak and stunted, but mentally alert, perhaps over-excited, finding an outlet for this according to character in the depravity of the beer-house and gin-shop or in the intellectual leisure of botany, music or reading. 'No county', noted Leon Faucher in 1844, 'buys so many books as Lancashire. Chamber's Edinburgh Journal, which circulates to the extent of 85,000 per week, is read principally in the manufacturing districts; and Lancashire alone takes 20,000 of them'.[10]

And yet, even in Lancashire, eroded as custom had been with respect to the number of hours worked and the weekly cycle of work, the traditional holidays were still observed. Under the 1833 Factory Act workers were entitled to eight half-holidays a year plus Christmas Day and Good Friday. But these statutory provisions were often ignored, not only by penny-pinching masters but also by workers who preferred to rely on custom. 'There are wakes and fairs, and so many customs of stopping', reported Factory Inspector Leonard Horner, 'that it amounts to more than the eight half days'. Even in a model mill like that of Henry Ashworth at Turton the mills were idle about four days a year 'for the wakes and holidays of that kind, which the people have been accustomed to enjoy'. As to Christmas Day and Good Friday, the workers had scant regard for these parliamentary but uncustomary holidays. Ashworth described in 1840 how no one was compelled to work on Christmas Day and Good Friday:

We have given them permission to work, and they have mostly accepted it; for instance, Good Friday occurred about a fortnight ago; we shut the mill doors in the morning when the hands collected at six o'clock to go in; the Act was read to them, stating that they were entitled to have a holiday, and that they were at liberty to accept of a holiday; they immediately began to debate the propriety of taking or not taking the holiday proposed to them; eventually it was concluded, that as Easter Monday was following so soon after, and they could not afford to have a holiday each week, that is to say to lose both Easter Monday and Good Friday, they would exercise a choice, and they put it to the vote who were for Good Friday and who were for Easter Monday, and the vote was unanimously carried in favour of Easter Monday . . . the same with regard to Christmas-day; in our part of the country Christmas-day is not esteemed a workman's holiday, but New-Year's day is, and the same process has been gone through of informing them that they were entitled to a holiday on Christmas-day, and they have uniformly expressed a desire to take New-Year's day in lieu of it.

Even in the cotton mills, then, where the effects of the Industrial Revolution had had their greatest impact, custom retained some force. But it affected holidays more than the crucially significant questions of hours of work and regularity of work; and even with holidays the workers can be seen carefully balancing the possible enjoyment of a holiday against the financial loss it would entail – for there was no question of holidays with pay. The workers were disciplined and rational, not blind followers of custom. The masters too had changed. They no longer believed as they did when arguing against a shorter hours bill in 1816 that 'in the lower orders, the deterioration of morals increases with the quantity of unemployed time'. Some, like Ashworth, in addition to the legislative requirement of eight half-holidays, gave permission to the work people to take a week or more of holiday and 'they will go to Ireland or London, or Scotland, wherever the coach or the steam-boat will carry them, and spend their time rationally . . .' Even in their holiday habits the cotton operatives were beginning to enter a new world of leisure, and to discern a new relationship between work and leisure. By mid-century custom was only dimly, if nostalgically, remembered.[11]

If it was the machine and its demands which killed custom for the cotton operatives, for others it was their own lack of organisation and bargaining power. Chief amongst these must be counted the agricultural workers who shared with textile workers the sharpest deterioration in hours and conditions of work in the early nineteenth century. In the occupation above all others in which the seasons seemed to dictate an accustomed rhythm of work, the proletarianisation of the farm labourer coincided with a tightening-up of his work routine. Obelkevich has described how in South Lindsey traditional festivities – 'hopper feast', clipping supper, harvest supper — were suppressed, and the day labourers, who formed the majority amongst farm workers, worked six days a week with only Good Friday and Christmas as holidays. As Assistant Hand-Loom Commissioner Joseph Fletcher stated before the Health of Towns Select Committee in 1840, 'the agricultural labourer is as much tied to regular hours as the factory labourer'. In such a situation customary leisure opportunities were sharply curtailed, and the relatively short hours of the agricultural labourer in the eighteenth century were but a dim memory.[12]

Amongst outworkers and in the sweated trades, too, lack of organisation and bargaining power led to very long and at the same time irregular hours. The number of workers involved was large, growing and increasingly female, the work itself frequently seasonal. In an overstocked labour market (outworkers were the classic reserve army of labour), workers had to endure quite exceptionally long hours of labour in order to scrape a living. Marx, in a brief section of *Capital* entitled 'Branches of English Industry in which there is no legal limit to Exploitation', is as good a guide as any to the situation as it existed as late as the 1860s. Very long hours of work, for children as well as adults, are reported in the Nottingham lace trade, in the Potteries, in lucifer match-making, in the manufacture of wallpaper, in baking, and amongst milliners and blacksmiths. No sense of custom protected, no leisure existed, for Mary Anne Walkley, milliner in London, who worked on average 16½ hours daily, and during the season sometimes for 30 hours at a stretch. When such as she were not working, they were not enjoying leisure, but enduring unemployment.[13]

General labourers, after agricultural workers the largest single group of employees, probably retained more links with custom. Those men who did that sheer physical hard labour which, as J.F.C. Harrison has stressed, was so important in the early Industrial Revolution, had an essentially task-oriented attitude to work.[14] Employed by subcontractors, they would work very hard in short bouts and then enjoy a period of leisure until their earnings were exhausted. Those who worked as labourers for artisans perforce followed the irregular work patterns of the latter — that is to say, Monday in particular would often be taken as a holiday.

The artisans were perhaps best equipped both to prevent an increase in hours worked and to maintain a customary relationship between work and leisure. Their efforts to keep down working hours to ten per day are imperfectly recorded, and any generalisations made about them will conceal a multitude of differences between localities and trades.

What seems to have happened is this: pressure by organised workers secured a reduction of the long hours of the seventeenth century so that by the mid-eighteenth century a ten-hour working day had become the norm in most handicraft trades. The building trades had achieved this earlier, by about 1720, and coal-mining hours were shorter than the norm, only six to eight hours a day. In the early nineteenth century, workers had to fight hard to maintain this norm. Engineers, builders and printers in the 1830s, for example, successfully reaffirmed 6 a.m. to 6 p.m. (i.e. ten hours' actual work) as a normal day. In the London printing trade there was clear workshop control over output and hours. According to J.C. Hobhouse in 1825, 'ten and a half hours and in some cases eight hours in winter, was an ordinary day's work for machine makers, moulders of machinery, house carpenters, cabinet makers, stone-masons, bricklayers, blacksmiths, millwrights and many other craftsmen'. In the 1840s, before the passage of the Ten Hours Act, 'To talk to a mechanic or an artizan of London, Bristol or Birmingham of working more than ten hours a day was to risk being set down as a madman.' In most occupations trade union activity achieved what was due to legislation in the case of the cotton industry.[15]

Control over the number of hours worked was not the only achievement of the better-organised trades. With varying degrees of success they also maintained a customary irregularity of work and the right to the enjoyment of traditional holidays. Here again each trade, each locality has to be considered on its own. Amongst coal miners, for example, there was a wide variety of experience. Normally the Monday after pay day, itself usually fortnightly but sometimes weekly, was a holiday. In some areas but not in others there was no recognised starting or ending time for the day's work.[16] Besides the regular Mondays the amount of holiday taken varied considerably. In Warwickshire, as we have seen, in the 1840s, a prize-fight would lure the men away from the pit five or six times each summer. In Lancashire, Joseph Hatherton (an underlooker at Messrs Foster's mine at Ringley Bridge) reported,

> They have a fortnight at Christmas, a full week at Whitsuntide, three or four days at Ringley Wakes, about the same at Ratcliff Wakes, and at odd times besides. The wages are paid every fortnight; and they are never expected to come on the Monday after pay . . . and when they come on a Tuesday they are not fit for their work. Christmas and New-Year's-Day are universal holidays in the district, and generally the wakes or feasts of the different villages, and the races in

their respective neighbourhoods – for example, at Worsley, Eccles Wakes, at St. Helen's and Haydock, the Newton Races, the Manchester Races also, which occur during Whitsuntide, attract an immense number of colliers from Clifton, Bolton, Leven, Outwood, Middleton, Worsley, and the whole surrounding district.

Against this luxurious amount of holiday time taken by miners in Lancashire and Cheshire has to be set the much more restricted time enjoyed by those in Wales or Scotland, and, universally, the amount of enforced but probably unwelcome holiday through short time. As the 1842 Royal Commission for Inquiry into the Employment and Condition of Children in Mines and Manufactories put it, 'in general the colliers have a considerable portion of idle time, because there is not a sufficient demand for their labour to occupy them every day in the week, winter and summer'.[17] The control which the miners exercised over their own hours and conditions of work, achieved through the force of custom and the maintenance of the subemployment and butty system, helped to create a distinctive leisure culture, but part of the cost to be paid was a tradition of short-time working.

Although miners in general maintained greater control over their work than cotton workers, it would be wrong to suggest that they avoided the pressures towards more regular work associated with the advance of capitalism. Sometimes the pressures were self-generated, as with Methodism, which found mining areas fruitful ground in which to till. But the exertion of authority by employers, particularly at times when labour was overabundant, could result in major changes. In the Cornish tin mines, for example, where in the late eighteenth century there was evidence of high leisure preference, in the early nineteenth century the process of erosion of holidays was in full swing. By 1817, according to one observer, 'the spirit of sport has evaporated, and that of industry has supplied its place. The occupations in the mining countries fill up the time of those engaged in them too effectively to allow leisure for prolonged revels, or frequent festivities'. The Cornish tin miner was undergoing the same process as the Ashton-under-Lyne hatter or weaver. Similarly in the isolated lead mines of the northern Pennines a disciplinary paternalism on the part of the employers, combined with a surplus of labour in the early 1830s, led to a major reduction of drink outlets, and the imposition of a regime of fines, punishments and dismissals which any factory employer would have been proud to emulate. By 1832, as the historian of the miners notes, the London Lead Company could 'make its employees obey almost any regulation it chose to lay down'.[18] Where labour power was weak, custom could be smashed.

A customary irregularity of work and an enjoyment of traditional holidays was best maintained in those handicraft industries where trade unions were able to control the supply of labour, or, as in the West Midlands and Potteries, where small masters, uninfluenced by modern notions of progress, held sway. The pattern of working described of the weavers in the eighteenth century who used to 'play frequently all day on Monday, and the greater part of Tuesday, and work very late on Thursday night, and frequently all night on Friday' had very deep roots, roots which grew when machinery was absent and labour power exerted. Thomas Wright wrongly claimed in 1867 that the custom of celebrating St Monday was 'a comparatively recent one'; but he quite correctly saw its spread as a consequence of the bargaining power of skilled workers. The latter continued to have a strong leisure preference, and provided their work was not dependent on steam, there was little anyone could do to break the St Monday habit. As E.P. Thompson has noted, St Monday appears 'to have been honoured almost universally wherever small-scale, domestic and outwork industries existed'.[19] Some of these St Mondayites, it is worth remembering, were involuntary worshippers, labourers for whom there was no work because of the absenteeism of their artisan superiors. Similarly we need not suppose that the potters necessarily enjoyed the debased paternalism of their employers as Charles Shaw described of the 1840s:

> These gentlemen [i.e. employers] exhibited their inferior tastes, especially at the fag end of an annual Wake. When the bulk of the people had spent their money in fun and fury, and in riotous living, these gentry and publicans would subscribe for sack-races, for eating boiling porridge, for eating hot rolls dipped in treacle, suspended on a line of string, eight or ten competitors for a prize standing with gaping mouths, swaying bodies, and their hands tied behind their backs. Then as dusk came on, and the excitement flagged, these 'gentlemen', with their glasses of whisky, sitting at the second-storey windows of the hotel or the 'Lamb', threw shovelfuls of hot coppers among the frantic crowds.

Such an account is a reminder that not all employers were active proponents of the new work ethic; and with such employers it is hardly surprising that the celebration of St Monday and sometimes St Tuesday flourished, and that there was drinking and cooking on the job. Free from the tyranny of the machine and the labour discipline of the model employer, the potter clung with success to what he thought of as custom.[20]

The experience of the potters reminds us, too, of the intimate connection between work and leisure. Work, we have suggested, was essentially instrumental, a means to the support of life and to the enjoyment of leisure. But it was work which dictated the hours that were available for leisure, and more important the content and meaning of that leisure was always intimately related to the experience of work. In clinging to custom men and women were resisting any untying of the interconnection between work and leisure. Just as reformers were well aware that rationally pursued leisure was a necessary precondition for a model workforce, so their opponents knew that if they were to enjoy their leisure in their own way then they must also control their conditions of work.

The evidence of song perhaps provides the clearest indication of the customary interplay between work and leisure. It is true that only a minority of songs were directly about work, but even where the subject-matter was love or patriotism, the imagery was normally taken from the experience of work. Some of these songs were so full of technical terms that they must have been unintelligible to anyone outside the trade in question. Consider part of 'The Bury New Loom', described by A.L. Lloyd as 'A characteristic early piece of the erotic imagery of the industrial age', and first printed on a broadside in 1804, then reissued many times by printers in the north-west:

'She took me and showed me her loom, the down on her warp
did appear.
The lam jacks and healds put in motion, I levelled her
loom to a hair.
My shuttle ran well in her lathe, my tread it worked up
and down,
My level stood close to her breast-bone, the time I was
squaring her loom.[21]

The imagery of work was as apparent in the other great area of industrial song-making, the north-east, as it was in the cotton manufacturing areas of the north-west. The image of Bob Cranky, hard-living, hard-drinking, cheeky, perky, patriotic, was inseparable from, indeed derived from, the hard but independent working life of the collier. The songs themselves could be quite directly about events in the pits, or about poverty.[22] They demonstrate without leaving room for argument the very close interplay between work and leisure. Not only did people seek their leisure in occupational groupings, but also their leisure activities were infused with the experience of work. There was a widespread song about a young man who visited his girl, wearing, depending on the version, a billycock, a cattle-smock, a leather apron, navvy boots and so on; whatever happened to the hero he never removed the badge of his standing or trade. The last verse of the miners' version runs:

> Come all you young maidens wherever you be,
> Beware of them colliers who are single and free,
> For their hearts do run light and their minds do run young,
> So look out for the fellows with the pit boots on![23]

Sexual prowess was clearly linked to occupation.

Rivalling sex in the imagery of most occupations was drink. Drinking was the most time-consuming, expensive and frequently-indulged leisure activity. And like song, with which of course it was connected, it was not divorced from but intimately linked with work. Different occupations had their own elaborate drinking codes. As John Dunlop, the Scottish temperance advocate put it, 'almost every trade and profession has its own code of strict and well-observed laws on this subject'. He described the different drinking customs of the joiners and cabinet-makers, of the herring-fishers, and in the ship-building yards. In England, he believed, 'there are fewer usages, but still there are a good many'.

Drinking on the job was frequent. Francis Place in 1833 could 'remember the time when in almost every printing office there was a bottle of rum, and the workmen served themselves with it, and kept a score against themselves; I remember when almost every tailor's shop in London had a bottle of gin, and the man who kept the score for the publican was paid by having a glass out of a certain quantity'. Rum for the printers, gin for the tailors, each occupation with its separate custom. Place believed that these customs had ended. Lovett, too, 16 years later, thought that 'in the workshop . . . a great improvement has taken place among the working classes; their footings, fines and drinking bouts are now almost done away with'.[24] These opinions may be more a sign that Place and Lovett had removed themselves from the ambience of work-based drinking than that they were objective, for there is much evidence pointing to the continuance of such habits. Charles Manby

Smith's recollections of London printing shops suggest that drinking and practical joking remained lively traditions. Charles Shaw, looking back to his early days in the Potteries in the 1840s, described not only drinking and eating, but also elaborate ritualised sanctions against anyone who stepped out of line. A socially superior thrower, for example, who produced ware which the turners could not work with, had a mock funeral directed against him; 30 workers placed his poor workmanship in a 'coffin' and after a funeral procession through the workplace tumbled the contents onto the thrower's head.[25]

Drink and the ritualised customs that often went with it — mock funerals, mock weddings — survived, it seems, in the workshops of England throughout the first period of the Industrial Revolution. And off the job, drinking by occupation was common. The London turners were reported in mid-century to 'amuse themselves in the public-houses near where they work'.[26] And the very names of pubs — Bricklayers' Arms, Carpenters' Arms, and so on — suggest that it was normal for people to drink in pub or beer-house during their leisure hours in occupational groupings. Of course not all drinking was occupation-specific, but a significant proportion of it was. And such drinking, consciously or not, was a defence of customary ways of doing things against those who wished to reform both the work and the leisure of the working man.

Songs and drinking habits point to a close connection between work and leisure, but the richness and complexity of that connection needs to be explored further if we are to understand the full weight of the custom which was threatened by any challenge to them. Consider the cultural world of the Spitalfields weavers as it existed in the early nineteenth century. A solicitor who had lived among them for 30 years, stated in 1840:

> The Spitalfields Mathematical Society is second in point of time to the Royal Society, and still exists. There was an Historical Society, which was merged in the Mathematical Society. There was a Floricultural Society, very numerously attended, but now extinct. The weavers were almost the only botanists of their day in the metropolis. They passed their leisure hours, and generally the whole family dined on Sundays, at the little gardens in the environs of London, now mostly built upon, in small rooms, about the size of modern omnibuses, with a fireplace at the end. There was an Entomological Society, and they were the first entomologists in the kingdom. The Society is gone. They had a Recitation Society for Shake-

spearean readings, as well as reading other authors, which is now almost forgotten. They had a Musical Society, but this is also gone.
There was a Columbarian Society, which gave a silver medal as a
prize for the best pigeon of a fancy breed . . . They were great bird
fanciers, and breeders of canaries, many of whom now cheer their
quiet hours while at the loom.[27]

By 1840 of course these 'quiet hours' were longer and much less re-
warding than previously for the Spitalfields weavers. Inevitably their
culture collapsed along with their means of livelihood; by 1840 this
vigorous flourishing of working-class culture was dead.

There was the same delicate balance between work and leisure in
other trades. That 'intellectual culture' of the artisans which E.P.
Thompson has so vividly described, with its avidity for literature, for
theatre and for print, was dependent on a defence of the work situation
which each individual trade had fought for and won; not only in terms
of hours of work, but also of restriction of entry into the trade. Indeed
thoroughly political as that culture was, its participants could not but
be aware of the threads which bound together their work and their
leisure. Any dilution of the 'honourable' section of a trade by the 'dis-
honourable' spelt doom for a culture which was dependent both on
keeping the labourer in his place as well as extracting every possible advantage from the employer; indeed the advantages could be won only if
the honourable status of the trade was maintained.[28]

Even within this artisan culture there were clear distinctions between
trades. No one was better equipped to observe them than Mayhew at
mid-century. Of the West End cabinet-makers it could be said that
'They are not much of play-goers, a Christmas pantomime or any holiday spectacle being exceptions, especially where there is a family. "I
don't know a card-player," said a man who had every means of know-
ing, "amongst us. I think you'll find more cabinet-makers than any
other trade members of mechanics' institutes and literary institutions,
and attenders at lectures." ' In contrast among the declining fancy
cabinet-makers the chief recreations seemed to be 'card-playing, dominoes, and games that are carried on without bodily exertion'. The
nature of the coopers' work encouraged quite different forms of recreation: 'Coopers are generally fond of manly exercises, such as cricket.
There are very few skittle-players among them. Cards are played sometimes in the public-house on Saturday night, but not generally . . . The
theatre and the public gardens, I am told, are, however, the principal
recreations of the coopers'.[29] Each trade had its own culture based on

an intimate linkage between work and leisure. This did not mean that they could not all, in some degree, share in a wider culture, but such participation was built on and dependent on the trade-based link between work and leisure.

For some perhaps, so dominant were the values of the occupation, that it provided the focus for all leisure, and stimulated a degree of sectionalism which was as apparent in leisure as in work. This seems to have been the case with the costermongers. Street-selling encouraged a leisure time spent away from home, whether in the beer-shop, 400 of which, according to Mayhew, were resorted to by costermongers and principally supported by them, or in the dancing room where at twopenny hops 'the band is provided by the costermongers, to whom the assembly is confined', or in the theatre where the costermongers dominated the galleries of the theatres on the Surrey side. With their devotion to sparring and boxing, to dog-fighting and pigeon-fancying, with their own language, and with their willingness to cheat at cards when playing with non-costers, the costermongers had developed a culture which was inseparable from their whole working way of life, and in which their amusements as much as their work made them a distinctive group.[30]

Such customs were not necessarily old, and if they were they may have changed considerably over time. What was significant to the worker was not to be able to trace deep historical roots for his customs, rather his sense that those customs were somehow natural, rightly and properly interconnected with work, and, most important, a fixed and stable point in a threatened world. Whereas in Continental Europe historians have noted the coincidence of social protest and customary festival, in England, where the vigour of popular ceremony had been broken at the time of the Reformation, the celebration of custom was itself meaningful. People clung to customs whose original meaning had been lost.[31] Bamford described how in Middleton on Easter Tuesday, some intoxicated fellow was 'elected' lord mayor; with his face daubed with soot and grease, his hair dusted and a pig-tail stuck on, and dressed in a woman's kirtle, he was taken round demanding dues. The custom was similar to one in Ashton-under-Lyne. Both, according to Bamford, seem to have been held in derisive commemoration of some member of the Assheton family, but Bamford did not pretend that the custom was infused with any of its original meaning; it was simply an enjoyable occasion, rooted in custom, when it was legitimate to ask the wealthy to be charitable.[32] The Lord of MisRule was alive, mocking the distinctions of power and sex, but in a way which seemed to have little meaning for the people beyond the celebration of custom. But that itself was important. The defence of custom linked one generation to another, gave a known rhythm to the work week and the work year, and provided moments of community when community was under stress. Those who tried to work at times of special festivals or in holidays might find the rituals of skimmington or riding the stang directed against them. Custom was used to enforce solidarity.[33]

The defence of custom, then, was a key bargaining factor for workers in a threatened world. It gave legitimacy to resistance to the machine or to the alien ways of new model employers. It might well have the sanction of the smaller master, or, at a very different level, of the Tory romantic. It could indeed exploit that split within the ruling class which we have identified. The language and tone of such a pamphlet as Lord John Manners's *A Plea for National Holy-Days* (1843) might be far removed from the world of the embattled worker defending his way of life, but the sentiment behind both was the same — a desire for a return to custom. Even those whom one might identify as spokesmen of middle-class ideals were by no means immune to the pull of custom. Strutt's celebration of *The Sports and Pastimes of the People of England* (1801) was to have many imitations, not least from radicals like William Hone who produced a new edition of Strutt and added a vast corpus to the tradition with his *Every-Day Book* (1825-7), *Table Book* (1827) and *Year Book* (1832). Hone, the scourge of middle-class religious susceptibilities in 1819, revealed a hankering for a paternalist past in his dedication of the second volume of the *Every-Day Book* to the Earl of Dartington 'as an encourager of the old country sports and usages chiefly treated of in my book, and as a maintainer of the ancient hospitality so closely connected with them, which associated the Peasantry of this land with its Nobles, in bonds which degraded neither'. Later those improving publishers, the Chambers brothers in Edinburgh, added their own *Book of Days* (1863-4) in celebration of the more refined customs of the past. From the 1830s and 1840s when the full horrors of an industrial civilisation burst upon all classes, and when many believed that such a civilisation might be short-lived, the appeal to custom and tradition was a potent one.

For most of these middle-class commentators custom meant the more colourful leisure traditions of the past, not its work habits. Working people could make no such distinction. They were defending a whole way of life, a culture against the demands of capitalism. A defeat in one realm had its clear repercussions in the other; most obviously, more regular work, or longer hours, or an erosion of holidays meant the abandonment of certain leisure customs. And a reform of leisure, such as a restriction on drinking habits, meant inevitably a change in conditions of work. Whereas the middle class could happily separate out and celebrate the customs of leisure without perceiving their relationship to work, for the worker the intimacy and intricacy of the relationship between the two was all too obvious.

There was another problem for the working class in the defence of custom in that some customs were less than praiseworthy. Whereas for the middle class there was no hesitation in carefully discriminating amongst the customs of the past, and recommending only those which were in accordance with the moral values of the present, for working-class people there was more difficulty. Take drink, for example. For the middle class, instinctively, lower-class drinking habits, whether of the past or the present, were to be condemned. Working-class spokesmen were in more of a quandary. From one perspective, that of Place or Lovett, drink could be seen as a main cause of the political and social subordination of the class as a whole. From another drink was a right, a custom and a necessity, and to defend the working man's right to it was at the same time to champion his claims to independence and to a relationship between work and leisure based on something more than the cash nexus.[34] Other customs, such as the brutal sports, found fewer vocal supporters among the working class. Customary they might be, but to defend them was to ally oneself with reaction.

Even for working people, therefore, the defence of custom had its ambiguities and difficulties. The tension embedded in the defence of custom, lying in the fact that custom implied turning one's back on the future, became greater as time went on. Until mid-century, however, that tension could be contained. The new forms of leisure, whose rise we documented in the first chapter, could all be absorbed into a customary relationship between work and leisure. They occurred episodically, and were designed to fit customary annual cycles of work and leisure. By mid-century, however, for those workers in industries where the machine or a new work ethic had come to dominate, custom was ceasing to have much value. And at the same time the entrepreneurs of entertainment were beginning to see new commercial possibilities in a world where leisure was both more regular and more separate from work.

Notes

1. A. Clayre, *Work and Play* (New York, 1974), pp. 142-68; K. Thomas, 'Work and Leisure in Pre-industrial Society', *Past & Present*, no. 29 (1964), pp. 50-62;

1. Blanchard, 'Labour Productivity and Work Psychology in the English Mining Industry, 1400-1600', *Economic History Review*, 2nd ser., vol. XXXI (1978), pp. 1-24.

2. E.P. Thompson, 'Patrician Society, Plebeian Culture', *Journal of Social History*, vol. VII (1974), pp. 384-7.

3. M.A. Bienefeld, *Working Hours in British Industry* (London, 1972), pp. 8-40; E.P. Thompson, 'Eighteenth-century English Society: Class Struggle without Class?' *Social History*, vol. III (1978), p. 153.

4. S. Pollard, 'Factory Discipline', p. 256.

5. R.G. Kirby and A.E. Musson, *The Voice of the People* (Manchester, 1975), pp. 346-406; G. Langenfelt, *The Historic Origin of the Eight Hours Day* (Stockholm, 1954), pp. 3, 53-126; J. Foster, *Class Struggle and the Industrial Revolution* (London, 1974), pp. 110-11.

6. Quoted in J.T. Ward, *The Factory Movement 1830-55* (London, 1962), p. 152.

7. R. Guest, *A Compendious History of the Cotton Manufacture* (London, 1968), pp. 38-9; P. Gaskell, *Artisans and Machinery* (London, 1968), pp. 18-19, 23, 181-4.

8. F. Engels, *The Condition of the Working Class in England* (London, 1969), esp. pp. 37-9; W.H. Chaloner (ed.), *The Autobiography of Samuel Bamford* (1st edn 1848-9, London, 1967), vol. I, pp. 131-2.

9. P.E. Razzell and R.W. Wainwright, *The Victorian Working Class*, p. 185; Children's Employment Commission, App. to 2nd Report of Commissioners (Trade & Manufactures), PP 1843 (431), vol. XIV, p. 642.

10. L. Faucher, *Manchester in 1844* (London, 1969), p. 122.

11. Select Committee on Mills and Factories, Minutes of Evidence, PP 1840 (203), vol. X, qq. 384-5, 392, 4047-53; 1816 quote from Ward, *The Factory Movement*, p. 24.

12. J. Obelkevich, *Religion and Rural Society* (Oxford, 1976), pp. 57-9, 69-70; Select Committee on Health of Towns, Minutes of Evidence, PP 1840 (384), vol. XI, q. 1257; Bienefeld, *Working Hours in British Industry*, p. 30.

13. D. Bythell, *The Sweated Trades* (London, 1978); K. Marx, *Capital*, vol. I, pp. 244-59.

14. J.F.C. Harrison, *The Early Victorians* (London, 1971), pp. 39-45.

15. Bienefeld, *Working Hours in British Industry*, pp. 20-81; Hobhouse quoted in J. Clapham, *Economic History of Modern Britain*, vol. II (London, 1932), p. 448; *Ten Hour Advocate*, 13 October 1846, quoted in M. Hodgson, 'The Working Day and the Working Week in Victorian Britain 1840-1900' (unpublished Univ. of London M.Phil Thesis, 1974), p. 36 and passim for a most helpful discussion of these issues; C.M. Smith, *The Working Man's Way in the World* (London, 1967), pp. 184-7; S. and B. Webb, *Industrial Democracy* (London, 1920), p. 352 n.1.

16. R. Samuel, 'Mineral Workers' in Samuel (ed.), *Miners, Quarrymen and Saltworkers* (London, 1977), p. 51.

17. R.C. on Children in Mines and Manufactories, PP 1842, vol. XV, pp. 122-5.

18. J.G. Rule, 'The Labouring Miner in Cornwall *c.* 1740-1870' (unpublished Univ. of Warwick PhD Thesis, 1971), pp. 73-80; C.J. Hunt, *The Lead Miners of the Northern Pennines* (Manchester, 1970), pp. 224-7.

19. For weavers see S. Pollard, 'Factory Discipline', p. 256; T. Wright, *Some Habits and Customs of the Working Classes* (New York, 1967), pp. 108-30; E.P. Thompson, 'Time, Work-Discipline, and Industrial Capitalism', *Past & Present*, no. 38 (1967), p. 74; cf. D. Reid, 'The Decline of Saint Monday 1766-1876', *Past & Present*, no. 71 (1976), pp. 76-101.

20. C. Shaw, *When I was a Child* (Caliban Books, Firle, Sussex, 1977), pp. 31, 47-54.

21. A.L. Lloyd, *Folk Song in England* (London, 1969), pp. 321-3.

22. R. Colls, *The Collier's Rant*, pp. 14-56; Lloyd, *Folk Song in England*, pp. 351-3.

23. A.L. Lloyd, *The Iron Muse, a Panorama of Industrial Folk Song* (Topic Records, London).

24. S.C. on Inquiry into Drunkenness PP 1834 (559), vol. VIII, qq. 4610-98, 2006-12, 2036; S.C. on Public Libraries, PP 1849, vol. XVII, qq. 2783-4.

25. C.M. Smith, *The Working Man's Way*, pp. 249-58, 304; Shaw, *When I was a Child*, pp. 71-3, 76-8; cf. W.E. Adams, *Memoirs of a Social Atom*, p. 84.

26. Razzell and Wainwright, *Victorian Working Class*, p. 147.

27. Quoted in J.L. and B. Hammond, *The Skilled Labourer 1760-1832* (London, 1919), pp. 212-13.

28. E.P. Thompson, *The Making of the English Working Class* (London, 1963), chs viii and xvi, esp p. 711; cf. G. Stedman Jones, 'Class Expression versus Social Control? A Critique of Recent Trends in the Social History of "Leisure" ', *History Workshop*, no. 4 (1977), p. 169.

29. Razzell and Wainwright, *Victorian Working Class*, pp. 135-6, 149.

30. H. Mayhew, *London Labour and the London Poor*, 4 vols. (London, n.d. [1861-2]), vol. I, pp. 13-22.

31. P. Burke, *Popular Culture in Early Modern Europe*, pp. 203-4; Thompson, 'Patrician Society', p. 394.

32. W.H. Chaloner, *Autobiography of Samuel Bamford*, pp. 138-43.

33. E.P. Thompson, ' "Rough Music": Le Charivari anglais', *Annales*, vol. 27 (1972), pp. 285-312.

34. B. Harrison, 'Teetotal Chartism', *History*, vol. 58 (1973), pp. 193-217; W. Godwin, *Thoughts on Man* (New York, 1969), pp. 177-80.

3   PUBLIC LEISURE AND PRIVATE LEISURE

For much of the eighteenth century in both town and country most people had access to some kind of public space: space which they might use individually — to walk on, to pursue game in, to graze animals on — or collectively — as the forum for political activity or communal entertainment. Such space was public in the sense that it was owned communally and belonged to everyone; hence everyone had equal rights to it. In the later eighteenth century the wealthy tried, successfully in many instances, to appropriate these public spaces for their own exclusive use, to privatise them. At the same time, and as a corollary to it, they frowned on and became suspicious of public gatherings of the lower orders for whatever purpose. The result was that leisure became increasingly class-bound. The leisure class retreated to the home or to those fenced-off private enclosures where they might look at pictures or botanical specimens, or listen to music, safe in the knowledge that they would meet only their own kind. And those thus excluded sought new patrons in publicans whose upper rooms or backyards could host a variety of entertainments unseen by their social superiors. The privatisation of property, that is, entailed for all classes a privatisation of leisure, privatisation in the sense that leisure became class-bound and impenetrable for those outside the class in question.

By the end of the first quarter of the nineteenth century, some members of the middle class had become alarmed at this process and guilty at their own class's role in bringing it about. They sought to create a new kind of public leisure to counteract it: with leisure space and leisure facilities provided by government or by charity, patronage could be renewed, and the leisure of the people would be visible and controlled. This kind of public leisure they called rational recreation.

We can sense something of the earlier public and communal leisure in the description of Middleton at the turn of the century which Samuel Bamford recorded in the 1840s. In Bamford's memory this already industrial village with a population of some 3,000 expressed itself as a community through its leisure. On Easter Wednesday, 'White Apron Fair', it was the custom for 'the young wives and mothers, with their children, and also for the young marriageable damsels, to walk out to display their finery, and to get conducted by their husbands, or their sweethearts, to the ale-house, where they generally finished by a dance, and their inamoratos by a bottle or two, and their consequences, bruised hides and torn clothes.' And at the Wakes on the third Saturday in August there was rush-bearing to the church. Each hamlet sent its own rush-cart, and there were often fights between the different carts. Everyone wore new clothes, and the carts were accompanied by their own musicians and sometimes morrice dancers. The women's role was to help prepare the rush-cart.[1] Leisure involved strife, it was age-specific, sometimes sex-specific, but it took place within a context of community and in public. Ideally, perhaps, it expressed the harmonious solidarity of a community, with the rich offering their benevolent patronage, but it might also be a way by which the conflicts within a community could be worked through whether by the ritual fights between the different hamlets or by some reversal of roles in which for a day the poor took on the attributes and power of the rich.

In evoking this customary world in the second quarter of the nineteenth century the romantics were in some sense creating a myth. But like all myths it bore some relation to reality. For the attack on popular leisure in the late eighteenth century, together with the growth of class-specific sports and pastimes such as spa-visiting, shooting and hunting, sapped the strength of the tradition of public and communal leisure. As the rich developed a leisure life of their own they became increasingly intolerant and suspicious of the remnants of that leisure which they had once patronised but now abhorred. What had once been harmless customs could become perceived as, and be the occasion for, class conflict; not some tension-reducing ritual, but a state of permanent strife. Even in Bamford's Middleton we can see this process occurring when a much-frequented bowling green on one side of the church 'was broken up and the games put a stop to, chiefly, it was said, because the late steward under the Suffields could not, when he resorted to the place, overawe, or keep the rustic frequenters in such respectful bounds as he wished to do'.[2]

The public, annual and often customary sports, those which ranged through a whole community, were the most obvious target for reformers. They offended against the privatisation of property, against the business life of a community and any sense of work ethic, and against notions of decorous behaviour. The best known of these sports is the Stamford bull-running which came to an end in 1840 only after a protracted struggle since 1833 involving the Home Office, the metropolitan police, the army and the RSPCA as well as local interests. The custom involved running the bull through the town onto the bridge and then heaving it into the river. The bullard's song suggests some of the commotion which might be caused in such a busy thoroughfare as Stamford:

> Come, take him by the tail, boys,
> Bridge, bridge him if you can;
> Prog him with a stick, boys,
> Never let him quiet stand.
> Through every street and lane in town
> We'll chevy-chase him up and down.'

It was when the citizens began to count the cost of the bull-running that they decided it was time to bring an end to the custom.[3]

In Derby it was the Shrove Tuesday and Ash Wednesday football that became the centre of controversy. In 1845 the clergy, tradesmen, manufacturers and a large portion of the working classes sent a requisition to the Mayor claiming that the game gave rise

> to the assembling of a lawless rabble, suspending business to the loss of the industrious, creating terror and alarm to the timid and peaceable, committing violence on the persons and damage to the properties of the defenceless and poor, and producing in those who play moral degradation and in many extreme poverty, injury to health, fractured limbs and (not infrequently) loss of life . . .

If in this one senses a certain exaggeration it is because it was the expression of a clash of cultures. Popular recreation, as Tony Delves points out, was in general 'public, improvised and inconclusive', much of it taking place in the street, whereas that of their opponents was increasingly regular and privatised. In Derby, interestingly, there was a third party, the 'liberal recreationists', who opposed the forms rather than the very existence of popular recreation. Rather than simply suppress football they tried to counter its popularity by promoting in opposition to it first athletics, and then, more successfully, horseracing. Racing took place under the control of the rich in a defined area where there was no likelihood of the business of the town being interfered with; rather it might be enhanced.[4]

It was again in the 1840s that the Leicester practice of 'whipping toms', another annual Shrove Tuesday occasion, came under attack. According to Throsby, who described the sport in 1791 'two, three, or more men, armed with cartwhips, and with a handkerchief tied over one eye, are let loose upon the people to flog them, who are, in general guarded with boots on their legs and sticks in their hands. These whip-men, called *Whipping-Toms*, are preceded by a bell-man, whose shake of his hand-bell gives a token or authority for whipping the legs of those who dare to remain in the Newark'. Ironically the custom seems to have been originally instituted by the dwellers in the Newark in order to drive away the rabble. It became a general threat to the business and decorum of the town. A local Act was passed against the practice, but this did not prevent serious clashes in 1846 and 1847 between the people who were anxious to continue the sport and the police.[5]

In all these cases there was a quite violent dispute at the end of the first phase of the Industrial Revolution about the use of space. Space which formerly had been thought of as common and public, a centre for communal activity, was now being commandeered for use by (or according to the moral standards of) one class only. The growth of towns entailed class segregation and a breakdown of any customary sense of community. Although this can be demonstrated most dramatically by looking at these conflicts over customary annual sports, its impact may have been felt more harshly in day-to-day recreation.

Consider swimming. Naked bathing seems to have been a popular sport amongst working-class youths, but its practice in river or canal was increasingly hazardous. In London 'from a desire to promote public decency', bathing had been prohibited and 'the poorer classes bathe in the canal from Limehouse to Bromley at their peril, being sometimes taken into custody for it'. The police, reported a London coroner,'drive the children now from points where they were accustomed to go, and where they understood the depth of the water; and in order to avoid them they get into deeper water and are frequently drowned; that has been repeatedly the case in sports in the river Lea.' There, a decade later, 500 or 600 boys aged 16 to 17, might be seen swimming. In some towns there seems to have been prolonged skirmishing between the desire of the working class to bathe in ways in which, as the Borough-reeve of Manchester put it, 'the sense of shame is very frequently taken away', and that of authority keen to protect the respectable from the distressing sight of proletarian nudity. It was reported in 1833 that working men and boys in Birmingham 'generally bathe in the canal in the summer, which is very offensive to women walking along the towing path. The practice is now forbid by the proprietors of the canal, although it is continued'. And a Sheffield doctor, keen on bathing, was nevertheless anxious not to 'allow them to bathe in the more frequented districts of the town as they do at present, to the great annoyance of respectable females'.[6]

The problem of space, we can see, was as much social as geographical; that is to say, one of the effects of the Industrial Revolution was
to create towns where the rich wanted to demarcate zones for their
exclusive use. They achieved this in part by creating their own suburbs,
but they needed also to establish their own standards in any part of the
town with which they might come into contact. Increasingly they chose
to do this by commandeering parts of towns which were formerly
public to their own private and exclusive use. 'The loss of playgrounds',
which the Hammonds rightly lamented,[7] was not an inevitable consequence of urbanisation and industrialisation; it was the outcome of
decisions to enclose this piece of land here, to stop up that footpath
there, to exclude the poor from this or that facility.

Nor was this simply an urban problem. The privatisation of property
was as apparent in open country and in villages as in the towns. The enclosure of open fields and the game laws had quite as great an impact
on long-established communal rights as the sprawling buildings of the
new towns. Muriel Ashby describes the processes at work at Tysoe in
Warwickshire:

> Land had formerly been like the falling rain, free alike in some
> measure to the just and the unjust. On foot or on your pony you
> could thread your way by balk and headland over to any village in the
> neighbourhood, but some of these were set miles further away by
> the new private fields. Now the very Red Horse itself had been
> penned up within hedges, without even a footpath past it. The old
> Whitsun Games were never held again. The enclosure of the open
> fields was a visible sign and symbol that rampant family and indi-
> vidual power had gained a complete victory over the civic comm-
> unity.

As to the game laws, a grandfather in Wreyland in Devonshire in 1854,
wrote thus:

> In my growing up we heard nothing of game preserving hereabout,
> and game was in abundance; and at certain seasons you could see at
> times all classes of people out for a day's sport. They would kill but
> little; but then it was an amusement, and a day's holy-day, and
> apparently an unrestricted right to go where they liked unmolested:
> so they enjoyed a right old English liberty, and came home tired and
> happy, not caring whether they had game or not. But since the game
> is preserved,and they are restrained from killing it in the old way,

they appear determined to kill it some way or another. Consequently game is not so plenty now as heretofore.[8]

All over the country the closure of footpaths was deeply resented. An Act passed in 1815 allowed footpaths to be closed by any landowner who could obtain the sanction of two JPs and the confirmation of the next Quarter Sessions. This of course left the poor with very little chance to assert their rights. By 1833 D.W. Harvey, MP, was complaining that 'the arbitrary power lately assumed by Magistrates enclosing footpaths had engendered much discontent among the poorer classes, who were thereby shut out from all means of wholesome recreation'. In the following year Edwin Chadwick reported how 'In the rural districts, as well as in the vicinities of some of the towns, I have heard very strong representations of the mischiefs of the stoppage of footpaths and ancient walks, as contributing, with the extensive and indiscriminate inclosure of commons which were play-grounds, to drive the labouring classes to the public-house'.[9]

It was undoubtedly in towns that the loss of space was most frequently commented on. The problem was first apparent, naturally enough, in London. Strutt complained in 1801 that 'The general decay of those manly and spirited exercises, which formerly were practised in the vicinity of the metropolis has not arisen from any want of inclination in the people, but from the want of places proper for the purpose: such as in time past had been allotted to them are now covered with buildings, or shut up by enclosures . . .' The pressure on space increased. In evidence before the Select Committee on Public Walks in 1833, John Stock, magistrate, stated that 'the humbler classes are now deprived of all the means of athletic exercises, from having no place to exercise themselves'. He remembered 'the fields at the back of the British Museum being covered every night in the summer by at least from one hundred to two hundred people, at cricket and other sports', and the site of the West India Docks being formerly a popular bathing place 'to which hundreds resorted every summer's evening'.[10]

Pressure of space had also hit a favoured and favourite form of recreation for the working class, allotments. In London, as we have seen, the Spitalfields weavers had found their allotments taken away from them. In Birmingham in 1833 it was the custom 'for the working men to have gardens at about a guinea a year rent, of which there are a great number round the town, and all the better parts of the workmen spend their leisure hours there; a considerable portion of land in the immediate vicinity of Birmingham is let at 12 l. an acre for these small gardens'. Families spent their evenings and Sundays in these little gardens with their summer houses. By 1849 all had changed: 'the expansion of the town on all sides has almost swept the whole of them away, and the goods station of the London and North-Western Railway occupies the site of many scores of them. Only a few now remain, in the neighbourhood of the two Vauxhalls; and it is likely that these will be speedily swept away by the rapid extension of streets, factories, and railway stations.'[11]

Public open spaces were being lost. Many years ago the Hammonds described how in Oldham and in Gateshead enclosures were carried out without any land for recreation being set aside; how in Coventry land on which the weavers had been accustomed to spend much of their leisure time in 'football and quoits, and bandy, and cricket' was now enclosed and part of the property of the Marquis of Hertford. Town after town in the 1840s could produce evidence of open spaces which had been shut up. 'In Sunderland', reported D.B. Reid, 'as in other towns visited, a strong impression was conveyed to me that the public are deprived of rights which at former periods they have been accustomed to enjoy . . .'[12]

This loss of public rights, the rich began to realise, was due less to any economic rationale than to class consciousness. George Offer, a London magistrate appearing before the 1833 Select Committee on Public Walks, 'often regretted the places, when I was a boy, where I used to play and amuse myself, are now entirely shut up, and devoted either to buildings or to *places of promenade for the higher classes*'. Great Tower-hill, for instance, had been enclosed, 'and none but the aristocracy are permitted to come in'.[13] Formerly public areas were being set aside for the private recreation of the rich. A sense of shock, of anger, can be detected in the writings of the more sensitive middle-class writers as they face the enormity of what has been done. Here is William Cooke Taylor, the Anti-Corn Law Leaguer in his *Tour of the Manufacturing Districts of Lancashire* (1841):

Hitherto nearly all our legislation on the subject of the amusements of the poor has been penal and restrictive; while a sour, jealous, and selfish spirit has led to a series of encroachments on their comforts and enjoyments which has far outstripped the intentions of the legislature. The commons on which the labourers indulged in healthful sports are enclosed; policemen guard the streets and keep the highways clear; high walls enclose demesnes, and even the high palisades that surround ornamental gardens are jealously planked over to prevent the humble operatives from enjoying the verdure of the foliage or the fragrance of the flowers. It is quite enough to say that a 'Footpath Protection Society' exists in Manchester: the necessity for such an institution at once establishes not merely the want of sympathy for the pleasures of the poor, but something like a determination to deprive them of their pleasure by robbery and usurpation.[14]

Indeed in the 1830s and more strongly in the 1840s the middle class began to realise that many of its efforts at cultural advancement had been for itself alone, and often at the expense of the working class. The zoological and botanical gardens, the libraries and museums, the Athenaeums and art galleries which had become features of any self-respecting town in the late eighteenth and early nineteenth centuries were almost exclusively private ventures, run for profit or financed out of subscriptions which were beyond the means of working people. True the latter might occasionally be admitted, but it was on sufferance, not as of right. In 1760 The Society of Arts opened its exhibition to the public, but quickly regretted the experiment, as the room was 'crowded and incommoded by the intrusion of great numbers whose stations and education made them no proper judges of statuary or painting and who were made idle and tumultuous by the opportunity of a show'. 'Until the eighteen thirties', writes C.P. Darcy, 'a definite mercantile and upper class bias pervaded provincial aesthetic enterprises.' And even after that date, one may add, a certain lack of realism surrounds attempts to broaden the social base of their enterprises. The Manchester Art Union, for example, in 1840 wanted 'all classes to become acquainted with, and likewise possessed of, works of art, which will greatly assist in forming a chaster and more correct taste in all ranks of life, but especially among the artisans and others employed in our various manufactures.' Since the Union's annual subscription was one guinea one may question the likelihood of it succeeding while noting the condescension of its aims.[15]

One consequence of the blocking off of public rights, it came to be believed, was that the poor became increasingly driven to the beer-houses for their recreation. And the latter were quite definitely not places which the respectable could patronise. Cooke Taylor ended the passage quoted above with this sentence: 'Excluded, partly by law, but chiefly by the spirit of class, from nobler pleasures, he [the mechanic] is driven, by a force not less stringent than any natural power in the universe, to seek the joys of gin and brandy, to find exercise for his mental energies in the impure dreams of intoxication and the miserable distractions of debauchery.'[16]

This was a world that the respectable could only observe with dismay from the outside. For just as middle-class leisure became privatised so inevitably working-class leisure had to follow suit. Driven from the public domain by the withdrawal of patronage and by law, the animal sports found refuge in the upper rooms and backyards of pubs. So did much else. As Brian Harrison has shown, the pub was a supplier not only of a drink comparable in price to tea and coffee, and safer than water or milk, but also of light, of heat, of lavatories, of newspapers, of books and of companionship.[17] Competition amongst drink-sellers led to an expansion of the facilities offered; as John Finch, iron merchant of Liverpool and temperance advocate, complained in 1833, the publicans and beer-house keepers

> institute clubs of various kinds, benefit societies, political societies, money clubs, clothing clubs, watch clubs, clock clubs, furniture clubs, building, or a hundred other clubs; they also get up what they call in the country wakes; once in the year, bull-baiting is also resorted to, for the purpose of increasing the sale of intoxicating liquors; also quoit-playing, bowling, wrestling, running, boxing, horse-racing, gaming, card-playing, etc.

Friendly societies nearly always met in pubs. In Nottingham there were libraries in pubs, in Leeds theatre clubs. Musical life was often pub-centred, even classical and religious music.[18] In Pudsey in the 1820s, as Joseph Lawson recalled, 'there were only two places to go in spending spare time away from one's own home − the church or chapel, and the alehouse; the former was seldom open, while the latter was seldom closed.' The pub was open and welcoming, not too concerned about the dress or manners of the customers, and hence *terra incognita* only to those with standards to maintain. For most people there was nowhere else to go; for if the inhabitant of Pudsey had travelled to a larger centre like Leeds he would still have found, according to Thomas Beggs, that before the foundation of the first Mechanics' Institute there was 'no amusement, no recreation that a man could resort to except it was connected with a public-house'.[19]

The private world of drink-based entertainment was expanding; of that contemporaries were in no doubt. And the cause was not only the aggressive competition of drink-sellers, or the withdrawal by the wealthy from the open patronage of entertainment; it lay also in legislative changes. By a supreme irony the free traders, the campaigning spokesmen of the middle class, seemed to have paved the way for the drink-sellers. In 1825 in England the spirit duty was reduced, and despite predictions that if drink like bread was easily accessible and cheap there would be less demand for it, the revenue from spirits rose, and so did the number of spirit-retailing licences. The era of the gin palace began. It was in large part in the hope of halting its spread that the beer trade was emancipated. From 1830 any householder assessed for the poor rates could obtain from the excise, for the sum of two guineas a year, a licence to sell beer on or off the premises. Although the effects of this on consumption were probably not more than immediate and temporary, they were widely thought to have been so. Moreover by removing authority for licensing from the magistrates, the Act helped to emancipate popular culture from upper-class control. From 1830 onwards the temperance and then the teetotal movement tried to counteract this growing world of drink-based entertainment, moved no doubt in part by a sense that it was the middle and upper classes who were responsible for its existence.[20]

Similarly the abuse of Sunday leisure seemed to many to be the outcome of the efforts of the Sabbatarians. The attempt to enforce Sunday observance had a long history in England. The Society for the Suppression of Vice, like Societies for the Reformation of Manners in the eighteenth century, concentrated its efforts on the proper observance of Sunday. Sabbatarians were perhaps mainly concerned with preventing economic activity on Sundays, but they were also and increasingly alarmed at the amount of commercialised leisure on that day, in particular the river excursions from the big towns. Lower-class Londoners headed downstream to Gravesend or upstream to Richmond. The Gravesend Company ran two or three boats every Sunday, competing with its rival, the Margate Steam-boat Company, which carried up to 1,000 passengers. To a non-Sabbatarian there was something positive in all this, certainly nothing offensive; as the agent to the Gravesend Company put it, 'you generally find that they disembark at Gravesend, walk up to the Windmill, and you generally find them spreading their little cloths, and taking their refreshments on the grass; but I must say that I have never seen anything like a tumult or anything like disorder'. The agent, however, was on the defensive, putting the case for his Company before the Sabbatarian 1831-2 Select Committee on the Observance of the Sabbath Day.

It was in 1831 that the Lord's Day Observance Society was formed, and it was soon followed by attempts to persuade Parliament to pass stricter Sunday Observance laws. These, sponsored by the Recordite

Evangelical, Sir Andrew Agnew, all failed, but not without causing much alarm to their opponents. One of the latter was Charles Dickens who, like the Gravesend Company's agent, found the Sunday excursionists 'neat and clean, cheerful and contented', but recognised that there was also another side to Sunday. 'In some parts of London, and in many of the manufacturing towns of England', he wrote, 'drunkenness and profligacy in their most disgusting forms, exhibit in the open streets on Sunday, a sad and a degrading spectacle'. The cause of this, he believed, was not the inherent wickedness or lack of religion of the poor, but the refusal of the Sabbatarians to allow respectable but secular entertainment on that day. Moreover the efforts of the Sabbatarians, he believed, were directed exclusively against the poor.[21]

Dickens was not alone in so thinking. The Sabbatarians were driving the people to drink. 'The more rigorously the Sabbath is observed', wrote Leon Faucher, 'the more frequented are the public-houses and gin-shops'. Joseph Paxton could point to a specific example. Chatsworth had traditionally been open on Sundays, and up to 800 people from Sheffield would come to visit. In the 1840s it was closed, and almost the same number of people came 'to revel at the public-houses, and create great disturbances'. The Duke of Devonshire then reopened the house, and since that time, said Paxton, 'there has been no difficulty about the public-house nuisance on Sunday in our district at all'. The Select Committee on Public Houses of 1853-4 to which Paxton was giving evidence called 'attention to the fact of how few places of rational enjoyment are open to the great mass of the population on Sunday, which serve as a counter-attraction to the public-house. They have it in evidence that wherever such opportunities have been provided, they have been eagerly seized upon, and have led to the decrease of intemperance'. Open the British Museum and the National Gallery on Sunday afternoon, people claimed, and there would be an immediate reform of manners. It was a cry uttered with confidence in the 1830s: 'It would appear that the doors were purposely closed against the lower classes', wrote James Hogg: 'would it not be good policy to throw open these interesting halls on the Sundays, and during Christmas, Easter, and Autumn, every day, and all day long, by which the orgies of the gin shop, and the saturnalia of Bartholomew's and Greenwich fairs might be superseded?' So great, however, was the opposition of the Sabbatarians that it was not until 1896 that Hogg's objective of Sunday afternoon opening was achieved.[22]

During the second quarter of the nineteenth century middle-class reformers came increasingly to believe that it was their own class which was to blame for much of the dissoluteness and drunkenness of working-class recreation. By the laws which they had passed and by their own class exclusiveness they were driving the poor to the private world of drink and drink-based entertainment. They felt both guilty and alarmed.

But it was not merely these clearly unrespectable forms of leisure which alarmed the middle class. Other forms of leisure, stemming from the religious and the secular radical culture, were equally privatised. In 1799 the Lincolnshire clergy expressed their alarm at 'those more private assemblies, which are generally known by the name of classed meetings, and at which those persons preside who do not take upon themselves the name of Teachers or Preachers'. As W.R. Ward comments, 'The meetings which were fully public to the village labourers were "more private" to the clergy; their worlds had moved apart'. And within the secular radical culture the Chartists and Owenites created an elaborate culture of leisure which at least in some areas was also an assertion of working-class independence. With their celebration of the birthday of Owen at Whitsun, with their habit of behaving with maximum hilarity at the most solemn times in the Christian year, and with the halls which they built in at least twelve towns in 1839-40, the Owenites were creating a leisure life for their communities, but one which excluded their social superiors.[23] If the kind of order in which the middle class believed was going to be achieved some challenge had to be offered to such overt claims to independence on the part of the people.

From the late eighteenth century onwards middle-class reformers sought to counteract this increasing privatisation of working-class leisure. Their first gambit was to re-emphasise paternalism. In 1787 Sheridan and Windham had been associated in projecting a society for the encouragement of ancient games.[24] Nothing seems to have come of this, but the fact that the idea was mooted is indicative of an awareness that patronage might need to be organised, that it might no longer flow naturally from the very structure of society. On the local level such attempts at organisation continued and had more success. At Necton in Norfolk in 1817 Col Mason established a guild or festival for rural sports. Ten years later Mason was to receive the approval of Hone in his *Every-Day Book*: 'Arranged under his immediate patronage, and conducted by his principal tenantry, it soon became, and still continues, the most respectable resort of Whitsuntide festivities in Norfolk.' Similarly Charles Tomlinson reflected favourably on the Hungerford Revel in 1820: 'I think it may be generally allowed that Wiltshire, and the western counties, keep up their primitive customs more than any counties. This is greatly to the credit of the inhabitants; for these usages tend to promote cheerful intercourse and friendly feeling among the residents in the different villages, who on such occasions assemble together.' The activities on these occasions were deliberately tradition-al — the maypole, backsword and single stick.[25] The aim was clear — to recreate or to preserve a world in which leisure was a public expression of social harmony and rural hierarchy. Examples of such activity are relatively rare, but they provide a thread of continuity between the trad-itional patronage of rural sports in the mid-eighteenth century and the full-scale revival of rural paternalism in the mid-nineteenth century.

Paternalism could also be attempted in an urban context. In West Bromwich in the 1840s the Earl of Dartmouth lent four acres 'for the use of the poorer inhabitants, at wakes and festivals, who enjoy them-selves, under the management of a committee of subscribers, in ath-letic sports, races, and rustic exercises'. 'I have reason to believe', com-mented Robert Slaney, 'this nobleman adopted this plan to wean the people from bull-baiting and other cruel amusements, by substituting something better in their place. He seems to have succeeded complet-ely in his laudable object . . .'[26] In towns a 'committee of subscribers' might play the role of the rural 'principal tenantry' but the aim was the same, to counteract the tendency towards the privatisation of the leisure of the poor, to make it once again public, open and communal.

There was a second and quite different approach to the problem of reforming lower-class leisure, and once again it was first evident in the later eighteenth century. This was to refine the privatisation of leisure by centering it in the home as a place of family affection and quiet pleasures. Wilberforce lamented that the man of irregularity and excess 'has no fireside comforts'. 'Firesides' — it is an evocative word, redolent of tradition, but of a cosy and sober tradition, not the tradition of rural sports, of climbing greasy poles. 'Happiness', wrote the Quaker William Howitt in 1838,

> does not consist in booths and garlands, drums and horns, or in capering round a May-pole. Happiness is a fire-side thing. It is a thing of grave and earnest tone; and the deeper and truer it is, the more it is removed from the riot of mere merriment . . . the more our humble classes come to taste of the pleasures of books and intel-lect, and the deep fire-side affections which grow out of the growth of heart and mind, the less charms will the outward forms of rejoic-ing have for them.

Tradition, community itself, could henceforth be celebrated not on the village green but round the fireside with a book, in private. Such was the intention of Robert Chambers as he made clear in the preface to *The Book of Days* (1863-4):

> It has been his desire as Editor, while not discouraging the progressive spirit of the age, to temper it with affectionate feeling towards what is poetical and elevated, honest and of good report, in the old national life; while in no way discountenancing great material interests, to evoke an equal activity in those feelings beyond self, on which depend remoter but infinitely greater interests; to kindle and sustain a spirit of patriotism tending to unity, peace, and prosperity in our own state, while not exclusive of benevolence as well as justice, towards others. It was desired that these volumes should be a repository of old fireside ideas in general, as well as a means of improving the fireside wisdom of the present day.

In this comforting imagery there was a certain amount of cant, as Mayhew was quick to recognise. 'It is idle and unfeeling', he wrote, 'to believe that the great majority of a people whose days are passed in excessive toil, and whose homes are mostly of an uninviting character, will forego *all* amusements, and consent to pass their evenings by their *no* firesides, reading tracts or singing hymns'.[27] To many it was the fireside of the pub which beckoned, and it was precisely that which the reformers wanted to damp down.

Perhaps no one believed in the fireside as a total solution to the problem of leisure. Wilberforce had this much in common with Windham that he did not object to the 'innocent amusements' of the common people, 'their festivals, their gambols, their athletic exercises'; he did not disown the condescending language of patronage. And from a different and unpatronising stance Howitt could wish 'Joy . . . to all fairgoers!'[28] What they did believe, however, was that a contented home was the only possible foundation for a real enjoyment of public and communal activity, and that it was the proper alternative to the increasingly private leisure of the drinking place.

Neither the revived patronage of rural sports nor the celebration of the fireside were adequate solutions to the problem of leisure as it was perceived by reformers in the early nineteenth century. The real solution, they came to believe, lay in the provision by themselves of new kinds of public leisure appropriate to an urban and industrial society. Perceiving a danger to society in the class-specific and privatised nature of leisure they sought to create new forms of leisure where the classes

could mix in a controlled and public environment. In the first half of
the century and beyond an enormous amount of energy and initiative
was put into this attempt, and the outcome both in ideology and in
material form was to have an abiding influence on the future shape of
leisure. The museums, the public parks, the libraries, the musical life
of the nation, the belief that leisure time should be spent in some
improvement of self and society, all owe much to this movement which
contemporaries came to call 'rational recreation'.

Rational recreation was not something invented by the middle class
for imposition on the working class. Its roots lay in middle-class experience itself, in the problem felt by that growing eighteenth-century
leisure class which had an excess of time on its hands and yet wished to
avoid aristocratic dissipation. Rationality implied both order and control. Jane Austen conveys to us its early nineteenth-century meaning in
writing of Charles Musgrove in *Persuasion* that '. . . a woman of real
understanding might have given more consequence to his character, and
more usefulness, rationality, and elegance to his habits and pursuits. As
it was, he did nothing with much zeal, but sport; and his time was
otherwise trifled away, without benefit from books, or anything else'.
Sport, with its aristocratic connotations, was not rational, books were.
So too was music. The middle-class Miss Iremonger recorded in 1786
how 'every evening my Pianoforte takes its share with the two Violins,
and we form a concert which, I think, a delightful rational amusement'.
She had found a happy solution to that search for forms of leisure
which filled the vacuum of time in an improving and yet non-utilitarian
way.

Entrepreneurs were alert to the requirements. The Norwich newspapers were advertising 'Rational Amusements' as early as 1775. In
1800 a Mr Lloyd advertised a series of lectures on astronomy in the
Bath Journal as 'An amusement so rational, upon an apparatus so
voluminous, explanatory and expensive', and in 1815 the Bath Literary
and Philosophical Society reassured anxious parents that the Society's
activities 'will afford a desirable opportunity of weekly rational recreation for their sons'.[29]

Until the 1820s rational recreation was a movement of and for the
middle class. The institutions it created – the circulating libraries, for
example, or the Assembly Rooms or the subscription concerts – were
class-specific, excluding by their fees and their social tone any members
of the lower orders. As a culture it was deliberately exclusive. Within it
leisure activities should be controlled, ordered and improving; they
should confirm and enhance one's social status; and they should be

essentially secular, consonant with religious belief, but not themselves intrinsically religious. They were rational because they implied a distrust of the emotions, and a supremacy of mind over body. It was the former not the latter which required recreation.

Guilty at their own exclusiveness, worried about its consequences, middle-class missionaries began to preach rational recreation to the working class. The enemy against which rational recreation was now posing itself was not vacuous idleness or aristocratic dissipation but the popular culture with its emphases on drink, on spontaneity, on emotional involvement, on physical contact. Ordered, disciplined, improving, educational leisure was what the rational recreationists hoped for. More than this they wanted leisure to be uplifted from its privatised class-specific locations, and become once more public and communal. They had to create new space for leisure, space where the classes could meet with both decorum and social ease.

It is easy to represent the rational recreation movement as a somewhat crude attempt at social control — an attempt to impose middle-class values and norms on a resisting working class. It would be foolish, indeed impossible, to ignore this side of rational recreation. But there is another side. Rational recreation as it came to be preached to the working class had its origins in guilt as well as in fear; in consequence there was a positive urge to open up to the working class cultural and aesthetic experiences from which it had previously been excluded. Books, museums, exhibitions, music, all these cultural goods from the middle-class repertoire were in a sense to be laid at the feet of a presumably grateful working class; but to the latter it was in many ways a poisoned gift, for it was tied with the strings of class. Along with the cultural good had to come an acceptance of middle-class patronage. Social control reasserted itself, but in a more subtle and insidious way.

There was no rational recreation movement, no Exeter Hall type headquarters. Rather what seems to have happened is that in the late 1820s and in the 1830s quite a number of people began to perceive working-class leisure as a problem, and to think of the expansion of rational recreation ideals from their own ranks as a solution. Frequently they differed amongst themselves as to what should be offered and how. The debates within particular movements, such as the mechanics' institutes, or between teetotallers and temperance advocates or Sabbatarians and secularists, all in their different ways offering rational recreation, could be extreme. But that said it is not only the advantages of hindsight that enable us to see a wide-ranging attempt to reform working-class recreation in a rational way in the second quarter of the century and beyond. Contemporaries too commented on what was happening, evaluated successes and failures, the more articulate amongst them perhaps thinking of themselves as leading a campaign.[30]

The privatisation of property, as we have seen, was one of the main causes of the privatisation and class-specificity of leisure. Not surprisingly one of the first and most enduring efforts of the rational recreationists was to provide more public space. In 1833 Robert Slaney, reformer and friend of Chadwick, chaired a Select Committee on Public Walks. The evidence which the Committee collected was carefully designed to bring it to the bleak conclusion that many towns had no open spaces for public use, and none had enough. The solution was obvious: provide some. But how?

First the Committee set out to persuade the public of the utility of providing public open spaces. It felt

> convinced that some Open Places reserved for the amusement (under due regulations to preserve order) of the humbler classes, would assist to wean them from low and debasing pleasures. Great complaint is made of drinking-houses, dog fights, and boxing matches, yet, unless some opportunity for other recreation is afforded to workmen, they are driven to such pursuits. The spring to industry which occasional relaxation gives, seems quite as necessary to the poor as to the rich.

Moreover the very lack of public space, they claimed, was leading to an increase in trespass and damage to property 'requiring a stricter and more expensive Police, and laws of additional severity'. Public walks would help stop trespass, improve the health of the working class, keep them from the drinking shops, make them cleaner and neater in personal appearance, and altogether were of first importance 'in promoting Civilisation, and exciting Industry'.

Having made a case for public walks, the Committee then turned to the problem of implementation. Here a certain caution was evident. The Committee suggested that Parliament might legislate to facilitate exchange of entailed or corporate property so as to encourage proprietors to form public walks, 'as much by a wish to increase the value of their circumjacent Property by the Improvements, as by a desire to promote the Public Good'. Secondly they recommended an Act to enable people to dedicate and bequeathe land for public walks. And thirdly an Act to ensure that future Turnpike Acts concerning large towns should set land aside for recreation. As to finance, the key, the

Committee appealed to the self-interest of proprietors, but also recognised that a public grant, voluntary subscription or low rate might be necessary. They allowed themselves one radical flourish, arguing that 'when no Subscription or Donation can be raised, it seems the duty of the Government to assist in providing for the Health of the People by whose efforts they are supported'. They were reasonably confident, however, 'that, in many instances, the liberality of individuals, if properly assisted, would furnish all that is necessary, when their attention is directed to the importance of the subject'.[31]

The Select Committee probably did not expect much in the way of government action. The Report was in large part a publicity exercise, as indeed were the efforts of the maverick MP James Silk Buckingham to secure the passage of a bill through Parliament in the following years.

Certainly the legislature began to show a new sensitiveness to problems of public space. In 1834 Lord Ellenborough's bill to facilitate enclosure was attacked in the House of Commons by J.C. Hobhouse, MP for Nottingham, on the grounds that if the bill was passed his constituents would be prevented from playing cricket and other sports on Lammas land. The bill was defeated 34-14. In 1835 Sir Robert Peel showed his interest in the provision of space for recreation by trying to insert in the Municipal Corporations Bill a clause returning rights over common land to the community, but the House of Lords threw it out. The General Enclosure Act of 1836 prevented enclosure of common land near large towns. In 1837 Joseph Hume secured the passage of a resolution 'that in all Inclosure Bills provision be made for leaving an open space sufficient for the purposes of exercise and recreation of the neighbouring population', and a similar resolution passed in 1839 afterwards became a standing order.[32]

The government also began to supply some money to secure public open spaces. In 1840 £10,000 was set aside for park provision. In 1842 the government purchased Primrose Hill in London from Eton College for £20,236. In 1846 Parliament voted £104,903 for the purchase of Battersea Park, and there was eventually an additional loan of £200,000 from the Public Works Loan Commissioners. The finance for a park in the East End, for which there was considerable public pressure, was provided by the sale of York House to the Duke of Sutherland and a grant of £115,683 from the Commissioners of Woods and Forests. These were large sums of public money, but they were being spent in London alone. Of the £10,000 voted in 1840, only £8,037 had been spent by 1858, £3,000 of it in Manchester, £1,500 in Bradford.[33]

London apart, the public parks of Victorian England owed their existence not to government assistance, but to a combination of philanthropy, self-interest and local initiative. Many towns owed much to the desire of the wealthy to perpetuate themselves in the memory of their townsfolk by giving land for a public park. Strutt, who presented an Arboretum to Derby in 1840, was perhaps the first to do so. Many followed his example, but mostly in the third rather than the second quarter of the century. Only in the 1850s, some 20 years after the urgent need for the provision of public land for recreation had become apparent, did philanthropy begin to make a major contribution. Self-interest, or the desire on the part of a speculator or corporation to make money or at least break even, seemed to hold out more hopes.

R.V. Yates in Liverpool showed the way. With 90 acres at his disposal, he set aside 50 for park and 40 for sale as building plots in the expectation that the favourable location overlooking a park would sufficiently enhance the value of the building plots so as to cover the costs of the 50 acres of park. On the other side of the Mersey Birkenhead carried out a similar scheme by Improvement Act: 226 acres were purchased, 125 of them being dedicated to public use in perpetuity, and the remainder disposed of as house plots. Officially opened in 1847, the park scheme was a financial success. The difficulty about this method of park provision was that it encouraged the development of parks in wealthy areas where property prices would be high. The attempt to construct Victoria Park in London's East End on the same principles was less than successful because of the low ceiling on house prices there.

Birkenhead was perhaps the most striking early example of a corporation taking the initiative in securing public open space, but it was not alone. As early as 1834 Preston Corporation had enclosed Preston Moor, but maintained its accessibility to the public. In 1836 a Health and Recreation subcommittee of the Council was set up, and in the 1840s and 1850s the Corporation purchased plots of land for recreation. In 1846 Liverpool Corporation purchased the Edge Lane gardens of the financially unsuccessful Liverpool Botanical Gardens Society. In Manchester, public interest rather than the Corporation raised enough money by a subscription to secure three parks at a total cost of £30,000.[34]

The provision of public parks was in many ways the most substantial achievement of the rational recreationists. For it was not only in the second quarter, but, as we shall see, with increasing tempo thereafter, that philanthropists and corporations began to set aside land for public recreation. There were, however, certain limitations on the achievement.

In the first place, at least in the 1830s, the concern was with walks. The movement to provide space was fired not only by a recognition of the growing pressure on space in urban areas but also by a distaste for such space that did exist in the form of the commercially-run pleasure gardens. Vauxhall, Ranelagh and their numerous provincial imitations had featured music, fireworks, balloon ascents and attractions of all kinds. At their height in the eighteenth century, their history in the nineteenth century was not simply one of decline, rather of a broadening in their social base. There were new foundations; in London, the Eagle Tavern Gardens in 1825, the Royal Surrey Gardens at Walworth in 1831, the Cremorne Gardens in 1843. Dickens described one of these tea-gardens in *Sketches by Boz*: 'What a dust and noise! Men and women — boys and girls — sweethearts and married people — babies in arms, and children in chaises — pipes and shrimps — cigars and periwinkles — tea and tobacco'. To Dickens the people seemed 'all clean, and happy, and disposed to be good-natured and sociable', but to the stricter kind of rational recreationist there was too much hearty vulgarity and open flirtation in such a scene.[35] Hence the early public walks and parks were quite deliberately formed in a different image. The park was to be improving, educational, a guide to nature but with 'due regulations to preserve order'. It was the combination of nature with order which commended the landscaping values of J.C. Loudon, planner of the Derby Arboretum. The careful display of individual trees, shrubs and plants would arouse people's interest and innate love of nature, and would both uplift them from their day-to-day concerns and dispose them to be sober, orderly and reflective. Until the foundation of the Birkenhead and Manchester parks in the 1840s there was no provision for games or sports. One went to a park to walk, and that alone. Some believed the civilising effects were remarkable. In Manchester by 1854 it was being claimed that the parks were drawing the working classes away from the public-houses, beer-houses and streets, and 'on Sunday, instead of loitering in the fields, dog-fighting, playing at pitch-and-toss, or being in the beerhouse, they go to some of those parks, they are also induced to dress better for the purpose of appearing in those parks'. Was this witness right, or should we give equal credence to another who claimed that on Sundays the people drifted from the park to the pub?[36]

The second limitation is concerned with the finance of these parks and their role as an object of pride to a local community and its benefactors. Not only was it easier to finance a park in a wealthy area than in a poor one; there was also a tendency to opt for the large, the grandiose and the imposing. This opened the parks to the kind of criticism brought against Victoria Park by a Middlesex magistrate in the 1850s; he 'regretted that those large parks should be formed at the public expense, in preference to squares of four or five acre pieces, in particular districts . . . The parks are too far off from the poor districts for them to avail themselves of them to the extent which they might otherwise do'. The parks were built in accordance with what philanthropists and corporations considered appropriate to their dignity, not with regard to what the customers of the parks might want.[37]

Thirdly, although Parliament was alert from the 1830s to the need to provide land for recreation, there were forces operating in the opposite direction which were equally powerful if not more so. In particular the General Enclosure Act of 1845, as the Hammonds argued, made it easier to convert land still available for public enjoyment into private property. Under the Act the consideration of enclosure schemes was no longer to be carried out by Committees of Parliament, but by local inquiries held by independent commissioners. In the case of enclosure of common or waste land the Act gave the Commissioners power to require the appropriation of an allotment 'for the Purpose of Exercise and Recreation for the Inhabitants of the Neighbourhood', but it did not insist that they should do so. *The Times*, a critic of the recreational side of the Act, envisaged 'a melancholy picture of the disregard of public interests by a department well-intentioned, but deficient in imagination and foresight, and untouched by any criticism'. In fact the Inclosure Commission acted on the principle that its main function was to facilitate enclosures. 'Many Commons', wrote Lord Eversley, 'were undoubtedly extinguished under its authority, where no public benefit whatever was conferred, by the increase of cultivation or otherwise, and where it would have been more to the advantage of the public that they should remain open.' Between 1845 and 1869 614,800 acres of common land were enclosed under orders approved by the Commission and sanctioned by Parliament, and of these only 4,000 were set aside for public purposes, 2,200 of them for garden allotments, a mere 1,742 for recreation grounds.

Thus if some new land for public purposes was coming into use by virtue of the activities of the rational recreationists, at the same time much old land, previously public, was becoming privatised. And this was not only a problem of the major cities. Constant vigilance was necessary if public rights were not to be infringed. In Rye, for example, in 1834 the Town Salts had been walled in, and a large meeting of the Freemen donated it to the town in perpetuity as a sporting field; in

1859 part of the land was let by the Council for building. The provision of public parks simply did not keep pace with the erosion of public rights through the privatisation of property.[38]

Parks, as we have seen, had an educational purpose. But the task of reforming the working class through improving leisure required more direct confrontation than parks could provide. The main instrument to which the rational recreationists resorted were the mechanics' institutes, along with other institutions for spare-time education, lyceums, mutual improvement societies and so on. These of course have been studied in depth and with expertise by historians, but generally within the context of the history of adult education. Here the task is to study them in the context of leisure, and it will be suggested that this implies a reassessment of their achievements. Generally the mechanics' institutes have been regarded as failures; they hoped to teach science to working men and they ended up teaching liberal arts to clerks. And there is enough truth in that account to confirm the opinion that from the point of view of those who set up the institutes they were a failure; for the clients however they may have met real needs.

The sense of failure stemmed from two sources. In the first place it became apparent in the late 1820s that there would be no fulfilment of the early hopes that the foundation of the institutes would lead to a diffusion of scientific education, to a release of the inventive power of the artisan, and to a spread of 'rational' information. The mechanics' institutes did have an educational role, but it was not that which had been envisaged. The education they provided was largely elementary. In 1852 the actual attendance at 59 Yorkshire institutes giving class instruction, containing 11,813 members, was 2,110 and of these four-fifths were in elementary classes. And if the education which was popular was elementary rather than scientific, it was also appealing to the young rather than to adults. In 1852 it was calculated that in 74 Yorkshire institutes over one-quarter of the male members and over one-half of the female members were under eighteen. In Manchester the majority of the members in the classes were aged between 14 and 21. The educational function of the mechanics' institutes was very largely to supply elementary education for young people; and the vast majority of members did not attend classes at all.[39]

The majority of members, too, it seemed, were not mechanics. 'The mechanics' institutes in the large towns', said Samuel Smiles in 1849, 'generally speaking, are not Institutes of mechanics; they are for the most part Institutes of the middle and respectable classes, and a small proportion, in some cases not so much as a half, of working men.' The language itself displayed a certain confusion: a half could hardly be described as a small proportion. And as Dr Royle has pointed out it was in fact no small achievement to have attracted as high a proportion as a half from the working class. Perhaps too there was little social cleavage between mechanics and the lower middle class whose presence in the institutes so worried the organisers, and was the second element in their sense of failure.[40]

Their response to this was to put increased emphasis on the recreational aspects of the institutes. From the very beginning the institutes had been seen as one answer to the problem of leisure. Timothy Claxton, the mechanic who in 1817 founded the 'Mechanical Institute' in London, hoped that it would among other things 'afford both rational and useful amusement' and 'a mode of passing our leisure time in a way which is much preferable to what is already practised by too many; it would make us better members of society; better for ourselves, our employers, and consequently to our families.' After a crisis for many institutes in the years 1829-31, when it became apparent that the original scientific objectives were not going to be achieved, an increased emphasis on social events became apparent.

This seemed to be the way to recruit members. In 1842 W. Newmarch, writing about York, concluded that the number of ordinary members 'has been in proportion to the number and popular character of the Lectures, and the frequency of the Excursions and social meetings'.[41] And an emphasis on recreation was certainly apparent in those institutions which remained relatively free of middle-class control. Rowland Detrosier, for example, leader of the breakaway Manchester New Mechanics' Institution, asserted in 1831 that 'to teach our youth how to spend their leisure time with profit to themselves, and advantage to others, has hitherto occupied the attention of the Committee of the existing New Mechanics' Institution'. In Huddersfield from 1844 onwards there was considerable provision for recreation and amusement: tea parties, soirees, a 'rural gala' in May, excursions, exhibitions. Counter-attractions were organised, similar in intention to those under middle-class aegis, but expressed in a different language, a gala and cheap trip being organised in order 'to give the rising generation a distaste' for 'large feudal orgies' such as took place at the time of the Henley feast. In Keighley, Halifax and Bradford, all starting under popular control, large soirees and excursions were organised, and there was an expansion of the social programme in the 1840s. At Stalybridge, again popular in origin, there was an amusement class on Saturday evenings. There can be no dissent from the conclusion of J.F.C. Harrison that '. . . by 1846 the conception of mechanics' institutes as centres for general cultural and quiet recreational activities was firmly established', and that by the mid-1850s the recreational objectives were being even more openly voiced.[42]

Middle-class reaction to these trends was not simply negative. With varying degrees of enthusiasm they came to accept, in the words of J.W. Hudson at mid-century, that one of the legitimate purposes of the institutes was

> The creation of intellectual pleasures and refined amusements tending to the general elevation of character. The frequent intercourse of men of different parties and grades of life, for the purpose of promoting one common intellectual object, gradually vanquishing those prejudices and jealousies which almost universally exist, even in cultivated minds, is unquestionably an object to be cherished and encouraged. By such means a taste for rational enjoyment may be produced, and those hours generally spent in listlessness and in foolish amusements, may be converted into periods rendered precious by the inculcation of enlightened and elevating principles. Habits of order, punctuality, and politeness would be engendered and flow from thence into all the other relations and departments of life.[43]

In this vision the mechanics' institute was to be the location for a programme of advancement for the working class under middle-class supervision. The absence of such a location had been sorely felt in the early nineteenth century. Neither class could meet with any pretence of social ease in their homes. From the middle-class point of view some public but supervised location was necessary, and despite the evidence that the imposition of middle-class norms, with regard to dress for example, was one major reason for working-class non-attendance, the mechanics' institutes came to seem to their middle-class promoters the ideal location for the achievement of class harmony. In 1843 Sir Benjamin Heywood publicly expressed his hope that the Manchester Mechanics' Institution would contribute to 'a more kindly intercourse between the different classes of people — more of mutual confidence and regard between the working man and his employer'. The Earl of Carlisle saw the Bradford Mechanics' Institute in 1846 as amongst other things a place where people of all classes could partake 'in innocent recreation'. In the mechanics' institutes and in the lyceums which were created in the later 1830s to cater for the factory workers, paternalism was reasserting itself. The lyceums had a much more openly recreational programme than the mechanics' institutes, and in the words of William Fairbairn, President of the Ancoats Lyceum in 1839, the hope was that the entertainment would 'afford evidence of the paternal care of the directors in providing for the amusement as well as the instruction of members'.[44]

The forms which this recreation took are indicative of the aims or at least *post hoc* rationalisations of the promoters. First, the recreation was to be primarily intellectual rather than physical. There was, at least in the early mechanics' institutes, a positive distaste for physical recreation. Thomas Latimer, 'The Cobbett of the West', attended the Mechanics' Institute in London as a young man; when he suggested that some physical recreation be included in the programme 'he received little sympathy: their hidebound intellectualism looked down on bodily culture as something relatively earthy and disreputable'. Latimer and some associates then set up an independent but short-lived London Gymnastic Society, designed as a counter-attraction to 'the unwholesome excitements of gin and gambling' but significantly failing to win enough commitment from the elite or the working class to expand into a national movement.[45] Even when there was elite support, for example from Benjamin Heywood in Manchester, the directors argued the prior claim of 'intellectual education' over a 'mere animal or physical one'. Gradually men like Dr Favell in Sheffield began to press for more outdoor games and gymnastics, and cricket and garden allotments started to appear under the auspices of the mechanics' institutes. But the more common emphasis was that of J.W. Hudson who in 1851 claimed the public attention for the institutes 'as a means of advancing morality and diminishing crime, by drawing men from those evil resources which the absence of intellectual culture is sure to lead to'.[46] As we shall see in a later chapter it required something of a revolution for the middle class to be able to absorb physical recreation into their cultural world; and that revolution had not occurred before mid-century.

Much of the recreation provided was deliberately counter-attractive, building on the models which the Sunday Schools and the Methodists had provided. The well-timed excursion could draw people away from the more insidious attractions of a fair or race-meeting. In Manchester, for example, in Whitsun-week 1837 'the oxy-hydrogen microscope and phantasmagoria were called into requisition, to assist various Sunday School visitors and teachers in their laudatory endeavours to amuse their scholars, and draw them from the scenes of immorality and vice, incident to the race-ground'.[47]

A third form of recreation was the exhibition, at least 50 of which were held under mechanics' institute auspices between 1838 and 1840. The exhibitions had two aims; first they were seen as a form of scientific education perhaps more acceptable to working-class audiences than the lecture, and secondly and most important, they had a financial object. It was central to the middle-class vision of the purposes of mechanics' institutes that they should provide a public location where leisure time could be spent, and as with the parks, that location had to be conceived in a style directly opposed to that of the pub, beer-house or incipient music-hall. The committees of mechanics' institutes therefore spent much time and effort trying to acquire suitable property, and then constructing an imposing and public-looking building. By 1858 at least 25 mechanics' institutes in Yorkshire had erected their own buildings. These were expensive ventures, and the exhibition proved to be an excellent way of raising money. Admission fees were relatively low, about 6d a day, and the crowds poured in, up to 200,000 visiting each of the four Manchester Mechanics' Institute exhibitions held between 1837 and 1842.[48]

Intellectual and cultural improvement, counter-attractive excursions, exhibitions could all be seen as only slight departures from the initial aims of the mechanics' institutes. But a final form of recreation which the institutes promoted suggests that they embodied hopes much more far-reaching than a general cultural uplift of the working class. The stern-faced historian of adult education may mention the institutes' Christmas party in a light aside, but he will not accord it any great significance except in so far as it is part of that move away from scientific education to the provision of recreation. But the Christmas party, as a study by Kathleen R. Farrar has shown, came to be of immense significance to the institutes. In Manchester for some 20 years from the early 1830s the Christmas party grew in elaboration and was attended by the elite of Manchester. In form it was a romantic attempt to re-create a socially-harmonious medieval past, and this in the city of free trade and the Manchester School.

Consider the party of 1848-9 when no trouble or expense was spared to make the party 'so far as our modern means avail a perfect representation of the customs . . . of the English Christmas of the olden time'. The Free Trade Hall was decorated to give 'as far as possible the appearance of an old Baronial hall of England', with evergreens, artificial flowers, 'vast numbers of banners, flags, old armour, armorial blazonings, spears, swords and antlers', heads of buffalo and ibex, and 'helmets, partizans and halberds' lent by the police. The processions formed the centrepiece of the party, with the Christmas Prince in ermine-trimmed robe, and a masque of the months recalling a rustic past with Maid Marian dancing with her maidens round a 30-foot maypole.

It was in such a setting that James Aspinall Turner, President of the Institution, could say how gratified he was to see 'assembled together in terms of equality and good fellowship, legislators and magistrates, merchants and mechanics, factory owners and factory operatives, masters and servants, – all mingling together in that spacious hall, forgetting for a time their various positions in society'. Here, in a public ceremony, with the reporters of the newspapers standing by, community could be reasserted and class conflict stilled. Properly managed, leisure time could be used not simply to civilise the working class, though that was necessary, but also to remake society, to halt that drift towards atomisation which so alarmed contemporaries. In 1853 at the last of the great Christmas parties Oliver Heywood took his audience back to the occasion when 'the members of the institution assembled together at their first Christmas festival when the plum pudding, and the boar's head, and the wassail were real, for the purpose of promoting a more kindly sympathy, and warmer concord amongst the various classes of the community'.[49]

The Christmas party had this disadvantage that it celebrated community on only one occasion in the year. Obviously more regular efforts were necessary, and many, both within the institutes and outside, put great faith in music as a force for good. It could however be the opposite. The directors of the Manchester Institution encouraged music from the mid-1830s, and were soon able to congratulate themselves on having helped 'to create a disrelish for those numerous entertainments wherein music has been used as a lure to the most objectionable associations and indulgences'. Music was in danger of being taken over by the entrepreneurs of leisure, by the publican and the beer-house keeper; secular – and on Sundays, sacred – music was being played and sung in that privatised world where alcohol was sold and drunk. Clearly music had to be rescued from evil associations, and the native tradition and innate love of music turned to good account.

In music, unlike other cultural and aesthetic experiences, it was not so much a matter of inculcating middle-class taste as of providing a suitable milieu. For there was gratifying evidence that musical tastes were not class-specific. Handel was reported to be popular among northern factory audiences as early as 1788; employers simply had to encourage and foster, and this they did. In Belper the Strutts, in Yorkshire and Durham the London Lead Company, and in Cheshire the Gregs all gave encouragement to the musical propensities of their employees. Of the cotton-spinners of Cresbrook in Derbyshire it was said in 1824 that 'their highest species of enjoyment, the highest that man can enjoy, is music; this delightfully intellectual source of pleasure is improved, encouraged, and scientifically taught at Cresbrook'.[50]

These efforts of employers to encourage music were sporadic and individual. In the early 1840s there began a more concerted effort to organise the music life of the nation as part of a total reform of the working class. In the Committee of Council on Education in 1840-1 J.P. Kay noted that 'The songs of any people may be regarded as an important means of forming an industrious, brave, loyal and religious working class.' They might 'inspire cheerful views of industry', 'associate amusements . . . with duties', and 'wean the people from vicious indulgences'. Music was to become a key part of the educational curriculum, and fortunately there was a new method of teaching it to hand in the Tonic-Sol-Fa method of Curwen and Hullah which, it was claimed in 1867, 'more especially addresses itself to the working class'. The inculcation of moral values was intrinsic to the Tonic-Sol-Fa method. Soon there were mammoth working-class choirs and working-class audiences. Faucher's Mancunian annotator noted in 1844 that

> . . . of the various styles of music, Sacred music has always enjoyed the especial preference of the working classes. The oratorios of Handel and of Haydn, are as household words, familiar to them from childhood; and no difficulty is ever found in selecting from amongst the factory operatives, choirs capable of doing justice to these immortal compositions.[51]

This of course was highly gratifying. As H.A. Bruce commented in an address at the Swansea Musical Festival in 1864, the promotion of music amongst the working classes 'has induced them frequently to desert the public-house, and to seek for some higher and better occupation. And no occupation surely can be purer, or free from anything like dangerous influences, or more successful in its results than the choral cultivation of music.' Only one thing more was needed to ensure that music was playing its fullest possible recreational role; that was to insist that it was performed and listened to in public not private and in such a manner as to reinforce notions of community rather than class. These ideas lay behind the establishment of the Saturday evening concerts in Lord Nelson Street in Liverpool in 1844. The elite of Liverpool presided — Rathbone or William Brown MP — and with the middle class occupied the reserved seats and side galleries. The operatives filled the body of the hall, and it was 'a common thing for the mechanics, with their wives and children making family parties, to attend these concerts'. The concerts served both to emphasise the social hierarchy and to re-assert the values of community and patronage. They acquired a national fame, were imitated elsewhere, and became a kind of fixed reference point, a model of what could be done: patronage was restored, the classes could mix, drink was absent, and music was enjoyed – indeed it was the music which allowed these other things to happen.[52]

For the remainder of the century commentators of all kinds praised music as a civilising force. H.P. Haweis in a book with the significant title, *Music and Morals*, believed that music in England was about to become what it had long been in Germany, 'a running commentary upon all life, the solace of a nation's cares, the companion of its revelry, the minister of its pleasure, and the inspired aid to its devotion'. George Gissing thought that only two things were necessary to humanise the multitude: 'an entire change of economic conditions', and then bringing 'to bear on the new order of things the constant influence of music . . . Destroy, sweep away, prepare the ground; then shall music the holy, music the civiliser, breathe over the renewed earth, and with Orphean magic raise in perfected beauty the towers of the City of Man.'[53] This romantic belief in the power of music to civilise stemmed from its ability to touch the emotions as well as the intellect. So much of what passed under the name of rational recreation seemed dry and lifeless; it might civilise but it would not inspire. Music, however, was not only rational but it had that inspirational quality which would enable people of all classes to rise above themselves and to be united in a sense of community. The repeated invocation of music by middle-class commentators brings home to us their yearning for a more simple and organic society.

Art, too, might civilise and humanise. During the 1830s and 1840s there was a fairly concerted effort, headed in Parliament by the Radical MPs Joseph Hume, William Ewart and Thomas Wyse, to open up art exhibitions and national monuments for the free inspection of the people. Hume presided over a 'Society for Obtaining Free Admission to Public Monuments' aimed particularly at Westminster Abbey, St Paul's and other cathedrals which were open only on payment of a fee: even ecclesiastical property had become privatised. In 1841 Hume chaired the Select Committee on National Monuments and Works of Art appointed 'to inquire into the present state of the National Monuments and Works of Art in . . . Public Edifices; to consider the best means for their protection and for affording facilities to the Public for their inspection, as a means of moral and intellectual improvement for the People.' The Committee assembled evidence to show that the people flocked to museums when they were open free of charge, and that there were no problems of public order. The National Gallery had over 10,000 visitors on certain holidays, while the British Museum, which had been open to the public during the Easter and Whitsuntide holidays only since the late 1830s, had 32,000 visitors on Whit-Monday. With such gratifying results in London to point to it was natural that the Radicals should seek to establish similar institutions in the provinces. The outcome was the Museums Act of 1845 which enabled councils of municipal boroughs with a population of over 10,000 to erect and maintain buildings for museums of art and science, financed out of a rate not exceeding one halfpenny in the pound, and with its admission charges not exceeding one penny per person. There was no rush to build museums, but the means to do so were now there, and the tide which had run so strongly towards the privatisation of art and culture was on the turn.[54]

The Radical MPs, particularly William Ewart, now turned their attention to books and the provision of public libraries. Concern about the lack of public libraries reached back into the 1830s, but achievements were limited until 1849 when Ewart joined forces with Edward Edwards of the British Museum to set up a Select Committee as the prelude to legislation. Public libraries, Edwards believed, would provide the means not only of instruction but also of 'rational amusement . . . I believe that want of some provision, from the public resources, of amusements of a rational and improving character, has led to the introduction, to a large extent in our towns, of brutalizing and demoralising amusements.' Libraries were one solution. As the Committee put it, in villages 'a taste for something better than mere animal enjoyment may be instilled into them through the instrumentality of well-chosen books'. The Act which followed in 1850 was on the same principle as the Museums Act of 1845 except that it eliminated charges, but also ruled that two-thirds of the local ratepayers must give their approval before the Act could be put into operation. Not surprisingly the ratepayers were less than keen to spend money for public facilities, and relatively few libraries were built in the early years.[55]

Public parks, public monuments, public museums, public libraries: nothing is more striking in the history of leisure in the 1830s and 1840s than the attempt, led in the main by Parliamentary Radicals, to reverse the trend towards the privatisation of all leisure facilities. The achievements look quite imposing on the statute book, though before 1850 they were scarcely visible on the ground. The significance of this second quarter of the nineteenth century lies in the fact that men and women were coming to recognise and deplore that process whereby leisure became privatised. In horror at what was happening they exaggerated the extent to which the working class was driven to the drinking place, for, as we have seen in Chapter 1, the working class and the entrepreneurs who aimed their wares at it had a resourcefulness and inventiveness which had led to the spread of many new forms of entertainment. But the belief was strong that because of middle-class exclusiveness as much as working-class immorality the working class had no pleasures other than those of drink and sex — both of these enjoyed in private, both dangerous to morality, neither in any way conducive to self-improvement or to the creation of a sense of community.

Moreover signs that the working class was trying to raise itself were far from comforting, for those efforts were leading in the direction of political radicalism, of Owenism, of socialism. In this crisis period of the Industrial Revolution it seemed that there was an urgent necessity to create new forms of leisure which might by their attractiveness draw the workers out of their privatised drinking places and Owenite halls, and which on the positive side might lead to the creation of a civilisation in which cultural goods were public property and hence class antagonism mitigated. Charles Kingsley perhaps expressed these hopes with greatest fervour. In the aftermath of the Chartist gathering on Kennington Common in 1848 he praised the British Museum 'because it is almost the only place which is free to English Citizens as such — where the poor and the rich may meet together . . . The British Museum is a truly equalising place, in the deepest and most spiritual sense; *therefore I love it*.'[56] United by a sense of national achievement the classes might come together in a public place to celebrate what they held in common.

This was the rhetoric of rational recreation. More prosaically it had to justify its claims on the purse strings of the wealthy by a resort to the crudest utilitarianism. Public parks, museums and libraries it was claimed would reduce crime, trespass and drunkenness and were therefore a contribution to the national economy. It is these utilitarian arguments which have most frequently impinged on the attention of the historian, and rational recreation has therefore seemed to be a blatant attempt at social control. In part it was, but even at its crudest it embodied an aspiration towards the creation of a new kind of society which would in some sense be one society, not two nations. After mid-century, as we shall see, the possibility of creating such a society became greater as leisure time itself became more clearly defined and increased in quantity; and in the third quarter of the century an even greater onus was to be placed on leisure as the means to the creation of a society in which the classes could meet in harmony, in public.

Notes

1. W.H. Chaloner, *Autobiography of Bamford*, vol. I, pp. 143-55; 1801 census.
2. Chaloner, ibid., p. 26.
3. R.W. Malcolmson, *Popular Recreations*, pp. 126-35; R. Palmer, *A Touch on the Times* (Harmondsworth, 1974), p. 112.
4. A. Delves, 'Popular Recreations and their Enemies', Paper to the Conference of the Society for the Study of Labour History (November 1975); Malcolmson, *Popular Recreations*, pp. 141-2.
5. J. Throsby, *The History and Antiquities of the Ancient Town of Leicester* (Leicester, 1791), p. 356; C. Hole, *English Sports and Pastimes* (London, 1949), pp. 58-9; Hone, *Year Book* (London, 1832), pp. 269-70; R.D. Storch, 'The Policeman as Domestic Missionary' *Journal of Social History*, vol. IX (1976), pp. 491-2.
6. S.C. on Public Walks, PP 1833 (448), vol. XV, qq. 113-14, 152, 344, 836, 892-3; R.C. for Inquiring into the State of Large Towns and Populous Districts, 1st Report, PP 1844 (572), vol. XVII, qq. 5207-10.
7. J.L. Hammond and B. Hammond, *The Age of the Chartists 1832-1854* (London, 1930), pp. 106-43.
8. M.K. Ashby, *Joseph Ashby of Tysoe 1859-1919* (London, 1961), pp. 281-2; C. Torr, *Small Talk at Wreyland* (London, 1918), p. 27; cf. E.J. Hobsbawm, *Industry and Empire* (London, 1968), p. 81.
9. Hammond and Hammond, *Age of the Chartists*, pp. 109-10, 116-17; S.C. on Drunkenness, PP 1834, vol. VIII, q. 325; S. and B. Webb, *The Parish and the County*, pp. 599-602.
10. J. Strutt, *Sports and Pastimes*, p. lxii; S.C. on Public Walks 1833, qq. 100-16.
11. S.C. on Public Walks 1833, qq. 364-5; P.E. Razzell and R.W. Wainwright, *Victorian Working Class*, pp. 319-20; Hammond and Hammond, *Age of the Chartists*, pp. 126-30; cf. Howitt, *Rural Life*, vol. II, pp. 305-11.
12. Hammond and Hammond, *Age of the Chartists*, pp. 111-15; R.C. on Large Towns 2nd Report 1845, p. 203; see also for loss of open spaces in Norwich and Portsmouth, pp. 285, 291.
13. S.C. on Public Walks 1833, qq. 133-9 (my italics).
14. W. Cooke Taylor, *Notes of a Tour in the Manufacturing Districts of Lancashire* (London, 1968), p. 133; L. Faucher, *Manchester in 1844*, pp. 55-6.
15. K. Hudson, *A Social History of Museums* (London, 1975), p. 15; C.P. Darcy, *The Encouragement of the Fine Arts in Lancashire 1760-1860* (Manchester, Chetham Society, 1976), pp. 4-5, 86; cf. R.D. Altick, *Shows of London*, pp. 25-9, 101-2.
16. Cooke Taylor, *Notes of a Tour*, p. 134.
17. B. Harrison, *Drink and the Victorians*, pp. 37-55.
18. S.C. on Drunkenness 1834, q. 3781; B. Harrison, ibid., p. 53; J.J. Rowley, 'Drink and the Public House in Urban Nottingham 1830-60', Paper to the Conference of the Society for the Study of Labour History (November 1975), pp. 14-17; S.C. on Public Houses, PP 1852-3 (855), vol. XXXVII, q. 5481; Faucher, *Manchester in 1844*, p. 49.

19. J. Lawson, *Pudsey*, p. 58; S.C. on Public Houses 1852-3, q. 5469.

20. See B. Harrison, *Drink and the Victorians*, pp. 64-126.

21. S.C. on the Observance of the Sabbath Day, PP 1831-2 (697), vol. VII, qq. 2881-2, 2921-3, 3270, 3316, 3323-6, 3394; 'Timothy Sparks' (pseud. Charles Dickens), *Sunday under Three Heads* (London, 1836), passim.

22. Faucher, *Manchester in 1844*, p. 53; S.C. on Public Houses, PP 1854 (367), vol. XIV, q. 3095, and Report, pp. xxi, xxiii; J. Hogg, *London As It Is* (London, 1837), pp. 320-1.

23. W.R. Ward, *Religion and Society*, p. 51; Eileen Yeo, 'Robert Owen and Radical Culture' in S. Pollard and J. Salt (eds.) *Robert Owen* (London, 1971), pp. 84-114.

24. W. Sichel, *Sheridan* (London, 1909), vol. I, p. 79; *Parliamentary History*, vol. XXXVI (1801-3), p. 851.

25. Hone, *Every-Day Book*, vol. II, pp. 335-8, 604-6, 700-2.

26. R.C. on Large Towns 1845, p. 7.

27. R.I. and S. Wilberforce, *The Life of William Wilberforce*, vol. II, p. 449; Howitt, *Rural Life*, vol. II, pp. 150-1; R. Chambers, *The Book of Days* (London, 1863-4), preface; H. Mayhew, *London Labour*, vol. I, p. 44.

28. *Parliamentary History*, vol. XXXVI (1801-3), p. 847; Howitt, *Rural Life*, p. 255.

29. J. Austen, *Persuasion*, 1st edn 1818 (London, 1956), p. 36; Hole, *English Sports and Pastimes*, p. 92; E.A. Goodwyn, *Selections from Norwich Newspapers 1760-1790* (Ipswich, n.d.), p. 62; P.M. Wadsworth, 'Leisure Pursuits in Nineteenth-century Bath' (unpublished Univ. of Kent MA Thesis, 1975), pp. 72, 78.

30. See further R.D. Storch, 'The Problem of Working-class Leisure: Some Roots of Middle-class Moral Reform in the Industrial North: 1825-50', in Donajgrodzki, *Social Control*, pp. 138-62.

31. S.C. on Public Walks 1833, Report.

32. Hammond and Hammond, *Age of the Chartists*, pp. 121-6.

33. G.F. Chadwick, *The Park and the Town* (London, 1966), pp. 121-31; PP 1854 (408), vol. LXVII, pp. 339-48; PP 1857-8 (15), vol. XLVIII, pp. 347-50.

34. Chadwick, *Park and the Town*, pp. 67-71, 97-9, 121-2; A.L. Gallagher, 'The Social Control of Working-Class Leisure in Preston, *c.* 1850-*c.* 1875' (unpublished Univ. of Lancaster MA dissertation, 1975), pp. 24-5; J.G. Branston, 'The Development of Public Open Spaces in Leeds during the Nineteenth Century' (unpublished Univ. of Leeds MPhil thesis, 1972), p. 16.

35. C. Dickens, *Sketches by Boz*, scenes, ch. IX.

36. Chadwick, *Park and the Town*, pp. 53-64, 71, 99; S.C. on Public Houses 1854, qq. 3524, 2251.

37. S.C. on Public Houses 1852-3, qq. 7606-14; G. Godwin, *Town Swamps and Social Bridges* (Leicester, 1972), pp. 92-3.

38. Hammond and Hammond, *Age of the Chartists*, pp. 13-43; Lord Eversley, *Commons, Forests and Footpaths* (London, 1910), p. 16; *Clark's Guide and History of Rye* (Rye, 1861), p. 70.

39. J.F.C. Harrison, *Learning and Living* (London, 1961), p. 130n; M. Tylecote, *The Mechanics' Institutes of Lancashire and Yorkshire before 1851* (Manchester, 1957), pp. 164, 260; S.C. on Public Libraries 1849, App. 2, pp. 306-9.

40. S.C. on Public Libraries 1849, q. 1956; E. Royle, 'Mechanics' Institutes and the Working Classes 1840-1860', *Historical Journal*, vol. XIV (1971), pp. 305-21.

41. Tylecote, *Mechanics' Institutes of Lancashire*, pp. 11, 77; J.F.C. Harrison, *Learning and Living*, pp. 71-2.

42. R.G. Kirby, 'An Early Experiment in Workers' Self-education: the Manchester New Mechanics' Institution, 1829-35' in D.S.L. Cardwell (ed.), *Artisan to Graduate* (Manchester, 1974), p. 93; Tylecote, *Mechanics' Institutes of Lancashire*, pp. 191-245; J.F.C. Harrison, *Learning and Living*, p. 74.

43. J.W. Hudson, *The History of Adult Education* (London, 1969), p. 55.

44. Dame Mabel Tylecote, 'The Manchester Mechanics' Institution, 1824-50' in Cardwell, *Artisan to Graduate*, p. 66; J.F.C. Harrison, *Learning and Living*, p. 73.

45. R.S. Lambert, *The Cobbett of the West* (London, 1939), pp. 22-6; Hone, *Every-Day Book*, vol. I, pp. 10, 327-9, 658-62.

46. Tylecote, 'Manchester Mechanics' Institution', p. 70; Tylecote, *Mechanics' Institutes of Lancashire*, pp. 110-11; Hudson, *History of Adult Education*, p. vi.

47. Tylecote, *Mechanics' Institutes of Lancashire*, p. 183.

48. Ibid., pp. 178-9; Toshio Kusamitsu, 'Great Exhibitions before 1851' (Paper to Art and Society History Workshop, London, June 1978); J.F.C. Harrison, *Learning and Living*, p. 58n.

49. K.R. Farrar, 'The mechanics' saturnalia' in Cardwell, *Artisan to Graduate*, pp. 99-117.

50. Tylecote, 'Manchester Mechanics' Institution', p. 72; E.D. Mackerness, *Somewhere Further North, a History of Music in Sheffield* (Sheffield 1974), p. 20; Mackerness, *A Social History of English Music*, pp. 130-2; G. Hogarth, *Musical History, Biography, and Criticism* (New York, 1969), pp. 172-3.

51. Kay quoted in R. Johnson, 'Educational Policy and Social Control in Early Victorian England', *Past & Present*, no. 49 (1970), p. 110; Mackerness, *Social History*, pp. 161-4; J.M. Ludlow and Lloyd Jones, *Progress of the Working Class 1832-1867* (London, 1867), p. 191; Faucher, *Manchester in 1844*, pp. 49-50.

52. *Lectures and Addresses by the Right Hon. Henry Austin Bruce, First Lord Aberdare* (London, 1917), p. 209; [H. Shimmin], *Liverpool Life* (Liverpool, 1856), p. 10; for their national fame, S.C. on Public Houses 1854, Report, p. xxvi.

53. H.P. Haweis, *Music and Morals*, 13th edn (London, n.d.), p. 498; G. Gissing, *The Nether World* (Brighton, 1974), p. 109.

54. J. Minihan, *The Nationalization of Culture* (New York, 1977), pp. 41-92; R.D. Altick, *The Shows of London*, pp. 416-19, 440-5.

55. S.C. on Public Libraries 1849, q. 452, Report, p. xi and passim; T. Kelly, *A History of Public Libraries in Great Britain 1845-1965* (London, 1973), pp. 5-15.

56. *Politics for the People*, no. 11 (July, 1848), p. 183.

4 CLASS AND LEISURE IN MID-VICTORIAN ENGLAND

Charles Kingsley's hopes that leisure might serve the social function of bringing the classes together seemed to receive some confirmation as the Great Exhibition of 1851 ushered in a period of relative social harmony. Historians have affirmed the same theory, arguing that there was an alliance of the respectable within all classes against the joining together in unrespectable leisure of the aristocracy and the poor.[1] Certainly, there was a colossal investment of time and effort in the attempt to bring the classes together in leisure, an investment of such an extent that it constituted the dominant ideology of leisure in the mid-Victorian years; an investment, too, whose chances of success were all the greater because the sponsors were now willing and anxious to include physical recreation amongst the respectable leisure activities. Nevertheless, for a number of reasons, the return on that investment was minimal or non-existent. Class and not the divisions within classes continued to be of prime importance for an understanding of leisure. This chapter will explore the ideology of class conciliation in leisure, and seek to explain its failure.

Historically at mid-century the hope that the classes might be brought together in leisure had two distinct roots. On the one hand were those who had opposed the attack on popular leisure in the later eighteenth and early nineteenth centuries, arguing instead for a paternalist patronage of the people's customs and sports. These, they claimed, brought the classes together, prevented effeminacy and promoted patriotism. The attack on popular leisure seemed to them motivated by class interest. The Cruelty to Animals Bill of 1809, said Windham, was 'A Bill for harrassing and oppressing certain Classes among the lower Orders of His Majesty's Subjects'.[2] And this kind of argument appealed not only to Tory traditionalists but also to middle-class people with a social conscience and radical disposition. On the other hand there was rational recreation which was a first if hardly explicit admission on the side of reformers that there was something to Windham's accusations. The remedy they proposed of course was quite different. They advocated not the preservation of the past but the creation of new institutions and activities. Within these, they argued, the respectable of all classes could meet in harmony. Thus it was a commonplace in the 1840s to argue that mechanics' institutes, or Sunday School excursions, or music, or art, or any improving rational recreation would amongst other things bring the classes together.

These two traditions, distinct and opposed to each other as they were, carried on a kind of dialogue in which each tried to appropriate the strong points of the other's argument and language. Sportsmen made claims for the rationality of their pastimes. 'Intellectual pursuits may gain the ascendancy', wrote the *Sporting Magazine*, 'but they will never exclude other means of rational enjoyment.' Shooting, claimed Blaine in 1840, once 'constituted the healthful and rational recreation of thousands'. Popular entertainment, too, made the claim to be 'rational', as in mid-century advertisements in Hartlepool for Smith's Royal Music Saloon and the Royal Casino, Dock Hotel.[3] On the other side the process of appropriation demanded nothing less than a turnabout. The hostility to physical recreation, the notion that there was a split between mind and reason on the one hand and body and animality on the other, remained strong at mid-century. It was a split exemplified by George Combe in the 1847 edition of his popular *The Constitution of Man*, in which he wrote about the labouring population:

> Life with them is spent to so great an extent in labour, that their moral and intellectual powers are stinted of exercise and gratification; and their mental enjoyments in consequence are too much confined to the pleasures afforded by the animal propensities: — in other words, their existence is too little *rational*.

This kind of instinctive distaste for physical recreation owed much to the history and associations of sport. The drink-seller and the bookmaker were its organisers and inspirers. Many popular sports, such as pugilism and cock-fighting, involved not only drinking and gambling, but also excited the worst lusts of mankind — violence, and cruelty to fellow-men and to animals. Moreover sportsmen inhabited a peculiar world of their own, the world of 'the Fancy' with its own language, its own literature, and its own meeting-places. Even the more liberal sections of the middle class found this a totally alien world. In Dickens's journal, *Household Words*, G.A. Sala described 'The Sporting World' in 1852, and did so by outlining to his readers the contents of *Bell's Life*, a journal dominated by horse-racing and prize-fighting. Yet these sports, Sala insisted, however distasteful, 'are bound up with us . . . they are bone of our bone, and flesh of our flesh — they are crackling cinders at almost every Englishman's fireside'. Clearly, though, not

at the firesides of his readers. These were sports which the respectable
could not countenance. But Sala in 1852 did not reject all sport: he was
hopeful for the future, and had glimpses of a world in which sport
might be the pride and property of *his* world, and no longer of the
Fancy's. 'I hope', he continued

> I have not said a word in ridicule or depreciation of the athletic
> sports of England — the sports that send our lads (from Eton to
> charity schools) forth to do yeomen's service all over the globe. Nor
> can I end this paper without recognising the hopeful good that edu-
> cation, steam, cheap printing, cheap pictures, and cheap schools have
> done towards discouraging and discountenancing that brutal and
> savage wantonness in our sports, which was, until very lately, a scan-
> dal and disgrace to us as a nation.

Apply the traditional nostrums of the middle class, it is suggested, and
sport can render real service to the nation; it will produce a breed of
'yeomen' — the process of appropriation has begun.[4]

That process is most clearly evident in the history of cricket. In the
early nineteenth century cricket was morally suspect. We can see why if
we look at Miss Mitford's famous description of a country cricket
match in the 1820s. She carefully distinguishes the type of cricket she
is writing about from others:

> I doubt if there be any scene in the world more animating or delight-
> ful than a cricket-match — I do not mean a set match at Lord's
> Ground for money, hard money, between a certain number of
> gentlemen and players, as they are called — people who make a trade
> of that noble sport, and degrade it into an affair of bettings, and
> hedgings, and cheatings, it may be, like boxing or horse-racing; nor
> do I mean a pretty *fête* in a gentleman's park, where one club of
> cricketing dandies encounter another such club, and where they
> show off in graceful costume to a gay marquee of admiring belles
> . . . No! The cricket that I mean is a real solid old-fashioned match
> between neighbouring parishes, where each attacks the other for
> honour and a supper, glory and half-a-crown a man. If there be any
> gentlemen amongst them, it is well — if not, it is so much the better.

Cricket, like so many other sports, was 'noble', but liable to be degraded.
And even in this idealised village cricket match the morally sensitive
would note that money is passing hands, and that for lack of gentry

patronage, it was the publicans who organised the game. In less idealised form, and at much the same period, cricket at Pudsey was unknown

> except as played mostly in the lanes or small openings in the village
> — with a tub leg for a bat, made smaller at one end for a handle, a
> wall cape, or some large stone, set on end for a stump (called a
> 'hob'), and a pot taw or some hard substance covered with listing
> and sometimes sewed on the top with twine or band. They were all
> one-ball overs if double cricket was played; no umpires, and often
> those who cheated the hardest won.[5]

It was from these suspect origins, much more than from the gentry-
sponsored games of the south, that cricket emerged as a popular spectator sport in the first half of the century. In 1824 there were 17,000
spectators at a match in Sheffield, and in 1835 20,000 working-class
men, women and children watched the Nottingham versus Sussex
match. These and other less notable games were reported in that journal
of the Fancy, *Bell's Life in London*, and there was only pardonable
exaggeration in its editor's claim in 1844:

> I attribute the Extension of the Game of Cricket very much to the
> Paper of which I am the Editor. Having been the Editor Twenty
> Years, I can recollect when the Game of Cricket was not so popular
> as it is at the present Moment; but the Moment the Cricketers found
> themselves the Object of Attention almost every Village had its
> Cricket Green. The Record of their Prowess in Print created a Desire
> still more to extend their Exertions and their Fame. Cricket has
> become almost universal . . .[6]

Indeed, but under auspices which must make the respectable shudder.
And probably more important than the journals of the Fancy was
something equally worrisome, the role of the professional. As Mandle
has written, 'In England, cricket, hitherto a game for gentry and their
servants or a knock-about recreation for self-employed Midland weavers,
entered national life through the itinerant efforts of William Clarke's
All-England Eleven from 1846 on.' Clarke was a Nottingham man, a
bricklayer by trade, a fine bowler, and an astute manager; he paid each
of his men £4 a match, and took the balance of takings for himself. He
soon had rivals. In 1852 John Wisden formed the breakaway 'United
England Eleven', in 1858 Sherman and Chadband organised a 'New All
England Eleven', in 1862 Fred Caesar was responsible for 'Another New

All England Eleven' and in 1865 for the United South of England Eleven. These were touring professional teams, and as Altham and Swanston acknowledge, 'were truly missionaries of cricket, winning to knowledge and appreciation of the game whole districts where hitherto it had been primitive and undeveloped'. In 1859 there occurred the first overseas tour, all professional, to America and Canada, and in 1861 the first, again all professional, to Australia. In the light of these developments there can be no dissent from the conclusion of C.L.R. James that in the development of cricket 'The class of the population that seems to have contributed least was the class destined to appropriate the game and convert it into a national institution. This was the solid Victorian middle class.'[7]

The process of appropriation owed something to a change in the rules in 1864, legalising over-arm bowling, but much more to the achievements of one man, W.G. Grace. In the early 1860s county cricket, the key to upper- and middle-class control, was in a most rudimentary state. It was only in that decade that the county cricket clubs of Hampshire, Lancashire, Middlesex and Yorkshire came into being. Grace, entering the first-class scene in 1864, was an immediate and spectacular success. His achievement, helped by the legalisation of over-arm bowling, was to reverse the trend whereby the professionals dominated the game, and he did it by outplaying them; of 40 matches between the Gentlemen and the Players between 1865 and 1881 the Gentlemen won 27 and lost only 5. Through these victories the amateurs could reassert their control over the game, and reduce the professionals to a subordinate position. As James writes, 'It is not possible that cricket would have reached and held the position it did among the upper classes if the Gentlemen, that is to say the products of the public schools and the universities, had been as consistently and cruelly beaten as they had been by the professionals before W.G. began.'[8]

By the late 1860s the Eton versus Harrow match had become an important part of the London season. By 1870 the counties were ranked according to performance, and in the course of that decade the last book-makers were removed from Lord's. The MCC after a period in the doldrums began to revive. Upper- and middle-class control was being asserted, and on the basis of it the moral qualities of cricket could safely be preached. Christians now exalted in their prowess at the game, rather than denied it. And in Pudsey those primitive beginnings were but a dim memory from the past; in the 1880s Joseph Lawson could write that cricket has had a most wonderful influence for good on the young men of Pudsey — not only on the players, but on the spectators as well. By cricket, players are taught patience, endurance, precision and courage. They are taught self-respect and gentlemanly conduct in bowing to the decision of the umpires, and derive physical benefit as well. The discipline taught by the game of cricket is great and invaluable. . .

With such a comment, we may safely say, the process of appropriation was complete.[9]

The appropriation of sport was all the more urgent because of its traditional importance in the public schools. Now, with the foundation of new middle-class-oriented public schools — Cheltenham, Marlborough, Rossall and Radley all in the 1840s — the problems posed by sport had to be faced. Some of the older schools, Harrow in particular, and then Winchester in the mid-1830s through the influence of the old Harrovian Charles Wordsworth, had given a serious purpose to games-playing in the first half of the century, but equally common was the attitude of Butler, Headmaster of Shrewsbury 1798-1836, who saw football as 'only fit for butcher boys'. And traditionally it was in games above all that the boys asserted their independence of authority.

It was no part of Thomas Arnold's plans for the reform of Rugby that organised games should become as important as in time they did. But since they embodied that antagonism between masters and boys which he wished to overcome, he could not simply ignore them. He himself favoured individualistic sports, like gymnastics and throwing the spear, but the traditional games flourished. As McIntosh has written, 'the growth of athleticism at Rugby may be regarded . . . as the price paid by Arnold for the cooperation of the boys in maintaining discipline and effecting the reforms which he desired'.[10]

It was Arnold's disciples who began to see organised sport as a key means of asserting control and moulding character, while at the same time allowing boys some measure of self-government. Between 1845 and 1862 the seven main public schools committed their football rules to written form. Headmasters became advocates of organised sports. At Marlborough G.E.L. Cotton sent a circular letter to parents in 1853 extolling the 'healthy and manly' games of cricket and football as against

other amusements, often of a questionable character in themselves, or at least liable to considerable abuse, and which have no effect in providing constant and wholesome recreation for the boys. Many do not spend their half-holidays in the playground, but in wandering

about the country, some in bird's nesting, or in damaging property
of the neighbours, or other undesirable occupations.

The element of social control in the fostering of organised games could
hardly be more openly stated. In the following year Thring became
Headmaster at Uppingham, and not only preached the gospel of organised games but also participated in them. In the 1850s and 1860s
Clifton, Haileybury, Wellington and King Edward VI, Birmingham, all
had headmasters who had been pupils or masters under Arnold, and all
adopted the Rugby game. Official support for games-playing came with
the 1864 Clarendon Commission on the older public schools which concluded that 'the importance which boys themselves attach to games is
somewhat greater, perhaps, than might reasonably be desired; but
within moderate limits it is highly useful'.[11]

'Useful': that is certainly one reason why games-playing spread in
the mid-century period, for it became an essential part of the organisation and structure of the public schools. But it was not simply utility
which encouraged the growth, nor was that growth confined to the
public schools. There were other reasons, which take us back to the
process of appropriation, and which may best be appreciated by looking at Thomas Hughes's *Tom Brown's School-Days*, first published in
1857, and selling 11,000 copies within a year. In its celebration of public schools and games, the book is at the same time a criticism of industrial, commercial and urban life. As Hughes put it, 'The ideas and
habits which those who have most profited by them bring away from
our public schools do not fit them to become successful traders.'
Rather it was the life-style of the gentry which was held up for admiration, a life-style which could reconcile the middle class's urge for
social acceptance and its wish not simply to ape the aristocracy. In the
public school boys could acquire the new-model gentry values: unin-
tellectual, combative, manly, Christian and patriotic. As Tom says to
Arthur: 'I want to be A1 at cricket and football and all the other games,
and to make my hands keep my head against any fellow, lout or gentleman. I want to get into the sixth before I leave, and to please the
Doctor; and I want to carry away just as much Latin and Greek as will
take me through Oxford respectably.' These values, it is suggested, not
only now, but throughout English history have been at the heart of
the nation's achievement: 'Talbots and Stanleys, St Maurs, and suchlike folk, have led armies and made laws time out of mind; but those
noble families would be somewhat astounded — if the account ever
came to be fairly taken — to find how small their work for England has

been by the side of that of the Browns.' For Hughes, it seems, the process of appropriation must be facilitated by the rewriting of history so that the star roles are played by the Browns; and it was easy for the mid-nineteenth-century middle class to identify with the new-model gentry values of the Browns.

The appeal of *Tom Brown's School-Days* was enhanced by the fact that it was written in the aftermath of the aristocratic mismanagement of the Crimean War, a war which also had the effect of bringing Englishmen face to face with the role of force and of fighting in industrial and urban communities. The war created the myth of the Christian hero, and Tom Brown was that same hero in fiction. Both were living proof that 'old English' virtues could survive in an industrial and urban civilisation, and that their social location now lay within the gentry, not the aristocracy. War, and its nearest approximation, sport, also served as a bulwark against two other insidious and connected threats: tractarianism and effeminacy. Puseyism, as David Newsome has commented, was the greatest stimulus to muscular Christianity. Games-playing was English, Protestant and masculine. 'Fighting with fists', wrote Hughes, 'is the natural and English way for English boys to settle their quarrels.'[12] How often had Pierce Egan and others said the same in the heyday of prize-fighting? Now the argument, and the sport, was being taken away from the Fancy and appropriated for the benefit of the public schools and the respectable middle class.

The implications of the book and of its popularity seem inescapable. Sport, said Veblen at the end of the century, was an atavistic survival of the old barbarian virtue of prowess. 'The ground of an addiction to sports', he wrote, 'is an archaic spiritual constitution – the possession of the predatory emulative propensity in a relatively high potency.'[13] And however modernised the sports became – defined space and time, set rules and so on – they retained something of the characteristic noted by Veblen. In its attempt to appropriate sport the middle class was seeking an escape from its own world, and an escape not into the future but into the past; the model which it held up before itself was that of the gentry – of what one might call a purposeful leisure class. In view of this it is hardly surprising that with the sports that they appropriated the middle class should also take over the ideological lumber with which they were encrusted. That included not only the arguments that sport promoted patriotism and prevented effeminacy, but also, and most important of all, that it effected a union of classes.

With this new acceptance of physical recreation and of sport the argument for class conciliation through leisure could be broadened from the rather restricting rational recreations of the 1840s. And in the 1850s, in the aftermath of Chartism, and in the rosy glow shed by the Great Exhibition, the moment seemed appropriate for a new initiative.

Hugh Shimmin in Liverpool in 1858, in a book dedicated to the officers and members of that quintessentially middle-class body, the National Association for the Promotion of Social Science, put the matter in historical perspective:

> Time was, when the distinction of classes in this country was not so strongly marked: then the upper appeared to take more interest in the pastimes of the lower. The rapid advance of manufacturing industry has totally changed the relation of the classes, and the labourers have been left to themselves in a great measure, so far as their recreation is concerned.[14]

The task was obvious: the upper class must once again take an interest in the pastimes of the lower class. What could not be predicted was the extent to which recourse would be had both to the sports and pastimes and to the language of those early nineteenth-century traditionalists, whose landscape was inhabited by the peer and the peasant.

The first sign that this language and its implications were meeting with some acceptance outside the ranks of their more obvious advocates may be seen in the 1844 House of Lords Select Committee on Gaming which, called to enquire into 'the extensive Frauds which have of late been perpetrated on the Turf' resisted the temptation to clamp down on racing, thinking it 'desirable that this Amusement should be upheld, because it is in accordance with a long-established National Taste; because it serves to bring together, for a common Object, vast Bodies of People in different Parts of the Country, and to promote Intercourse between different Classes of Society.' Nothing very remarkable here, it may be said, considering the aristocratic source of the comment; but it was an indication that these kinds of argument about the social function of leisure were beginning to be thought sufficiently weighty to be worth the consideration of government. Move ahead a quarter of a century, moreover, and we will find the same arguments, this time in defence of Derby Day, being put by a very different figure, the journalist Blanchard Jerrold:

> All classes are intermingled for a few hours on the happiest terms . . .
> It cannot be pretended by the keenest lover of the course and the
> hunting-field that racing promotes any of the virtues. On the other

hand it fosters a general love of gambling. But this Derby-day has its bright – even its useful side. It gives all London an airing, an 'outing'; makes a break in our over-worked lives; and effects a beneficial commingling of classes.[15]

In the intervening quarter of a century every form of leisure was assessed and weighed in terms of the contribution it could make to an improvement in class relations. Small events became pregnant with larger consequences. The annual flower show evoked this comment from the *Banbury Guardian* in 1866:

Floriculture and horticulture while being a health giving is also a pure and harmless recreation, which may be engaged in by individuals of either sex and of all stations of life – the peasant as well as the peer, the overtoiled man of business and the industrious artisan, on every imaginable scale from a single flower pot to the princely conservatory.[16]

Cricket was a more obvious example, and, once safely appropriated, its potential seemed vast. The local press had this to say on an 1869 match between Lord Monson's Burton Park Club and the Gentlemen's Servants Club:

This match strikingly shows that cricket recognizes no distinctions of class; that it is, and ever has been, one of the principal agents in bringing the different grades of society into contact, and showing that God's mental and moral as well as His natural gifts, are bestowed alike upon the peasant and the peer. Some thirty, or even twenty years ago, this match would have been ε social impossibility.

Elsewhere cricketers wore belts inscribed with the motto, 'The Prince and peasant by cricket are united'.[17] The Volunteer Force, founded in 1859, seemed for a time to offer even more than cricket. As Thomas Hughes put it in 1860:

The difficulty of finding a common standing-ground, anything in which we may all work together; where we can stand shoulder to shoulder, and man to man, each counting for what he is worth; the peer without condescending, and the peasant without cringing, is almost as great as ever. Here, in volunteering, we think we have found what may, when rightly handled, do much towards filling up this gap.

And in 1865 the *Pall Mall Gazette* was most impressed by the annual Wimbledon rifle shooting:

> The healthy mixture of all ranks at the butts and in the tents contin-
> ues to be one of the most valuable features of the gathering. Young
> marquises and earls and squires are there, shoulder to shoulder with
> strong hardfisted men, speaking every dialect, from the roughest
> Scotch to the softest Devonian patois. And though several of our
> English games are great levellers . . . we are inclined to think that
> this new sport of yesterday bears the bell in this respect, even from
> cricket.[18]

The tone and language of these comments is significant. It was not simply that mid-Victorians were hoping that the classes could meet in leisure; it was that they were doing so in the language of 'peer' and 'peasant'. In an urban and industrial society, and one in many ways dominated by middle-class values, the advocates of class conciliation in leisure use a language which bears no relation to social reality; England in the second half of the nineteenth century is not peopled by peers and peasants. How can we explain this language? What is happening, I suggest, is an attempt by the middle class to appropriate to itself the values of a refined gentry. And this in itself is symptomatic of a profound rejection of urban and industrial civilisation, and of a wish to escape back into a simpler patron-client kind of society.

The hopes of the mid-Victorian middle class may best be appreciated by looking at two advocates of class conciliation through leisure. The first is H.A. Bruce, a Peelite MP from 1852, and later a Liberal and Home Secretary in Gladstone's first government. His speeches in the 1850s give a sense of the weight and importance he placed on leisure. In an address in 1855 at the opening of the Cardiff Arts Exhibition he said, 'Next to the deep-pervading sentiment of religion, I know nothing of more importance to the well-being of a people than well-ordered amusements.' Five years earlier in a lecture at Merthyr Tydfil the language of religion had been applied to leisure; for, doubting the adequacy of education in making the working class 'more happy, contented and virtuous, better workmen, better citizens, better Christians', Bruce declared that for him 'the simplest, most natural, most efficacious instrument of redemption seems to be, to provide, or to assist the working classes to provide, those means of innocent pleasure, of social enjoyment, at which moral and mental improvement rather insinuate themselves than are enforced.' This was all the more important because of past failures, said Bruce: 'Of all the leading people of Europe, I grieve to say, those worst provided with the means of rational and manly amusements are the inhabitants of the British Isles.' Bruce hoped to achieve the redemption of the working class − redemption with its connotations of sin and a return to something better − through leisure. The sin was on both sides; the middle class should have provided something better, the working class should not so easily have succumbed to the temptations of the beer-house. However, in the provision of 'well-ordered amusements' by the rich for the poor, class conflict might be stilled, and the level of civilisation raised.[19]

The same kind of language was used by Henry Solly, the founder-secretary of the Working Men's Club and Institute Union, who after 20 years of trying to bring the classes together, came to believe that it might be achieved in the recreational ambience of the clubs. The benefits would be mutual and far-reaching. For Solly believed not only that the working classes were too inclined to resort to the beer-house, but also that the wealthier classes were becoming too effete and luxurious. It was therefore, as he put it, fortunate rather than otherwise that working men were generally unable to raise the funds for a club, 'as it gives wealthier people the occasion for rendering them help of an elevating nature, and of strengthening the bonds of good feeling between different classes'. A 'nobler life' would be rekindled among the middle and upper classes, the teachers would benefit as much as the taught, and society would once again be modelled on paternalist lines. For Solly had a vision of

the bearing of all such interchange of influence upon the elevation and refinement of the working classes, the extent to which it would eradicate class prejudices, and develop in them a sense of citizenship, of common national life, of oneness with the classes above them, the new and nobler links of gratitude by which it would bind them to those upper classes, the preparation it would give them for the wise and faithful exercise of political duties . . .[20]

Not only in sport, we can see, but on any kind of leisure occasion the meeting of the classes was coming to have a most far-reaching significance.

Solly was influenced by and in contact with the Christian Socialists, and it was probably within their ranks − F.D. Maurice, Thomas Hughes,

Charles Kingsley, J.M. Ludlow — that the hopes of what might be achieved through leisure were at their greatest. But it would be wrong to suggest that the aim of achieving class reconciliation through leisure was confined to a small if well-publicised group. If the Christian Socialists were the most articulate spokesmen of class reconciliation through leisure, there were many others who were groping in the same direction with less conscious awareness, perhaps, of what they were doing. Indeed in both rural and urban society the aim found institutional form.

It was easiest to achieve this in the countryside. As we have seen, the language of class conciliation was archaic, reflecting the social structure of a mythical rural past which, in so far as it had ever had any reality, had been destroyed by capitalist agriculture and the class relationships which were part of it. Now, in mid-century, there came a quite deliberate attempt to revive paternalism, to recreate community.

In Lincolnshire, for example, harvest suppers were revived in the late 1850s, sometimes associated with another innovation, a harvest festival in the parish church.[21] In the village it was easier than in the town to think in terms of community, and much of this revivalism of festivals and of 'rural sports' and fetes — occasions patronised and controlled by the wealthy and participated in by a deferential populace — was an attempt to reassert community over class values in a rural society increasingly riven by class. The new paternalism was most successful in its creation of ritual around the Friendly Societies which were more likely to be controlled from above in the village than in the town. This process probably began in the 1840s for it was then that Margaret Fuller in her study of West Country Friendly Societies found most evidence of participation by honorary members in the management of the societies. In Oxfordshire, too, there was a mid-century emphasis on control from above. At Whitsun, the keypoint in the Friendly Society year, the old brutal sports were replaced by order and moderation, and a public ceremony became an occasion for achieving class harmony. Indeed as with other institutions we have studied, for example the mechanics' institutes, these annual public ceremonies became more and more significant, often thrusting into the background the mundane day-to-day work of providing against sickness and poverty. Both the hopes and the self-conscious revivalism of these ceremonies are captured in the comment of a patron of a Wiltshire society in 1872, 'By means of what we call festivals (that is to say a jollification promoted in each parish where we have a branch) a vast amount of information is distributed, good fellowship and good understanding are promoted in different classes . . .' Accounts of such occasions leave one in no doubt that they were participated in and enjoyed by many in the lower ranks of rural society. But there was after all little else for them to enjoy, and even so the new paternalism was not established without some show of opposition. The more independent Friendly Societies were favoured by such a man as Joseph Ashby of Tysoe. And amongst some there was a distaste for childish sports; in 1872 in Lincolnshire the Primitive Methodists tried to persuade labourers not to 'befool' themselves by rustic antics such as sack races in which they had been encouraged by gentlemen of the parish.[22]

It was even more difficult to impose a new paternalism in the city, but the attempt was certainly made. As Gareth Stedman Jones has argued, the prescription for the problems of the East End in the 1860s was thought to lie in the creation of a resident gentry, 'a new urban squirearchy'. A one-class community, certainly a wholly working-class community, by definition could not be a healthy one; indeed it could hardly be said to be a community at all. Hence the proposals for settlements in the East End. They were designed to bring the classes together under the leadership of the gentry through the organisation of leisure activities and leisure time. Less ambitious institutions also came into being to serve the purpose of bringing the classes together through leisure, for example, the ubiquitous penny readings which had, as C.M. Davies wrote in 1875, 'a sound principle lying at the bottom of the movement, insofar as it was designed to bring about a fusion of classes; though, perhaps, it involved too much of an assumption that the "working man" had to be lectured to, or read to, by his brother in purple and fine linen'.[23]

All these deliberate attempts to improve class relationships through leisure were considered by optimistic reformers to be having some success. 'Brother Volunteers', enthused the Liverpool Volunteer, James Walter, on the coming of age of the Force in 1881, 'it is joyous to feel and know that there is a largely increasing sympathy between our various classes of society. This is one of the best signs of our time, and Volunteers have done much for it.' So too, others argued, had cricket, horticulture, friendly societies, mechanics' institutes, choral singing, penny readings, and a plethora of other organisations and occasions. Leisure time now presented not so much a problem as a hope, a hope that through its proper management it might lead to a reconciliation of classes, a recreation of community and a reassertion of paternalism.[24] In all these hopes there was a large degree of wish-fulfilment, but it is a testimony to the importance of leisure in mid-Victorian times that such

high hopes and expectations should be placed upon it; hopes and expectations which ultimately it could not bear, for reasons which we
must now examine.

Perhaps the most obvious reason was that noted by Hippolyte Taine
in his comments on Derby Day. Far from seeing, as Jerrold had, a
'beneficial commingling of classes', Taine was somewhat disgusted by a
familiarity between classes which clearly lasted only for a day:

> Good humour and unreserved merriment; classes mingle; P—, one of
> our party, has met his usual coachman at table with a gentleman,
> two ladies, and a child. The gentleman had employed and then
> invited the coachman; the coachman introduces P—, who is amicably
> compelled to drink port, sherry, stout, and ale. In fact, today it is
> hail fellow well met; but this lasts for a day only, after the manner
> of the ancient saturnalia. On the morrow distinctions of rank will be
> as strong as ever, and the coachman will be as respectful, distant, as
> is his wont.[25]

Derby Day was but a moment in the year, and the relaxation of social
tensions then was the condition for their normal strict observance. Such
occasions were indeed 'after the manner of the ancient saturnalia', a
momentary overturning of the social order which had the effect of
confirming it. It is true that on most of the other once-off annual leisure occasions that we have discussed there would be less overt familiarity between classes, but one cannot escape the sense that many occasions on which class conciliation was preached and to an extent practised — the Christmas party of the mechanics' institutes, for example —
were possible only because they were rare.

On occasions and in institutions where the classes met more frequently in leisure, such as the Volunteer Force, the maintenance of
social barriers was much more marked. Indeed it was one of the attractions of the Volunteer Force to its middle-class advocates that it repro-
duced the social structure of the workplace on the parade-ground;
middle-class officers, lower middle-class or upper working-class NCOs,
working-class rank and file. With at least a pretence of military discipline, undue familiarity could be resisted, while at the same time the
middle class could be active patrons of working-class leisure. The consequences which they hoped would flow from such a meeting of the
classes are instructive; the rank and file would in work as much as in
leisure become more obedient, more punctual, more respectful and
more valuable to their employers.[26]

Indeed it was a sense of the difficulty of achieving any kind of understanding between the classes in work which drove people to look for it in leisure. The more intensive use of labour which seems to begin in mid-century required more labour discipline not less, and hence made difficult any relaxation of class relationships at the workplace. Even optimists, even those creating working conditions most favourable to class co-operation, found themselves looking to leisure for its achievement. Solly hoped that the meeting of the classes in the Working Men's Clubs would 'prepare for that mutual good understanding in case of Trade disputes, perhaps for those mutual concessions or explanations, or that successful arbitration, which would give the best chance of fair play for all, and obviate the warlike proceedings of a Strike or Lock-out'. And Ludlow, instigator of many of the co-operative workshops, believed that it was easier to achieve class conciliation in leisure than in work. The students of the London Working Men's College, he said, went on many expeditions, 'bringing back with them, with invigorated health, a store of new memories and new ideas, and a power of assimilation to other classes which could never have been acquired within the four walls of the workshop'.[27] If it could not be acquired within the workshop, however, it was unlikely to be achieved elsewhere, for work is of primary importance in determining class relationships. The failure of mid-Victorians to recognise this was the second reason why the aim of achieving class conciliation in leisure was not fulfilled.

Closely related to it was the third reason, the fact that when the classes did meet in leisure they often interpreted the meaning of the meeting in different ways. The middle class hoped that the working class in leisure would accept and assimilate middle-class norms and values. Even someone like Ludlow, sensitive to working-class objectives, could write of them having 'a power of assimilation to other classes'. Others, less sensitive, hoped to achieve this in ways both patronising and authoritarian. It would be quite wrong to pretend that just because class conciliation was a new and dominant ideology of leisure, the older wish simply to suppress and control the leisure of the working class had evaporated. More interestingly, however, where the meeting of the classes was apparently on more equal terms and where the ideology was openly stated, the meanings attached to the experience were very different. And those meetings were likely in the nature of the case to be with the upper working class, with the aristocracy of labour. Until recently it might have been argued that the emergence of an aristocracy of labour at mid-century suggests a convergence of middle

and upper working-class values; or more crudely that the aristocracy
of labour accepted bourgeois values. The closely related and convincing work of Gray, Crossick and Tholfsen, however, has shown that a
simple assimilationist model does less than justice to the complexity
of the value system of the labour aristocracy, or, it may be added, of
other sections of the working class. Their argument is that although
the stated values of the labour aristocrats — respectability, thrift and
so on — look bourgeois in content they were in fact invested with
different meanings; in particular that they express the aspirations of a
group rather than of an individual. Gray thus argues that, for the labour
aristocracy, respectability 'is properly interpreted as a claim to status
recognition and citizenship on behalf of skilled workers as a corporate
group'.[28]

Armed with these insights we may see how the class-conciliatory
objectives embedded in many of the recreational institutions of mid-
Victorian England failed to be realised. The hope of achieving class
conciliation in the Volunteer Force, for example, was voiced by the
officers, not the men. For the former, it was the manly and patriotic
recreation within the Force, together with its semblance of military
discipline, which gave it such potency as a forum for achieving class
harmony. If the latter were stirred by patriotism at all, it was probably
of a more radical, Garibaldian kind than that of their officers, but
undoubtedly the main reason why they joined the Force was because
of their desire to enjoy the recreation available within it. The force of
this demand was strong enough to push officers into providing forms of
recreation within the Force which otherwise would not have occurred
to them. Moreover there is no evidence from below to suggest that
working men felt themselves to be any closer to their officers as a
consequence of this recreation; if anything the evidence suggests the
opposite. Quite simply, an ideology conceived by middle-class spokesmen for the Force met with neither understanding nor acceptance by
those working-class people who made up the bulk of the membership.[29]

The same is true of the Working Men's Clubs. Solly's aims and hopes
were to be rudely shaken, first over the issue of the admission of beer
to the clubs, and then more seriously when from the early 1870s the
clubs began to challenge the patronage of and financial dependence on
the rich. Finally in 1883-4, the clubs were victorious, freed themselves
from patronage, and became a true working-class organisation. Here was
irony indeed. For it had been a constant theme of the Union's middle-
class supporters, indeed in some sense the basic reason for their involvement, that the clubs should be instruments of class conciliation. As late

as November 1883 the *Club and Institute Journal* was claiming that

> The Union is in no respect a class institution; we have quite enough
> of those already. One of the best features of Union work . . . lies in
> the fact that it brings people of different grades and classes together
> and helps remove that idiotic and wicked class prejudice which are
> the bane and curse of society.

From the mid-1880s, however, if not before, many clubs were independent working-class organisations, and frequently radical and class-
conscious in their politics.[30] As with the Volunteers, the ideology
imposed from above had struck no roots. The classes met, but no new
understanding, far less camaraderie, resulted.

The history of football follows much the same pattern. In the conventional history of the game the public schools and Oxbridge are the
dominant force from the moment the public schools begin to write
down their rules, through the foundation of the Football Association in
1863 and up to that symbolic defeat of the Old Etonians by Blackburn
Olympic in the Cup Final of 1883, and the legalisation of professional-
ism in 1885. There is a period of amateur dominance, almost exactly
paralleling that in cricket. And during that period the middle class are
seen as missionaries, using football as, amongst other things, a forum
for class conciliation, and founding many of the clubs that dominate
the professional leagues today. Aston Villa, Bolton Wanderers, Wolverhampton Wanderers, Everton, all foundations of the 1870s, have their
origins, we learn, in religious organisations. Preston North End were
financed by their employers, Peel Hall Mill, and the committee of the
first Sheffield Football Club included the later chairman of the
Sheffield Forge Company and the future head of Vickers Engineering.[31]

This history is inadequate on two grounds. First, seeing things
through public school spectacles, it ignores the continuous history of
football as a popular sport. It is true that those local, traditional, annual
matches ranging over huge spaces and involving whole populations had
for the most part been abolished during the first half of the century.
But it seems highly likely that the more casual practice of kicking a ball
around, a practice much closer to the modern game of football,
survived. Irishmen, for example, were reported by Hone to play football on Sunday afternoons in open fields near Islington. And in the
West Riding coalfield, football as well as cricket and nor-&-spell were
played on wasteland by young miners in their relatively plentiful spare
time.[32] This kind of football, precisely because it was so casual, was

unlikely to leave behind it many records; that however is no indication
that it was rare. At this stage of historical research one can do no more
than speculate that the middle-class missionaries found it unnecessary
to spend time converting the working-class natives; the latter were
already enthusiastic lovers of the game.

This brings us to our second criticism of the conventional history.
Listing the ultra-respectable origins of the leading clubs implies that
middle-class ideology permeated the game and all its players. What
seems more plausible is that football as developed by the amateurs
required a defined space and some capital investment, and that such
access to land and money was beyond the working class. Hence they
needed sponsors, and the middle-class amateurs were sponsors more
than missionaries. As such, they might be little more than a respectable
façade to be cast aside when necessary. Aston Villa, for example,
although connected with the Bible Class of a Wesleyan Chapel, had
playing fields provided by a local butcher, and a dressing room supplied
by a local publican. Working men, anxious to play football, were perhaps none too concerned about the means by which they could trans-
late their aspirations into reality. The sponsorship and patronage of the
rich certainly did not imply a submission to their control and values.

Detailed examination of the development of the game, indeed,
suggests that the middle-class input was much less than one might
suppose. Geographically the 1860s and 1870s saw not only the flowering
of the southern public school tradition, but also the laying of the foundations of the game in Sheffield, Nottingham, Birmingham, the Black
Country and Lancashire. Contemporaneously with horse-racing, clubs
started charging for admission, Aston Villa leading the way in the early
1870s. County cups in Lancashire, Birmingham and Staffordshire
established forms of competition, and in the 1870s the number of spectators was already substantial. All these developments owed much more
to the greater availability and regularity of time for leisure amongst the
working class than they did to the impact on the game of the public
schools.[33] We may conclude indeed that middle-class claims for their
own impact on the game have had more influence on the historiography
of football than they have had on its practice.

The suggestion we are making here is that the working class, for lack
of any alternative, was prepared to accept for as long as necessary, the
fact of middle-class sponsorship, but not its ideology. The demand for
recreation was great, and in this mid-Victorian period the commercialisation of it was only partial. Hence middle-class rational recreationists
had an apparent opportunity to achieve in leisure their supreme objec-

tive — a better understanding between the classes. They failed to realise that working-class people approached these recreational occasions without any such objective. They wanted simply to enjoy what was being offered, and as soon as financial constraints allowed they shook off what they perceived as heavy-handed patronage. Within the Working Men's Clubs and in football this had been achieved by the mid-1880s. Within the Volunteer Force it was never entirely possible, but after the 1870s experience brought home to the middle-class officers that the hopes of class conciliation which they had nourished at the time of the Force's foundation were unlikely to be fulfilled, and they quietly dropped the hope from their public statements.

These three forms of recreation, typical as they are of those espoused by the middle class in the search for class conciliation, were all exclusively male. And herein lies a fourth reason for the failure of the hopes. Class conciliation was intended to bring middle-class men into contact with working-class men, and to a lesser extent middle-class women with working-class women, but scarcely at all to let down the barriers of both class and sex. If the sexes were to meet in leisure it must be within class boundaries. The more liberal rational recreationists could be happy at the sight of working-class wives accompanying their husbands to the music-hall, but would not invite their own wives to observe such a scene. And on the other side of the class barrier, croquet and archery could, as Jerrold put it, beguile 'the hours of sentiment', but only because there was no danger of class mixing in them. Women began to hunt only in the 1850s when the social exclusivity of the sport had been firmly established.[34]

Leisure for women, it was assumed, posed little problem, for the solution to it lay in the home, and in the home, in the nature of the case, there could be no class-mixing. Although there was some unease that on the Saturday half-holiday the men might be free to enjoy themselves while the women scrubbed and cleaned, the answer was not that men should help, but that wives should not work. The proper task of women was that of home-making, one of particular importance among the working class. 'In no rank of society', wrote Thomas Wright, 'have home influences so great a power for good or evil, as among the working classes.' In any minutes spared from this almost unending task women might possibly engage in some self-improving occupation or join in a family excursion, but generally their leisure was confined within the bounds of home, family and class. This was the almost instinctive ideal of the middle-class rational recreationists, and as a result they gave little thought to the leisure of women. As Walter Besant wrote in

1884, 'As regards the women, I declare that I have never been able to find out anything at all concerning their amusements.' Almost exclusively they were men dealing with men.[35]

The sexual barriers could be crossed in class-conciliatory leisure only when the relationship was clearly one of authority, and the occasion therefore as far as possible asexual. Even in such circumstances there was a certain piquant novelty; in the mid-1860s the Working Men's College spawned a Working Women's College; A.J. Munby who taught there noted in his diary:

> One has to remind oneself that these are girls, sitting in front of one, writing or repeating their latin; that this is for oneself a new relation of the sexes; and after all tis hard to realize that it *is* new; it seems so natural, so independent of sex.

In any more relaxed setting the crossing of the sexual as well as the class barrier was fraught with difficulty. The general rule was that any woman in a public place of leisure, and unaccompanied by husband or other suitable male, was a prostitute. And if there was any real commingling of classes in recreation it was, ironically enough, where prostitute met client. The prostitute was evidently easily recognisable, and as a result not only particular places of entertainment, but whole areas of towns were no-go areas, at least at night, for respectable women. In London the Haymarket was the principal area for higher class prostitution, and a gentleman could make a choice between Kate Hamilton's, Lizzie Davis's, Sam's, Sally's and other more or less select supper rooms. No respectable woman would wish to be seen anywhere in the area, nor would she go near either of the two leading casinos, the Argyll Rooms and the Holborn, or Cremorne Gardens. Acton, who visited the latter in the course of duty, described it as frequented by some 700 men of the upper and middle classes, none of them looking as though they were enjoying themselves; and though decorum reigned, he 'could have little moral doubt' of the character of the female visitors.[36]

Music-hall, and to a lesser extent theatre, were also suspect because of the presence of prostitutes. Although in giving evidence before the 1866 Select Committee on Theatrical Licences and Regulations, the police and magistrates stressed the decorous behaviour of the prostitutes who frequented the halls, they would perhaps have agreed with the sentiments of Benjamin Webster, Proprietor and Manager of the Adelphi Theatre who when asked, 'Do you think that a person must lose cast by going to a music hall?' replied, 'Yes; even if my son went there I should not like it; and as to taking my wife and family there I should think I was a scandalous person if I did so.'[37] The awkward fact, however, remained that only in such places did middle-class men meet working-class women in leisure, a meeting which was vitiated by the fact that for women this was work.

In almost every society it is one of the functions of leisure to provide an opportunity for sexual encounters. An ideology of leisure which ˜tries to prevent that is saddling itself with difficulties. The ideology of class conciliation through leisure did precisely that, and it did it, it may be argued, not because of some unrelated ideology of sex, but precisely because that ideology was bound up with the compulsions of class. The perfect lady of the mid-Victorian years, removed not only from worldly concerns, but also from household ones, was a symbol of her husband's wealth and status. She was part of the leisure class, but in somewhat the same way as an unemployed man was – by compulsion. And while in the latter case the opportunities to be enjoyed in leisure were cruelly curtailed by lack of money, in the former they were restricted by a concern for the maintenance of status. Conspicuous leisure and conspicuous consumption were a mark of status, their utility for purposes of reputability lying in the element of waste common to both – waste of time and effort, or waste of goods. Dress for women, therefore had to be both expensive and impractical for productive labour; designedly uncomfortable, it testified in a general way to woman's economic dependence on man, and specifically to the status of a particular man. These concerns with status led, as is well known (and was much deplored at the time), to late marriages, so that the husband, well set in his career, could keep his wife in the manner which she had been led to expect as daughter. And this in turn encouraged a boom in prostitution as young middle-class men, unable for financial reasons to marry, sought an outlet for their sexual urges.[38]

Significantly the cash transaction of prostitution was somewhat less horrifying to contemporaries than any non-commercial cross-class liaison. A.J. Munby, a barrister employed by the Ecclesiastical Commission and the lover and eventually secret husband of a servant girl, was made even more than usually aware of this when in 1863 he attended the Eton versus Harrow match at Lord's in his role of eligible middle-class bachelor:

The conversation turned on Lord Robert Montagu's recent marriage with a housemaid. Other cases of the kind were mentioned, and that with due contempt and abhorrence, by the ladies: and at length Miss

Williams drew me into a keen tête à tête discussion on the subject of
such mésalliances, which lasted nearly all the time we were there. If
she had known how nearly the question troubled me, and how all I
said had a secret reference to a certain maid of all work, I fear that
the respect and preference with which she has lately honoured me
would quickly disappear. For she spoke with such bitterness and
scorn of all servant maids and suchlike, that I half fancied she had
some private reason for doing so. She refused to believe that any
such woman could by possibility be refined in nature, or be com-
panionable for a man of education. She knew them by experience:
their faces might be pretty and their manner modest, but within,
they were full of baseness and vulgarity.[39]

There were many like Miss Williams, and she as much as Munby's 'maid
of all work' was trapped in a class role. It is true that towards the end
of the century women of all classes gained more autonomy in the pursuit of leisure, but in the mid-Victorian period, in the heyday of the
ideology of class conciliation through leisure, it might be said that
women of all classes, though in different ways, were confined in a
world where they were more the objects than the subjects of leisure. As
such neither they nor their menfolk could contemplate any lowering of
both sex and class barriers except when the relationship was overtly
authoritarian or patronising.

There was one further reason, and a most important one, for the
failure of the attempt to achieve class conciliation in leisure: there was
a thrust in the opposite direction, within the middle class, towards the
creation of sports and other leisure activities from which the working
class was excluded. This took three forms. First, middle-class infiltration into the previously exclusive leisure world of the aristocracy.
Secondly, the appropriation and imposition of a middle-class ethos on
sports and other leisure activities which might previously have been
described as popular. And thirdly, the invention of new leisure activities which were designedly class-specific.

The infiltration of the leisure world of the aristocracy was part of a
widespread emulation of aristocratic life-styles by the wealthier sections
of the middle class. From this encounter both sides gained. The middle
class brought much-needed cash to the more exclusive pastimes and in
return received a boost in status. The timing of this challenge to aristocratic exclusiveness varied. In concert life, for example, it was as early
as the 1820s that the upper middle class began to show signs of dissatis-
faction with a musical life centering on the aristocratic private salon.

Seeing their hold threatened, the aristocracy responded by expanding the salons into large-scale private concerts, featuring the most popular musicians and emphasising the exclusiveness of the gatherings. These, however, proved too expensive, and the outcome was a compromise whereby the formal and public concert replaced the salon. By the 1840s this coming together in musical life of the aristocracy and the upper middle class was symbolised by the creation of the Musical Union which replaced both the aristocratic Concerts of Ancient Music and the upper-middle-class Philharmonic concerts. High-status classical music now had an institutional form suited to the needs of a new elite which was both aristocratic and upper middle class.[40]

In hunting the challenge came a little later. The first step was to dispel any lingering ideas that it was a sport for all classes. In the 1840s Surtees was attacking publicans who for their own profit got up hunts of bag foxes for what he called the 'riff raff of the countryside', and Scrutator in 1861 hoped 'not to see any revival of that state of things which existed in the latter part of the eighteenth century, when few manufacturing towns were without a subscription pack, kept up by a club of clerks and apprentices, to the great loss of their time, injury to the surrounding country, and general demoralisation of the neighbourhood'. The poor were now firmly excluded, not that they had ever played much part in the sport, but the middle class was accepted. What happened in the age of the railway was an influx of middle-class capital, and greater participation by middle-class and frequently urban people. As Trollope wrote in the 1860s, hunting,

> open to all classes, has the effect of making all classes for a time equal in the country. We do not mean to imply that this operates on rustic labourers, or on any body of men who are paid by wages; — but it does operate very widely on all above that standing. The non-hunting world is apt to think that hunting is confined to country gentlemen, farmers, and rich strangers; but any one who will make himself acquainted with the business and position in life of the men whom he sees around him in an average hunting-field, will find that there are in the crowd attorneys, country bankers, doctors, apothecaries, — the profession of medicine has a special aptitude for fox-hunting, — malsters, millers, butchers, bakers, innkeepers, auctioneers, graziers, builders, retired officers, judges home from India, barristers who take weekly holidays, stockbrokers, newspaper editors, artists, and sailors.

There were, it must be said, more exclusive fields than this, but the participation of even a proportion of such men marked a change in the social function of hunting. It was no longer bringing together 'peer' and 'peasant', but rather melding together the middle class and the aristocracy into a new imperial ruling class.[41]

In yachting there was no problem of excluding the poor; it was the sport of the wealthy *par excellence*. 'Yachting will always be a tolerably select, if not an exclusively aristocratic sport', wrote Trollope. Just what that statement meant was revealed a little later, when the passage continues:

> The Yachting world is perhaps more heterogeneously composed than any other of our numerous sporting confederations. From a Lord Chancellor to a fashionable music-master, all sorts of conditions of men have belonged to it. Parliament and Downing Street, the Stock Exchange, the clergy, the bar, the medical profession, the army and navy, the civil service, the fine arts, literature, commerce, Manchester, and country squires, may all be found side by side in the club lists.

Clearly, as with hunting, a sport which could be described as almost 'exclusively aristocratic' contained a large leavening of the upper middle class. And the sense of unified status must have been enhanced by the peculiar visibility of the sport. As Oliver Westall has written of yachting on Lake Windermere, 'The rest of society massed to watch an elite demonstrate their distinctive economic and social position; yet despite the crowds and the bustle, the members of the "offcomer society" were carefully protected in their launches, yachts and lakeside enclosures.'[42]

The second way in which one can see a thrust towards the exclusion of the poor lay in the appropriation of sports which were previously popular. Rowing, for example, had been described by Strutt at the beginning of the century as 'exceedingly popular', attracting large crowds, and it remained so in 1844 when the editor of *Bell's Life in London* described rowing matches as 'among the most popular Sports we have in the Neighbourhood of London', a particular feature of them being that all classes participated.[43] Athletics was even lower in social tone, being associated with the pub and gambling. A young solicitor in the 1860s had to break off his engagement when his fiancée's mother discovered that he took part in athletics. Precisely at this time, however, there was a determined attempt at appropriation of both sports by the middle class. In 1866 rules were drawn up excluding not only those who made a profit or living from them, but also anyone who 'is a mechanic, artisan or labourer'. It was a ruling which lasted only some 15 years, and the middle-class ethos was never fully imposed on either sport.

The attempt to do so, however, should not be underestimated, and that it had some success may be seen in the complete and lasting change in the meaning of the word 'amateur'. Its use at the beginning of the century is indicated in a passage from Pierce Egan recording how when Richard Humphries fought Martin the Bath Butcher at Newmarket in 1786 'the whole of the amateurs rallied, and the *set-to* was witnessed by his Royal Highness the Prince of Wales, Duke of York, Duke of Orleans, and most of the French nobility at that time in England'. Nor were those amateurs above making money on the fight, for some £30,000-40,000 was sported. By mid-century this meaning of amateur as upper-class patron of and enthusiast for a sport was nearly obsolete. An amateur was now an upper- or middle-class participant in a sport confined to those classes.[44]

It was not only in sport that the middle-class appropriation of leisure was occurring. It was in mid-century that the upper- and middle-class reclamation of the theatre began to meet with some success. Charles Kean's nine-year management of the Princess's Theatre, starting in 1850,

> really marked the beginning of the end of a drama based upon the support of popular audiences, without significant participation from the fashionable, the socially respectable and the intellectually cultured segments of the population. This participation, when it occurred, led ultimately to the problem play, the middle and upper-class settings and themes of Jones, Pinero, Wilde and Shaw.

The Queen began to patronise drama, prices — which had fallen in the first half of the century — began to rise again, and theatres were remodelled, with stalls replacing the formerly rowdy pit. 'By 1880', writes Michael Booth, 'the middle-class conquest of the theatre auditorium, and consequently of the drama itself, was complete.' Soon it became difficult to remember that theatre in England could be in any sense popular.[45]

The third form taken by the thrust to exclude the working class was the invention of new, designedly class-specific leisure occasions. Once again this is most obvious in sport. It was in these years that mountaineering, tennis, cycling and golf were founded as elite recreations. Cycling, for example, in the 1870s was 'a middle-class male pastime with a sprinkling of aristocratic participants'. The class nature of the new sports was apparent too in the development of golf. The major period of growth in England came at the turn of the century, but in its Scottish homeland, and in England as it developed after the founding of the first specifically English club at Westward Ho! in 1864, it was marked by strong class distinctions. The clubs formed in the 1870s and 1880s in Lancashire, Kent and elsewhere were either on private land, charging high fees, or more contentiously on common land — in the London region on Clapham Common (1873), and on common land at Epsom, Epping Forest and Tooting Bec. Such courses led to disputes with other users of common land. As Cousins writes, 'in 1887 golf in England was played by only a few people, all belonging to the upper classes, and was regarded with indifference, if not with suspicion and aversion, by the uninitiated majority'.[46]

There can be little doubt that the desire for exclusivity was the most important reason for the failure of the hope that class conciliation might be achieved in leisure. Quite simply the Industrial Revolution had created what Trollope in 1868 described as 'the largest and wealthiest leisure class that any country, ancient or modern, ever boasted'. As a class which gained at least part of its identity from its possession of leisure, the spending of that leisure in exclusive and status-enhancing settings was of paramount importance. Not only in the three ways we have discussed but in others too the class showed considerable ingenuity in securing for itself the desired exclusivity. In the seaside resorts, for example, it appropriated to itself fashionable seasons within the year as well as whole areas of towns. In all this it behaved no differently from the leisure class of early modern times; indeed it was this very behaviour that confirmed that it was indeed a class.[47]

For centuries it had been traditional in European society to see an occasional recreational release for the populace as necessary in the interests of social control. In the mid-nineteenth century in Britain, the emphasis was different; it was not to maintain the social order by allowing the people a modicum of those 'violent delights' which Jerrold thought typical of Londoners as late as 1870.[48] It was, in consciousness of the growth of class feeling in the first half of the century, to halt and reverse the process; not to abandon authority, nor allow it on occasion to be mocked, but to reassert its legitimacy by the class-conciliatory nature of the leisure that was offered. Some middle-class Victorians strove earnestly, through co-operative workshops and the like, to reform the experience of work. Many more, accepting as given

the nature and permanence of capitalism, strove to mitigate the hard-
ships it entailed for the working class by organising their leisure for
them, and doing it in such a way as to emphasise, they hoped, the spirit
of community not of class.

Their efforts were doomed to failure. Community can hardly be
created when the wish for it comes almost exclusively from one side of
the class barrier. It is even less likely to do so when some of the promoters of the ideal are concerned solely to assimilate, not to give and take.
In the class conciliation projects of the mid-Victorian years, the concern to establish authority was as evident as the desire for reconciliation. The building of community through leisure also bore the marks of
wishful thinking, of escapism, of retreat to an ideal, patriarchal, gentry-
dominated society. For respectable liberal middle-class Victorians to
whom revolution was anathema, and the cash nexus of capitalism
socially and morally distasteful, the reform of leisure, and at the same
time an emphasis on its importance, offered the best hope of a socially
harmonious civilisation.

The debates on leisure in the mid-Victorian years, then, have a
different tone from those of earlier decades. The aim set by the middle
class for itself was more ambitious and positive. It reflected the deep
concern about class division, and in seeing the solution to it in leisure,
it both inflated the importance of leisure and helped in the process of
delimiting it. Leisure had imposed upon it perhaps the supreme task
confronting the ruling Victorian middle class, that of improving class
relations, and there could be no greater testimony to its new stature
The task imposed upon it, however, was too great. If anything in the
third quarter of the century and beyond, leisure became more rather
than less confined by class boundaries as new class-specific entertainment flourished. And leisure itself proved to be something which could
not simply be utilised to serve the immediate purposes of a hegemonic
middle class.

Notes

1. See above, p. 11.
2. W. Windham, *Speeches in Parliament*, 3 vols. (London, 1812), vol. 3, p.
315.
3. *Sporting Magazine*, September 1832, p. 359; D.P. Blaine, *An Encyclopaedia
of Rural Sports*, p. 718; R. Wood, *Victorian Delights*, pp. 35, 39.
4. G. Combe, *The Constitution of Man*, 8th edn (Edinburgh and London,
1847), p. 288; *Household Words*, vol. VI (1852), pp. 133-9; P. Egan, *Book of
Sports*, p. 56.

5. M.R. Mitford, *Our Village*, p. 169; J. Lawson, *Progress in Pudsey*, pp. 62-3.

6. J. Ford, *Cricket, a Social History 1700-1835* (Newton Abbot, 1972), p. 123; W. Howitt, *The Rural Life of England*, vol. II, pp. 273-8; S.C. of the House of Lords to inquire into the Laws respecting Gaming, PP 1844 (604), vol. VI, q. 234.

7. W.F. Mandle, 'Games People Played: Cricket and Football in England and Victoria in the Late Nineteenth Century', *Historical Studies*, vol. 15 (1973), p. 511, and 'The Professional Cricketer in England in the Nineteenth Century', *Labour History*, no. 23 (1972), p. 2; H.S. Altham and E.W. Swanston, *A History of Cricket*, 4th edn (London, 1948), p. 88; C.L.R. James, *Beyond a Boundary* (London, 1976), p. 159.

8. R. Bowen, *Cricket* (London, 1970), pp. 106-19; James, *Beyond a Boundary*, pp. 157-84.

9. P.C. McIntosh, *Physical Education in England since 1800*, revised and enlarged edn (London, 1968), p. 55; Bowen, *Cricket*, pp. 113-14; P. Scott, 'Cricket and the Religious World in the Victorian Period', *Church Quarterly*, vol. III (1970), pp. 134-44; Lawson, *Progress in Pudsey*, p. 63.

10. D. Newsome, *Godliness and Good Learning* (London, 1961), pp. 80-1; McIntosh, *Physical Education*, pp. 20-33.

11. E. Dunning, 'The Development of Modern Football' in Dunning (ed.), *The Sociology of Sport* (London, 1971), p. 143; McIntosh, *Physical Education*, pp. 38-53.

12. T. Hughes, *Tom Brown's School-Days* (London, 1857). See also Hughes's *The Scouring of the White Horse* (London, 1858); Newsome, *Godliness*, pp. 207-8; O. Anderson, 'The Growth of Christian Militarism in mid-Victorian Britain', *English Historical Review*, vol. LXXXVI (1971), pp. 46-72.

13. T. Veblen, *The Theory of the Leisure Class* (New York, 1919), p. 255.

14. [H. Shimmin], *Town Life* (London, 1858), pp. 121-2.

15. S.C. on Gaming, 3rd Report, PP 1844, vol. VI, p. v; G. Doré and B. Jerrold, *London, a Pilgrimage* (New York, 1970), pp. 73-80.

16. Quoted in B. Trinder, 'Conflict and Compromise: Evangelicals and Popular Culture in Banbury 1830-1870', Paper to Conference of the Society for the Study of Labour History, November 1975, p. 16.

17. Quoted in J. Obelkevich, *Religion and Rural Society: South Lindsey 1825-1875* (Oxford, 1976), p. 91n; P. Cunnington and A. Mansfield, *English Costume for Sports and Outdoor Recreation* (London, 1969), p. 28.

18. Quoted in H. Cunningham, *The Volunteer Force* (London, 1975), pp. 27, 114.

19. *Lectures and Addresses by Henry Austin Bruce*, pp. 2-5, 22, 95.

20. H. Solly, *Working Men's Social Clubs and Educational Institutes*, 2nd edn (London, 1904), pp. 79-100.

21. Obelkevich, *Religion and Rural Society*, pp. 57-9; R.W. Ambler, 'The Transformation of Harvest Celebrations in Nineteenth-century Lincolnshire', *Midland History*, vol. III (1976), pp. 298-305.

22. M.D. Fuller, *West Country Friendly Societies* (Reading, 1964), pp. 21, 48-9; A. Howkins, *Whitsun in 19th Century Oxfordshire* (Ruskin College, Oxford, 1973), pp. 19, 23; M.K. Ashby, *Joseph Ashby of Tysoe 1859-1919*, pp. 68-74; Obelkevich, *Religion and Rural Society*, p. 247.

23. G. Stedman Jones, *Outcast London* (Oxford, 1971), p. 261; C.M. Davies, *Mystic London* (London, 1875), pp. 172-8.

24. Cunningham, *Volunteer Force*, p. 28; M. Browne, *Views and Opinions* (London, 1866), pp. 279-80.

25. H. Taine, *Notes on England* (London, 1876), p. 42.

26. Cunningham, *Volunteer Force*, pp. 27-30, 63-4.

27. Solly, *Working Men's Social Clubs*, p. 87; J.M. Ludlow and Lloyd Jones, *Progress of the Working Class 1832-1867* (London, 1867), p. 196.

28. R.Q. Gray, *The Labour Aristocracy in Victorian Edinburgh* (Oxford, 1976), passim, esp. p. 139; G. Crossick, 'The Labour Aristocracy and its Values: a Study of Mid-Victorian Kentish London', *Victorian Studies*, vol. XIX (1976), pp. 301-28; T.R. Tholfsen, *Working Class Radicalism in Mid-Victorian England* (London, 1976).

29. Cunningham, *Volunteer Force*, pp. 103-26.

30. R. Price, 'The Working Men's Club Movement and Victorian Social Reform Ideology', *Victorian Studies*, vol. XV (1971), pp. 117-47, esp. pp. 122, 128; J. Taylor, *From Self-Help to Glamour: The Working Man's Club 1860-1972* (Ruskin College, Oxford, 1972).

31. Dunning, *Sociology of Sport*, pp. 133-51, 357-8; P.C. McIntosh, *Sport in Society* (London, 1963), pp. 72-3; J. Walvin, *The People's Game* (London, 1975), pp. 44-5, 57.

32. W. Hone, *The Every-Day Book*, vol. II, p. 187; R.C. on Children in Mines and Manufactories, 1st Report, PP 1842, vol. XV, p. 123.

33. P.C. Bailey, *Leisure and Class in Victorian England*, pp. 138-9; T. Mason, *Association Football and English Society 1863-1915* (Hassocks, 1980).

34. Doré and Jerrold, *London*, p. 174; Cunnington and Mansfield, *English Costume for Sports*, p. 62; D.C. Itzkowitz, *Peculiar Privilege*, pp. 55-7.

35. T. Wright, *Some Habits and Customs of the Working Classes* p. 190, and *The Great Unwashed*, 1st edn 1868 (London, 1970), pp. 31-41; M. Anderson, *Family Structure in Nineteenth-century Lancashire* (London, 1971), p. 77; W. Besant, 'The Amusements of the People' in *As We Are And As We May Be* (London, 1903), p. 279.

36. D. Hudson, *Munby, Man of Two Worlds* (London, 1972), p. 215; H. Mayhew, *London Labour*, vol. IV, pp. 210-72; W. Acton, *Prostitution* (2nd edn 1870, repr. London, 1972), pp. 16-22.

37. S.C. on Theatrical Licences and Regulations, PP 1866 (373), vol. XI, q. 6882.

38. J.A. and O. Banks, *Feminism and Family Planning in Victorian England* (Liverpool, 1964), pp. 58-76; Veblen, *Theory of the Leisure Class*, pp. 57-187.

39. Hudson, *Munby*, pp. 167-8.

40. W. Weber, *Music and the Middle Class* (London, 1975), pp. 24-63.

41. R. Carr, *English Fox Hunting*, pp. 78, 152-5; A. Trollope (ed.), *British Sports and Pastimes* (London, 1868), p. 75.

42. Trollope, ibid., pp. 197-200; O.M. Westall (ed.), *Windermere in the Nineteenth Century* (Centre for North-West Regional Studies, Univ. of Lancaster, 1976), pp. 49-50.

43. J. Strutt, *Sports and Pastimes*, p. 89; S.C. on Gaming, PP 1844, vol. VI, qq. 218-27.

44. Bailey, *Leisure and Class*, pp. 131-40; P. Egan, *Boxiana*, p. 103.

45. M.R. Booth, 'The Social and Literary Context' in *The Revels History of Drama in English*, vol. VI, pp. 14-21; K. Barker, *Theatre Royal, Bristol*, pp. 135-6.

46. D. Rubinstein, 'Cycling in the 1890s', *Victorian Studies*, vol. 21 (1977), p. 48; G. Cousins, *Golf in Britain* (London, 1975), pp. 16-23.

47. Trollope, *British Sports and Pastimes*, p. 18; J. Walton, 'Residential Amenity, Respectable Morality and the Rise of the Entertainment Industry: the case of Blackpool 1860-1914', *Literature and History*, no. 1 (1975), pp. 62-78.

48. Doré and Jerrold, *London*, pp. 161-2.

5 THE MAKING OF LEISURE, *c.* 1850-*c.* 1880

There is widespread agreement that a new phase in the history of leisure opens in the mid-nineteenth century. 'The leisure patterns of modern industrial urban mass society now begin to take shape', writes Geoffrey Best of the mid-Victorian period. Nor is it only in leisure that these years seem a turning-point. They mark in general the end of the crisis period of the Industrial Revolution and the beginning of an era when in political, economic and social behaviour the working class begins to accept the permanence of industrial capitalism, and to seek small gains within it rather than its overthrow. The Great Exhibition of 1851, when all classes dutifully admired the artefacts of capitalism, was a symbol and sign of the coming of this new era. In visiting the Crystal Palace the working class seemed at last to be responding to the message of rational recreation; and amongst other things the Great Exhibition was celebrated as a vindication of the gospel that leisure, properly organised, could be civilising.

Within this general framework other events seem to reinforce the notion of a turning-point around 1850. New technology, in the shape of the railway, begins to make a marked impact on leisure habits. The self-proclaimed foundation of music-hall by Charles Morton with the opening of the Canterbury Hall in Lambeth in 1851 seems to open a new era of capitalist entrepreneurship in leisure. More profoundly this in turn is seen as based on a greater quantity of leisure time at more regular intervals for the mass of the people, the majority of whom were now urban dwellers, and higher wages which people were willing to spend on leisure goods. Leisure became more clearly demarcated from work, while at the same time still closely bound to it as the compensation for work.[1]

My argument will be that while these years were indeed a turning-point, they were no more than that. And they were a turning-point not in the sense of being a 90° still less a 180° turn, but rather a curving and permanent shift of direction, the outcome of which was the end of that popular culture which we identified in Chapter 1 and its super-session by a culture of leisure which was more remote from and less controlled by its participants. And whereas from the perspective of 1880, 1780 seemed a totally different and distant world, towards the end of the nineteenth century there had emerged a world of leisure

140

recognisable and familiar 100 years later.

Our task then in this chapter is to assess the degree and timing of change and the relative weight of the different factors that went into the making of leisure. And those factors, I shall argue, were not simply the market forces of supply and demand. Important as the latter were they were modified by the attachment of the working class to the forms of leisure created in the first half of the century, by the provision of facilities by government and charity, and by that ideology of leisure which we explored in the last chapter.

The outcome was complex. The strength of popular demand was such that many direct efforts to control leisure failed, yet that demand was contained within a world of commercialised leisure which provided its own controls. From the point of view of authority this commercialised leisure was increasingly acceptable, for if what was offered within it was hardly uplifting, at least it posed no threat. On the contrary, leisure was shorn of many of its political and social associations, and while the way it was spent might be individually damaging, it was no longer politically or socially dangerous. For this reason it could become legitimate. As Walter Besant wrote in 1884, there had been a gradual recognition of 'the great natural law that men and women, as well as boys and girls, must have play. At the present moment we have just arrived at the stage of acknowledging this law.'[2] In studying the making of leisure, then, we have to concentrate as much on the emergence of a new definition and role for leisure as on the growth of leisure time and leisure activities.

In trying to understand these processes I shall look first at leisure time and leisure money, then at the provision of leisure facilities, both by public initiative and by private enterprise, and finally at the new role of leisure as it began to emerge in the third quarter of the nineteenth century.

Leisure Time and Leisure Money

If the mid-nineteenth century is to be established as a turning-point we may expect to find more regular work patterns, a clearer demarcation between work and leisure (for example a decline in drinking on the job), and the achievement of shorter hours of work through a demand for leisure. It might also be expected that there would be greater national uniformity in patterns of work and leisure. Broadly speaking all these things did happen in the third quarter of the nineteenth century, but not in a straightforward or unambiguous way.

Holiday customs, for example, remained singularly resistent to change. There is evidence that in the North some wakes, fairs and races disappeared in the 1830s and 1840s without much sign of protest from anyone, but this was an indication that the form of the holiday, rather than the timing of it, was changing.[3] The *Manchester Guardian*, for example, noted in 1845 that 'The most remarkable feature of this Whitsuntide was the larger numbers leaving Manchester rather than spending the holidays in the traditional way at the Kersal Moor races'.[4] But they were still taking their holiday at Whitsuntide, and as we have seen, factory workers clung tenaciously to customary holidays and rejected parliamentary ones.

The truth is that regional and trade customs in the timing of holidays remained virtually unaffected by any pressures towards regularisation in the third quarter of the century. The Factory Acts of 1867 and 1874 extended to much larger groups of workers those clauses from the Act of 1833 which ruled against work on Christmas Day or Good Friday. But Good Friday in particular remained an unpopular and normally unobserved holiday. In 1876 the Royal Commission on the Factory and Workshop Acts heard how amongst Sheffield cutlers Good Friday is 'against the custom and feeling of the workpeople'; a scissor manufacturer there employed women who took no less than 40 half-holidays in the year, but wanted to work on Good Friday. The same message came from the Midlands: 'with the men all through South Staffordshire', claimed an ironfounder and hollow-ware manufacturer from West Bromwich, 'Easter has been as great a holiday as Whitsuntide is in Manchester and that district', but Easter Monday, not Good Friday. 'Good Friday is of no use to the hands', said a cape manufacturer from Tamworth, 'and they do not like forced play on that day . . . There are during the year certain popular holidays, such as the statute fair, club days, and occasional extra demonstrations, excursions, etc.' The customary holidays continued to be celebrated, in new ways perhaps, but at the old times, and as a consequence there was very little national uniformity. For to the regional differences – Manchester's preference for Whitsun as against that of the Midlands for Easter Monday – must be added trade particularities: the custom in clothing factories, for example, of giving two to three weeks' holiday after the busy season.[5]

Towards the end of the third quarter of the century there are indications that some success was being achieved in the attempt to 'rationalise' holidays. From the mid-1860s there were efforts made to bring some order to the multitude of different wakes weeks in the Potteries, and this led in 1879 to the Great Stoke Wakes, one annual festival for the whole district. This process was also occurring in Lancashire, where the emphasis was beginning to be put upon wakes week rather than Whitsuntide. And it was of course in 1871 that the Bank Holiday Act marked a significant step taken by the state in the recognition and regularisation of leisure. The immediate effects of the Act were somewhat limited, but its extension in 1875 to cover docks, custom houses, inland revenue offices and bonding warehouses made it much more likely that the parliamentary holidays would become nationally observed; as R. Baker, Factory Inspector, noted in 1876, 'the bank holidays are now becoming universal. People are shutting up their shops on those days, generally . . .'[6]

The weekly pattern of working changed almost as slowly as holiday customs. In the eyes of authority an ideal pattern had emerged by mid-century: people should work five full days, Monday to Friday, and one shorter day, Saturday. St Monday would be a thing of the past, and the half-holiday on Saturday would enable workers to do their shopping on that day, and hence make Sunday work unnecessary.

Three groups of people were working for the achievement of a Saturday half-holiday, each with very different aims in mind. The first were the Sabbatarians. The Early Closing Association, which had its origins in the late 1830s and became a force to be reckoned with in the 1840s, was to a large degree concerned to secure early closing on Saturday in order to be able to argue in favour of keeping the Sunday holy. The Association was concerned mainly with hours of work in offices, shops and warehouses, and it was amongst the employees here that Sunday had become a chief day of leisure. The leading Evangelicals, Lord Ashley and Sir Andrew Agnew, were among the Vice-Patrons of the Metropolitan Drapers' Association, formed in 1838, and a forerunner of the Early Closing Association: in the propaganda and resolutions of the latter there was no attempt to disguise the link with Sabbatarianism. Thus at a public meeting in the Guildhall in 1855 in favour of 2 p.m. closing of London shops on Saturdays, a resolution argued that elsewhere early closing had proved 'highly beneficial to large classes of society, socially, mentally, and physically; added to the most important effect of tending materially to a better observance of the Lord's day . . .' It may be doubted whether the employees felt like this. The Early Closing Association was very much a movement from above. As Whitaker has written, 'The strength of the parent ECA, as of others that had a transitory success, was in the wealth and influence of the employers who supported it. Its weakness was in the lack of solid support by the employees, and by the small shopkeepers.' Without any great pressure from below the Early Closing Association persisted until the late 1880s in arguing for a voluntary agreement to close early on Saturdays, but it did not enjoy any great success. Nor indeed did it achieve much in its attempts to bring a halt to work on Sundays.[7]

The second group in favour of a more regular working week, including a Saturday half-holiday, were manufacturers and in particular those who made use of steam power. Factory Inspector J.E. White reported the views of Birmingham metal manufacturers in 1864:

An enormous amount of time is lost, not only by want of punctuality in coming to work in the morning and beginning again after meals, but still more by the general observance of 'Saint Monday', which is shown in the late attendance or entire absence of large numbers on that day. One employer has on Monday only about 40 or 50 out of 300 or 400, and the day is recognized by many masters as an hour shorter than others at each end. On Mondays I found few works fully and some but very partially employed; and in a large well-conducted foundry the casters were getting to work for the first time in the week towards midday on Tuesday. Masters complain much of this, but say that it cannot be helped. Experience, however, shows that firmness on the part of the employer, and dependence on steam power, which would otherwise be wasted, have, in some cases, done much to overcome this difficulty. One employer told me that he had just locked out for the day 200 of his hands who had stayed away the day before on the occasion of a local *fête* without leave though he always gladly gave leave when it was asked, and that he had no doubt that by such means he should secure greater regularity for the future.

This report came some 15 years after the Saturday half-holiday had first been introduced to Birmingham, and it coincided in time with a determined effort by the larger employers in Birmingham to substitute the Saturday half-holiday for St Monday. Such a process was by no means all gain for the worker who lost a whole day's holiday and gained only a half, and moreover frequently had to work extra hours on the other five days in order to earn his half day on Saturday. But equally clearly the employers did not have things all their own way. In 1876 John Hampton, the manager of a firm of engineers and iron and brass founders in West Bromwich, complained that 'when the hours of labour were reduced to 54, our men agreed to work on Mondays if we would consent to them leaving at 2 on Saturdays; but we find more difficulty in getting them to work on Monday than before the alteration, in fact as wages have been advanced less time has been made.'[8]

The workers, it is clear, had some bargaining power, some ability to resist changes which employers thought desirable. And while some workers clung to the celebration of St Monday, others had come to see advantages in the Saturday half-holiday. As such they form the third, and probably the most important group agitating for an early stoppage to work on Saturday. The history of Saturday working habits is somewhat obscure, but what seems to have been a fairly regular holiday in medieval and early modern times was probably like other holidays under pressure in the eighteenth century. John Brand in 1777 commenting on his predecessor Bourne's claims for 'the present Custom of spending a Part of Saturday afternoon, without servile Labour', feared that

An Inference might easily be deduced from it in favour of Idleness. Perhaps Men who live by manual Labour, or have Families to support by it, cannot better spend their Saturday Afternoons than in following the several Callings in which they have employed themselves on the preceding Days of the Week — Industry will be no bad Preparation for the Sabbath.

How far such views came to prevail is uncertain. In domestic work Saturday appears to have been traditionally a holiday or handing-in day, and there is some evidence of early stopping on Saturdays in other work in the first half of the nineteenth century. Stopping at 4 p.m. on Saturdays was reported as general in the cotton districts in 1816. Against this is the very distinct sense that the Saturday half-holiday was something that had to be fought for anew from about mid-century. Dr Bienefeld's researches suggested that by 1843 short Saturday working was confined to Lancashire and the West of Scotland, to paper mills, and to parts of the West of England, and even in these areas and types of work it was by no means universal.[9] It was the Factory Act of 1850 which achieved the Saturday half-holiday for factory workers, and it is indeed from about mid-century that one can discern more and more workers campaigning for its achievement. The builders started to do so in 1847, and in London by the late 1850s they had gained the half-holiday, but only in return for acceptance of payment by the hour. Other builders began to achieve success in the 1860s, the engineers by the early 1870s, the Nottingham lace workers also in that decade. It is a confused story, not least because one person's half-holiday might start at 1 p.m., another's at 5 p.m. What is clear is that in the third quarter of the century significant groups of workers were campaigning with some success for a short day's work on Saturday; they might do so only at the cost of loss of wages, or making up time earlier in the week, but the evidence suggests that it was seen as a gain.[10]

It seems likely that the workers who campaigned for a Saturday half-holiday were those who traditionally did not enjoy St Monday. For the latter there was much less incentive to press for or to agree to a Saturday half-holiday, and in its traditional strongholds, London, the West Midlands and Sheffield, the celebration of St Monday continued unabated during the third quarter of the century. In Sheffield, for example, according to the United States consul in 1874

Every Monday is so generally a holiday, that it has come to be called Saint Monday. The streets are full on that day of men at leisure ... This Monday idleness is, in some cases, enforced by the fact that Monday is the day that is taken for repairs to the machinery in the great steel-works, during which the masses of the men employed in such establishments must necessarily be out of work. But this will account for but a small portion of the idleness on that day. It is, to a great extent, voluntary, and has become a settled habit and custom. And this holiday is, in thousands of instances, protracted through the next day, so that large numbers of the workmen, stopping work on Saturday noon, do not commence again until the following Wednesday.

In Sheffield the institution of the Saturday half-holiday did not lead to the abolition of St Monday. Monday remained the best day for a holiday. As the Adjutant of the Hallamshire Volunteers wrote to Lord Wharncliffe in 1863, Saturday was a bad day for a review:

Many will not come on account of having to draw their wages, and many again wont loose [*sic*] a day's work on a Saturday – and again 2 thirds of the corps (or more) subscribe to different money clubs, and if they are not there to pay their subscriptions by ¼ to 9 on Saturday night, they are fined, so those will make many of them stay behind. Monday would have been a much better day.[11]

Indeed as one examines the evidence about St Monday and the Saturday half-holiday in the third quarter of the century, what is striking is not so much the elimination of the former in favour of the latter as the fact that Monday was beginning to be enjoyed as a holiday in ways which would win warm approval from the rational recreationist. As one witness before the 1854 Select Committee on Public Houses put it, Monday was now 'a legitimate holiday. It was a holiday then of a depraving, bad character, now it is a holiday spent with their families, and benefiting both their health and minds.' Even as early as 1840 *Art Union* had rejoiced that the National Gallery had 'become the resort of the many-aproned sons of industry, not only on holidays, but on those Mondays dedicated of old to tippling and riot'. The working men who celebrated St Monday, as Thomas Wright described, were not all the sporting and drinking types, but also families sedately taking day trips to the seaside. It was a Monday that the Hartlepool Temperance Society chose for its trip to Middlesbrough Polytechnic.[12]

In the third quarter of the century, then, there is only slow and halting progress towards the establishment of a nationwide pattern for the working week. Unquestionably by the end of it more workers were enjoying Saturday half-holidays than at the beginning, and this largely through their own achievements. Equally clearly St Monday continued to be widely celebrated. But whether it was Saturday or Monday which was the chief day of leisure for a particular trade or region, that leisure was being spent in ways which were increasingly 'rational', routinised and regular. There was a much greater sense that a regular part of the week was set aside for leisure.

To a large extent this regularisation of the days of leisure came about because of a change in the daily hours of work and in the nature of work. 'Roughly speaking', E.J. Hobsbawm has written, 'the mid-century brought the beginning of the substitution of "intensive" for "extensive" labour utilization.' Employers began to realise that productivity might increase if hours were shorter, wages higher and the pace of work intensified. The latter could be achieved by stricter supervision of work, by encouraging piece-work, and by technological innovation so that the machine could more and more dictate the pattern of working. Admittedly the story is not one which allows of easy generalisations. Amongst the engineers, for example, the spread of piece-work slowed down after 1850, and in the 1860s probably only 10 per cent of the skilled men were employed on piece-work. But the general trend does seem to be towards piece-work; it was widespread amongst carpenters and joiners and almost universal amongst coal-face workers. In cotton, experiments in the 1840s showed that shorter hours might lead to higher productivity. As Marx wrote in 1867, basing his forecast on evidence in the Parliamentary Papers,

It is absolutely indisputable that the tendency of capital, as soon as a prolongation of the working day is once for all prohibited, to compensate itself by systematically increasing the intensity of labour, and the tendency of capital to make of every improvement in machinery a more effective means of getting the utmost out of labour power, will ere long lead to a state of things that will make a further reduction in the hours of labour inevitable.

By the time Marx wrote, employers, confident in their ability to intensify the pace of work, had shown themselves willing to accept and even welcome parliamentary legislation to restrict hours of work.[13]

It was in the third quarter of the century that legislation began to encompass workers other than those in textiles. The Factory Act of 1850 guaranteed the textile factory workers a Saturday half-holiday, but added half an hour to other days, leaving a 10½ hour day. It was in essence this Act which began to be applied to other trades: to bleaching and dyeing in 1860, to lace-work in 1861, and to earthenware manufacture, lucifer match-making, percussion cap-making, cartridge-making, paper-staining and fustian-cutting in 1864. Then in 1867 the Factory Act defined 'Factory' in such a way as to include most of the industrial enterprises of England and Wales, and at the same time a Workshop Act established regulations, less stringent and as it turned out easily avoidable, for those employing less than 50 workers. In 1874 an Act reduced the hours of work in textile factories from 10½ to 10 and from 7 to 6½ on Saturday, thus reducing the working week from 60 hours to 56½. This flurry of state activity perhaps had motives and consequences different from those which appear on the surface. In many industries the actual hours worked at the time the legislation was enacted were *lower* than that set down in the Acts. What in essence was happening was not so much a reduction of the hours of work by Act of Parliament, as a regularisation of the working week — hence many employers' willingness to accept the legislation.

Much more important than Acts of Parliament in reducing the hours of work was the action of organised labour. It was the builders who started the movement for a nine-hour day in the 1850s, meeting with some success, particularly in the North of England, but suffering defeat in other places. It was the boom of the early 1870s which brought success to the movement, and established a nine-hour day for most unionised workers. Although there were minor setbacks after the boom years, the nine-hour day may be said to have become established as a norm by the end of the third quarter of the century. Of course this did not mean that no one worked more than nine or even ten hours. Even in those trades which had achieved the employers' recognition of the nine-hour day, many workers continued to work overtime. And, much more important, there were still many workers whose hours were quite unregulated and scandalously long — agricultural workers, for example, or those in the sweated trades, or shop workers, the latter working up to 90 hours a week. Significant numbers of workers, however, had won a reduction in the hours of work, and hence an increase in the hours of leisure.[14]

It has generally been argued that the motivation behind the campaign for shorter hours was first and foremost to lessen the risk of unemployment.[15] Even though it is admitted that the reduction of hours normally occurred at times of full employment, the fear of unemployment to come and the memory of it in the past acted as a spur to use a favourable bargaining position to win a reduction of hours which would help to spread employment when the boom broke. No one with any knowledge of the insecurity of life in nineteenth-century industry could deny the *a priori* likelihood that a desire to reduce the risk of unemployment lay behind the campaign for shorter hours; insufficient evidence, however, has yet been produced to show that this was actually the case. And there is evidence on the other side to suggest that it was quite as much a desire for more leisure time as a fear of unemployment which led people to campaign for shorter hours.

In the first place workers could not but be aware that part of the price to be paid for the attainment of shorter hours was an intensification of the pace of work; hence shorter hours would do little if anything to reduce unemployment. There is, too, piecemeal but convincing evidence that some groups of workers wanted shorter hours even if that entailed a reduction of wages. In 1866, for example, Newcastle builders voted for a 50½ hour week with 27s rather than 55½ hours with 30s. Almost 20 years earlier, in 1848 Leonard Horner, the Factory Inspector, had interviewed 1,153 operatives about the Ten Hours Act of 1847. The results showed that 61.75 per cent preferred ten hours even at reduced wages, that 12.75 per cent preferred eleven hours even at reduced wages, and that only the remaining 25.5 per cent wanted to keep up the level of wages even if this meant continuing to work for twelve hours a day. In general the better-off workers, and men more than women, preferred the shorter hours. By December 1848 Horner was confident that people 'set a high value upon the increased leisure . . .' and there seems no reason to dissent from his opinion.[16]

There is some interesting if admittedly somewhat speculative evidence that during the period 1840-70 workers set a particularly high value on increased leisure as against increased income. On the assumption, which contemporaries shared, that leisure time represents income foregone, it is possible to compare the relative preference for income and leisure at different periods. Taking the periods 1840-70, 1870-1905, 1905-1930/1, and 1930/1-1953, it seems that the preference for leisure was at its highest in the period 1840-70. Now it may be argued that that preference for leisure represents a willingness to forego income in order to protect employment, but it seems more plausible to conclude, with John Myerscough, that 'It was natural that a high preference for leisure as against income should show in a period immediately following the experience of long and fatiguing hours of work during the high phase of industrialization.' For, as we shall see, there is much evidence that workers set considerable store by the increased differentiation between work and leisure and on the new leisure facilities that sprang up from mid-century. As the Inspector of Factories put it in 1859, arguing the benefits of the Saturday half-holiday, 'the distinction [is] at last made clear between the worker's own time and his master's. The worker knows now when that which he sells is ended, and when his own begins; and, by possessing a sure foreknowledge of this, is enabled to prearrange his own minutes for his own purposes.'[17] As leisure time and leisure facilities increased, work may have become increasingly instrumental, accepted as a cultural norm but only as a means towards the enjoyment of leisure. Thus the growing intensity and also the shorter hours of work brought with them a delimitation of leisure and an emphasis on the hours of leisure as those in which a person could attain some degree of freedom, and which, therefore, were the hours which made life most worth living.

But time was not the only ingredient necessary if leisure was to attain a new status. There had also to be money. And here the evidence for a break at mid-century is much less convincing. The notion that the mid-Victorian period was one of growing prosperity for all has now been severely modified. Only from the mid-1860s does a marked upward trend in real wages become apparent, and even that was more for the skilled than for the unskilled, and for mechanised industrial areas more than for backward ones. Both differentials in earnings between skilled and unskilled, and regional income differentials, seem to have increased.[18]

Taken together the evidence about leisure time and leisure money suggests that only the most unionised and skilled workers were breaking through into a new world of leisure in the third quarter of the century.

For the mass of the working class it was the last quarter of the century that was crucial in terms both of time and money. Hence when we turn to survey the provision of facilities for leisure we need to bear in mind that there was likely to be an increase in demand but also that that demand would be limited both geographically and socially. It was hardly likely to be of a character which could be described as 'mass'.

Facilities for Leisure

The movement to provide public facilities for leisure which had its origins in the early 1830s had had relatively little impact in terms of actual provision by mid-century. Parliament had awoken to a need, and important enabling legislation had been passed: the Museums Act of 1845, the Baths and Washhouses Act of 1846, the Libraries Act of 1850; but it was to take time before the hopes of the legislature were to be transformed into bricks and mortar. Similarly the concern to provide open spaces had resulted in public money being made available, but once again not very much had been achieved either by public initiative or private beneficence by mid-century. In all these areas of public provision the third quarter of the century was the period when the hopes of the pioneers began to be fulfilled. Movements which might have died out without a trace took solid root, and the provision of public leisure facilities became an accepted responsibility of government and a favoured object of charity.

It was in this third quarter of the century that many towns began to acquire public parks. Some benefited from donations. The Duke of Norfolk had presented Sheffield with its first public park in 1847; Sir Titus Salt was the driving force behind the opening of the first public park in Bradford in 1850, and was later to provide a park for his workpeople at Saltaire; the People's Park in Halifax was presented to the town in 1857 by Sir Francis Crossley, while Hull owed its People's Park to Z.C. Pearson, a man who as later bankruptcy proceedings were to show was scarcely in a position to be so benevolent. The Albert Park at Middlesbrough, however, opened in 1868, was built on the firm financial base of the Bolckow ironworks. In Preston and Oldham parks were built as a means of relieving distress during the cotton famine. And in Leeds the Corporation embarked on an ambitious policy of purchase. In the 1850s it bought the 63 acres of Woodhouse Moor for £3,000, made some more small purchases in the following decade, and then in 1872 spent no less than £139,000 in buying the 773 acres of Roundhay Park, a purchase which was supported by 60,000 signatures. Leeds and Liverpool, which acquired three new parks in the late 1860s and early 1870s, were the large towns with the best provision of public open space.[19]

In Leeds the movement to provide open space had the support and backing of the Commons Preservation Society. This had been established in London in 1865, and was the direct consequence of Earl Spencer's plan to sell part of Wimbledon Common and use the proceeds to buy up and extinguish the rights of the commoners. A Select Committee of the House of Commons on Open Spaces, which disputed his right to do so, instead of deterring lords of the manor, had the effect of spurring them on in their efforts to enclose commons and extinguish commoners' rights; as an immediate consequence Berkhamsted, Plumstead and Tooting Commons, and Bostall Heath were enclosed, and hundreds of acres of Epping Forest were fenced off and trees felled. This led to the formation of the Commons Preservation Society, a body which fought for the rights of the commoners in the law courts, and if necessary resorted to carefully directed destruction of property. In Berkhamsted 120 navvies were employed to take down two miles of iron fences which the lord of the manor had erected; the Society was vindicated in the courts. Similarly in Plumstead, enclosures erected by the lord of the manor, the Queen's College, Oxford, were forcibly removed, and the College lost its subsequent suit.

It was over Epping Forest that the Society fought its most long-drawn-out and ultimately successful action. The Forest was a traditional pleasure resort for East Enders, and the location of the famous annual hunt when a stag was let loose and pursued by the lovers of the chase in the metropolis. In 1848 a House of Commons Committee recommended the enclosure of Hainault Forest and that Epping Forest be disafforested with some land reserved for public recreation. The 1849 Royal Commission on Crown Lands opposed this recommendation, but it was the 1848 report which was implemented; in 1851 Hainault Forest was enclosed by Act of Parliament, and the various lords of the manor in Epping Forest started enclosing. The initiative in the campaign to reclaim the Forest for public use was taken by labouring men who were imprisoned for breaking down fences. The Society took up their case, the Corporation of London was induced to fight on the side of the commoners and after years of debate, inquiries and legal action, an Act was passed in 1878 whereby the Forest was to remain open and unenclosed for the enjoyment and recreation of the people, and illegally enclosed land was to be handed back. So far had the movement for the preservation of open land for public use advanced that when the Forest was thrown open to the public in 1882 it was the Queen who officiated at the ceremony.

By the 1870s indeed, the Society was the spearhead of a campaign which enjoyed wide public support. In 1869 the Society had raised questions about the operation of the 1845 Inclosure Act so far as it affected rural commons, and in 1876 an Act was passed which, though not perfect, set up a standing committee which was vigilant in their protection. In the same years the Society kept a close watch on railway companies, who frequently planned routes which would cut through common land.[20]

The history of these years is of course not one of uninterrupted success in gaining or retaining open land for public use. What is significant about them, as the amount of debate in Parliament indicates, was that public opinion at all levels of society was aroused to the importance of the subject. The force of the trend towards the privatisation of property was recognised and opposed. In nearly all the larger towns some land was set aside in these years for public use; it was as though the British had come to realise that their civilisation was an urban one, and that some measures had to be taken to make it a tolerable one to live in. Not only the Commons Preservation Society, but also Octavia Hill's Kyrle Society, founded in 1876, and the Metropolitan Public Gardens Association of 1883, were alert to the need to preserve every possible scrap of land for public use.[21] And it was in these years, too, that the alarm was sounded about the encroachments on land both rural and urban which for centuries had been enjoyed by the public. As a result action was taken which had as its quite specific purpose the preservation of space for public recreation.

If the park or common land was in a sense an attempt to create *rus in urbe*, there was an equal recognition that an urban society needed public buildings for recreational purposes. The most important of these were libraries. Certainly there was no great rush to make use of the 1850 Act; only 24 libraries were built under the Act between 1851 and 1867, and it was only towards the end of the century that public libraries funded by the rates became nearly universal. Between 1847 and 1886 an average of only three or four per annum were established compared with an average of sixteen or seventeen between 1887 and 1900. The truth was that ratepayers were less easily persuaded than parliamentary politicians of the value of expenditure on libraries. But if ratepayers proved reluctant, philanthropists were often willing to step in to fill the gap; the list of donations of libraries, as described by W.S. Jevons in 1881, was as impressive as that of parks:

Several Free Libraries have already been established more or less at the cost of individuals. The Liverpool Library was built at the expense of the late Sir William Brown, on a site given by the Corporation. The Paisley Library building was presented by Sir P. Coats. Mr. David Chadwick gave a building and books, all complete, to Macclesfield. Mr. Bass built the Derby Library. The Wigan Library building was erected by Mr. Thomas Taylor, while Mr. Winnard presented £12,000 for the purchase of books. The site of the Stoke-upon-Trent Library, together with a handsome sum of money, was given by Mr. C.M. Campbell, a local society presenting a library of books and a museum. At Reading the adoption of the Act was defeated seven years ago; but Mr. William Palmer, of the great biscuit firm, proceeded to open a library at his own expense, under the management of a lady-librarian. The library soon became so popular that when the ratepayers again voted there was only a single dissentient. Hereford, Coventry, and several other places, owe their libraries partly to benefactors, while in many cases valuable collections of books have been handed over to the public by individuals or societies.

As Jevons suggests in his last sentence public libraries owed much to their forerunners. The first public library under the Act of 1850, that in Manchester, was housed in the former Owenite Hall of Science. Many of the early public libraries took over the buildings and stock of mechanics' institutes or subscription libraries. Many of them, too, like the mechanics' institutes, tried to combine a variety of functions, housing museums, for example, or offering lectures. But there was a difference, for the new libraries were emphatically public and free; as Thomas Kelly has written, 'it is plain that public libraries, just because they were free, were much more successful than the old mechanics' institutes had been in attracting the lower ranks of the workers'. Parliamentary returns in the 1870s showed that in Leeds, for example, 81 per cent of the users of the library were working class.[22]

Another public facility which became available was the washhouse or bath. The Act of 1846 which permitted local authorities to raise rates to build these had a background of concern with public health. Parliamentary investigations in the 1840s contained hints, however, that the working class might think of baths as more than places for a wash. William Sowton, proprietor of private baths in Westminster Road, London, who charged 1s for the middling classes and 3d for the humbler, found that the vast majority of his customers fell into the latter category, and added: 'I am mortified to find that, instead of being used as matters of health, they have merely been used as matters of pleasure in a very great degree.'

Hugh Shimmin's description of the public baths in Liverpool, which had been opened in 1842, makes it clear that there too pleasure was uppermost; and once again it was the cheapest (and smallest) bath which was most popular: at 8 p.m. on a Saturday evening upwards of 100 boys, mostly nude, were swimming and diving in a pool measuring 41ft by 27ft. Many were to be found there in the mornings too, with consequences which Shimmin delighted to dwell upon. 'Persons who thus commence the day by purifying their bodies', he wrote, 'will not be found at the "cat hunt" or "dog race" as the day advances.' Perhaps the same might have been said of those teenage boys whom C.M. Davies found bathing in Victoria Park in London between 4 a.m. and 8 a.m. daily. Clearly there was a huge demand for swimming, and the public baths and washhouses which were built to improve the health of the working class also had the effect of providing them with relatively cheap recreation.[23]

Slowly, and boosted as much by local philanthropy as by state legislation, the towns of Britain began to acquire public facilities for recreation. At the end of the third quarter of the century there was still a long way to go; as late as 1885 only 23 per cent of the population had access to a public library. But no one could doubt the trend towards the recognition that recreation was a proper concern of government.

Why did this happen? With the partial exception of the provision of open spaces it was not due to demand. As Helen Meller has commented, 'One of the curious facts about the municipal provisions for leisure and pleasure was how little their development owed, in most instances, to popular demand.' It was not some irresistible pressure from below which led to the establishment of a library, museum and art gallery in any self-respecting town. On the contrary, the pressure came from the elites for whom this public provision was an enterprise in bringing civilisation to the people.[24] It was compounded of the same motives of guilt and fear which had been behind the movement for rational recreation in the second quarter of the century. It was a bid to direct the leisure of the working class into self-improving channels. And, in terms both of the amount provided and of the response to it, it was only very partially successful.

In one sense the public provision of leisure was a direct and deliberate counterweight to the commercialisation of leisure. It was an attempt to get the working man out of the pub and into the library. But in another sense public and private worked hand in hand – indeed it was difficult to say where one ended and the other began. Consider the Crystal Palace, public in Hyde Park in 1851, but privately operated with its reopening in Sydenham in 1854. In both places it was the highest expression of the Victorians' urge to combine enjoyment with cultural improvement. At the opening ceremony at Sydenham the Queen hoped 'that this wonderful structure, and the treasures of art and knowledge which it contains, may long continue to elevate and instruct, as well as to delight and amuse, the minds of all classes of my people'. There, inimitably, and in one sentence, is expressed the core of the philosophy of rational recreation. Equally inimitably, though at greater length, the *Illustrated London News* stated its hopes:

> When the Crystal Palace, revived with all the triumphs of taste and skill that are in contemplation, is removed to this park; when four termini of railways are close adjoining the silent highway of the Thames, and are ready to convey all classes to the garden wilderness for the cost of an omnibus fare – into the midst of flowers and rare shrubs in full bloom in winter, and fountains and shady walks in summer, away from the smoke and din of London, where all will be framed with the view of purging and instructing by the eye and the ear, and every debasing habit and association will be excluded – a new era in the public amusements will have commenced. The day of pot-house gardens, and the pot-and-pipe selfishness of husbands will soon pass away.

With its triennial Handel festivals from 1857 onwards and its pioneering Saturday concerts, the Crystal Palce was to play an important part in the musical life of the nation – and perhaps its moral life too. Even the sceptical Gissing could describe how Bob Hewett and his bride Pennyloaf were transformed when they could see

> the vast amphitheatre . . . Here at length was quietness, intermission of folly and brutality. Bob became another man as he stood and listened. He looked with kindness into Pennyloaf's pale, weary face, and his arm stole about her waist to support her. Ha! Pennyloaf was happy! The last trace of tears vanished. She too was sensible of the influences of music; her heart throbbed as she let herself lean against her husband.

With such expectations invested in it, it was not surprising that the Crystal Palace became the model for other 'Palaces', recreation centres for the masses: the Alexandra Palace, the Peoples' Palace in the East End. The Crystal Palace was an enduring ideal of what the nation's leisure might be; it could civilise, improve and unite the people. And although owned by a private company (and an unsuccessful one at that), the Palace seemed to have a place in the heart of the people as a public institution.[25]

It was the Great Exhibition which made people aware of the full potentiality of the railway, and its ability to transform the leisure of the nation. The impact of the railway is in some ways the strongest evidence that there was a turning-point in the history of leisure at mid-century, and scarcely any form of leisure escaped its influence. What the Great Exhibition did was to familiarise people with the notion of travelling considerable distances for the sake of leisure, and to give a great boost to the excursion business. Excursions have a long and important pre-history. As early as 1813 Richard Ayton described how poor people from the manufacturing districts came to Blackpool for three or four days, sleeping in very crowded conditions. By the late 1830s Granville could describe how the walls of Manchester were 'placarded with "Cheap travelling to Southport" — "Only five hours to Southport" — "Excursion to Southport"; and vociferations from a hundred throats to the same effect, are to be heard from the top of every species of vehicle in the principal streets'. At much the same time ironworkers with their wives and families were travelling from Merthyr Tydfil to swim in the sea at Swansea. Londoners, as we shall see, were quite familiar with the idea of excursions by water to Gravesend or Margate. And the excursion train predates the Great Exhibition by a decade; it was in July 1841 that Thomas Cook publicly advertised an excursion train from Leicester to Loughborough and back for 1s a head.

Thereafter the excursion train became familiar to members of mechanics' institutes, temperance societies and Sunday Schools, and the inhabitants of the great industrial cities could escape for a day to neighbouring beauty spots. In Birmingham by mid-century, it was reported, excursion trains

> run on all, or nearly all, their [working men's] holidays during the fine season, and convey them at almost a nominal rate to every popular place of resort in the beautiful county of Warwick, and sometimes into Shropshire or Wales, or as far as Liverpool to inhale the sea-

breezes of the Mersey, and to visit the novel spectacle, to an inland population of the splendid line of docks in the great seaport of the west.[26]

Working people used the trains not to get to work, but to travel for pleasure. Trains came to supplement boats and horse-drawn vehicles as a means whereby working people could escape for a day from the cities. The City of London Commissioner of Police described in 1853 how in the City 'Sunday is a sort of Zahara' and how at the railway termini 'you may see hundreds of families with their baskets of provisions, going to different distances in the country, and walking in the fields, and making the ground their table, who come home as soberly and as healthful as you could desire them to be'.[27] Trains did much to make this kind of short-distance travel more accessible; but they also of course made much longer journeys feasible. The Great Exhibition marks the turning-point here. Cook, it is true, had seen the potential, and had run an excursion to Scotland in 1846, but it was the Great Exhibition which revealed to the railway companies the highly elastic level of demand.

Cook was engaged by the Midland Railway Company, and competed with the Great Northern in running trains to the Great Exhibition, with a return fare from Leeds to London of only 5s. Working men from all over the country headed for London. In Birmingham the employees of Messrs R. Timmins and Sons in the heavy steel toys trade were trying to decide in 1851 whether to go on a gypsy party (a favourite form of leisure at mid-century) or to the Great Exhibition; it was reported that they would probably decide in favour of the latter. Even from rural areas — Oxfordshire for example — London and the Great Exhibition became accessible by train. The railway excursions of 1851 opened up new possibilities for working people, and in the next two decades they were to make full use of the opportunities that came to them to travel. In the 1850s the excursion train remained something special, by the later 1860s it had become routine and unremarkable, a known and essential ingredient in the leisure life of the people.[28]

Behind much of this travel, particularly in the early days, there was a search for self-improvement, and a quite deliberate turning away from traditional entertainments. The commercial exploitation of the working-class demand for travel was in its origin strongly imbued with the ethic of Nonconformity and temperance; so much so that it often seemed to be more public than private. 'The EXCURSION TRAIN', wrote Charles Knight, 'is one of our best public instructors. It is also one of the cheapest . . . From all the great manufacturing and commercial towns, Excursion Trains are constantly bearing the active and intelligent artisans, with their families, to some interesting locality, for a happy and rational holiday.' Many excursions were deliberately counter-attractive, designed to draw the people away to some safe venue at the time of the horse-races or the wake. And many people continued to believe in the morally beneficial effects of railway excursions; in Lancashire, Ludlow and Lloyd Jones could report happily in 1867, excursions 'have in a great measure superseded the "wakes", "fairs", "feasts", etc., formerly the only means of enjoyment for the worker outside of his own town'.[29]

But however public they might appear, excursions were run for profit. And in the pursuit of profit the rational was often laid aside. It could hardly escape even the most blinkered rational recreationist that the train was morally neutral. Certainly it cannot have escaped that typical representative of mid-Victorian earnestness, Samuel Smiles; for it was he, of all people, in his capacity as Secretary to the South Eastern Railway Company, who had to explain to the Home Office why his company had mounted special excursion trains to prize-fights in 1859-60. His answer was that the demand was irresistible. Commerce triumphed over morality, and not in this instance alone. The railway gave an enormous boost to unrespectable as well as respectable leisure. There were excursions to public hangings and to fairs. Croydon fair, for example, and more enduringly Barnet, flourished when the railway made them accessible to Londoners. In Oxford, writes Sally Alexander, 'St Giles's came of age with the introduction of the excursion ticket', the first special excursion for the fair bringing in 900 people from Banbury in 1850. Soon the catchment area extended to Cardiff, Gloucester, London and Birmingham.[30]

Prize-fights, hangings and fairs were once-off occasions, annual at best in their regularity. But the railway also helped to promote more regular but still unrespectable entertainment. Touring theatre companies, for example, came to depend heavily on the railway; by the end of the century there were no less than 142 special trains every Sunday in England and Wales to transport these companies. It was the railway, too, that made horse-racing a national spectator sport; the new enclosed courses of the 1870s were directly linked to railway stations, and railway companies themselves sponsored races. Slightly more respectable, brass band competitions, which became popular from the mid-1840s onwards, were possible only because of cheap rail fares; by 1888 there were 50 excursion trains for the Belle Vue contest in Manchester.[31]

Most spectacular of all, of course, and again morally neutral in its thrust, was the impact of the railway on the development of seaside resorts. We need to exercise some caution, however, if we are to measure that impact accurately. The seaside resorts have a long and important history before the coming of the railway; two points need to be made about that development. First, in so far as these pre-railway resorts were popular, in the sense of being accessible to the working class, they were necessarily close to large centres of population. Unquestionably the most important of them was Gravesend on the Thames estuary, easily reached from London by river. In 1825 it was described 'as the goal of every young Cockney's Sunday excursion ... The people of London, who may be observed every Sunday flocking down by hundreds in Steam packets and sailing vessels, have taken such a liking to Gravesend, that a company of rich capitalists have resolved to build an entire new town in its vicinity.' Certainly there was heavy investment; over £30,000 was spent on a pier opened in 1834, and this sum must have been well-spent for in 1835 over 670,000 passengers went by steamboat from London to Gravesend, which was over 60 per cent of the total national steamboat traffic from London.[32]

Gravesend was unique in the pre-railway age; popular demand was unmistakable, and the response was heavy capital investment to meet it and profit by it. Elsewhere, and this is our second point, development was aimed at attracting the rich. *The Times* in 1841 noted 'an increasing tendency of late years among all classes to find excuses for Holydays. *Among those who are well-to-do* the annual trip to the seaside has become a necessity of which their fathers, or at least their grandfathers never dreamt.' In the first half of the nineteenth century the seaside resorts were places for the leisured class; in varying degrees they were snobbish and exclusive. It required the inheritance of a fortune before Dickens's shopkeeping Tuggs's decided on a holiday and chose the relatively prestigious Ramsgate where they were socially out of their depth; but one doubts whether they would have been much more at ease in Margate. In the North just as much as in the South speculators strove to develop exclusive resorts. In the 1830s John Atherton, a speculative builder of Everton, and his son-in-law bought 170 acres of sandhills which they christened New Brighton and planned to develop into an 'attractive and fashionable watering place ... exclusively for the accommodation of the wealthier classes in and about Liverpool'. As Granville commented,

It must have required some courage to have planted the first dwelling-house on such a waste, and still more to have expected to attract others to follow the example. Nothing can equal the air of desolation which prevails around. The few clusters of houses and villas that have since been erected in this perfect desert, tend only to make the scene of barrenness still more striking, and suggest the idea of a modern village overwhelmed in ashes after some dreadful catastrophe.

New Brighton never quite overcame these desolate origins, and did not fulfil its makers' hopes that it could be 'the sea-bathing rendez-vous, *par excellence*, of the Lancashire people of note'. Lower down the social scale, but not very far down it, Crosby Waterloo and Bootle were being developed for 'the middle classes and the wealthy shopkeepers' of Liverpool, with little more evident success than at New Brighton, but with the same deliberate attempt at social exclusivity.[33]

Not all such developments, of course, were failures. Bournemouth, to which Granville was invited to see if it was a place 'suitable for the resort of the better classes of society', won his whole-hearted approval. As he put it:

An opportunity is now offered of establishing a real Montpellier on the south coast of England . . . for the upper and the wealthier classes of society, who ought to be encouraged and enticed to remain at home and spend their income in husbanding their health in England. They have been driven away from every point of the coast by the facilities afforded to the 'everybody', and the 'anybody', of congregating in shoals at the same watering-place, creating bustle, noise, confusion, and vulgarity.

Bournemouth grew as Granville would have wished. The landowners developed it as a high-class resort, and the railway was deliberately kept at a distance until 1868; the undifferentiated middle class, the 'everybody' and the 'anybody' whom Granville so disliked, were excluded. And in the pre-railway age the working-class visitor, the day tripper, was hardly even a cloud on the horizon in a place as distant from centres of population as Bournemouth.[34]

Before mid-century, then, before the railway, the seaside resorts were developing but they were not popular. It was after mid-century that growth became rapid. Population figures may help to make the point. It is true that between 1801 and 1851 the 'four principal inland watering places' – Bath, Cheltenham, Leamington and Tunbridge Wells –

together with eleven seaside resorts had a percentage population increase of 254 per cent which was higher than that for any other type of
town, but they started from a very low population base — 78,000 —
and by 1851 had an overall population of only just over 278,000; and
even with giant Brighton included the average population of the eleven
seaside towns was under 15,000. Twenty years later, in 1871, the census report listed no fewer than 48 seaside resorts, as against only 8
inland watering places, and the annual rate of increase of these seaside
resorts between 1861 and 1871 was 1.97 per cent. The average population of these resorts was admittedly small — under 11,000 — but in
total over half a million people now lived in them. And of course population figures tell only part of the story of the development of seaside
resorts. A small resident population might be the base for a vastly
greater number of visitors. Blackpool provides the classic example; its
population in 1871 was only just over 6,000 but it was already welcoming 600,000 visitors in the season.[35]

These visitors to Blackpool are testimony to a considerable level of
demand, and one might have expected investors to rush in to meet and
profit by it. This, however, was rarely the case. Deterred by class prejudice, by the wish to preserve resorts against the incursions of the
populace, and by a doubt that there was really money to be made in
such ventures, developers were cautious and hesitant. The coming of
the railway to Brighton illustrates these points very clearly. Brighton in
the 1830s was in a state of hiatus: the sustaining force of royal patronage was on the wane, while cheap sea travel to the Kent coast gave
those resorts an advantage. It was in the mid-1830s that schemes for a
railway emerged, and only after long debate that the direct route was
chosen rather than a circuitous one via the port of Shoreham, which
according to Stephenson its engineer was to be preferred among other
reasons because 'as Brighton, in common with other watering-places,
owes its present importance mainly to fashion, every security ought to
be taken that the line should be as much as possible removed from the
risk of caprice'. Holiday traffic, it was still believed, provided no firm
basis for financial success.

Events, indeed, seemed to prove this to be the case. The direct line
was chosen, opened in 1841, and the company was soon in financial
difficulties. The reason for this, however, was not lack of demand, but
the deliberate policy of the company in setting fares high in an attempt
to exclude the poor and attract what a director described as 'very superior traffic'. Financial failure led to a boardroom revolution, and the
new chairman, Rowland Hill, encouraged cheap fares and excursion

trains at Easter, Whitsun, at race week in August, and every Sunday. By 1850 it was possible to go to Brighton and back for 3s 6d. And it was these cheap fares which led to resumed growth in Brighton. It seems probable that the population of Brighton was virtually stagnant between 1831 and 1841. The census figures suggest an increase from 40,639 in 1831 to 46,661 in 1841, but the 1841 census was taken in summer and included visitors, probably some 5,500. By 1851 the population had jumped to over 65,000, and the number of lodging house and boarding house keepers rose from 136 in 1841 to 573 in 1851. Once fares were lowered the impact of the railway on Brighton was immediate and substantial.[36]

The coming of the railway did not always mean an increase in the popularity of a resort. It also had the ability to carry the well-to-do to social safety at distances beyond the reach of the working class, along the North Wales coast for example, or in the south-west. All over the country, resorts owed their development or their inception to the coming of the railway. The steamer was not eliminated, and played a major role in the development of the Kent coast resorts, and of Clacton, Walton-on-the-Naze and Weston-super-Mare. But the dominant influence in the third quarter of the century was the railway.[37]

Only rarely in that period, however, was there unrestrained exploitation of the demand which cheap travel released. Not only Brighton, but Blackpool and everywhere else tried to maintain a high social tone and exclude the day tripper. Their lack of success in doing so is testimony to the level of the demand. Eventually in Blackpool enough people − not the rich, but the cheaper boarding house and cafe proprietors, the beach entertainers, the street vendors, the gypsies and fairground operators − came to have an interest in catering to popular demand, and thus to push the town in the direction of catering for the masses, not the elite. As Professor Perkin has argued, this development was possible in Blackpool in part because land was divided into small lots and no one owner could impose his will in an attempt to maintain social tone. But even when land ownership was concentrated the force of demand could sometimes skew development in directions quite unintended by the developers. Skegness, for example, whose land was owned by the Earl of Scarbrough, was modelled in the 1870s on Bournemouth and Torquay with villas being built for the seasonal residence of the wealthy. But the demand for accommodation in boarding houses or hotels was such that the planners had to change their minds and bow to it.[38]

One must conclude, however, that in seaside resort development capitalists were slow to exploit the very considerable working-class demand. The truth was that, snobbery apart, and despite the evidence of numerous failures, it still seemed more profitable to develop a resort for the relatively wealthy rather than the masses. And if there was money to be made out of the working class, it would be made more by railway companies running excursions than by the landowners or the residents of the resorts. But there was some response to demand, and it is perhaps most dramatically evident in the building of pleasure piers in the 1860s and 1870s. These required considerable investment (an average cost of about £20,000 in the 1860s) and were a high risk, being peculiarly liable to destruction. The fact that they were built in such numbers suggests that, along with the excursion train and the growth in the number of people willing to invest their savings in seaside boarding houses, there was some response on the supply side to working-class demand in this third quarter of the century.[39] Unquestionably, however, it was only in the last quarter of the century that the commercial exploitation of that demand began to be fully developed. In the mid-Victorian period the foundations for that later development were laid, and they were laid sufficiently firmly, and there was a sharp enough break with the pre-railway age, for us to conclude that in this respect as in others it marks a new period in the history of leisure.

The caution of capitalists in their response to the demand for seaside holidays and entertainment was untypical. In other fields as diverse as music hall, circus, fairs, the production of literature for a mass market, and in horse-racing, the third quarter of the century sees both major injections of capital and a rise in scale with the large often swallowing the small. There was a clear recognition on the part of suppliers that a new mass market was coming into being.

Charles Morton's opening of the Canterbury Music Hall in Lambeth in 1851 is conventionally taken to mark the beginning of the history of music-hall, and as such it confirms our argument that the mid-century inaugurated a new period in the history of leisure. But here, as with our account of the development of seaside resorts, caution is necessary, for it is rather too easy to set on Morton's achievements the values which he himself did. In fact the music-hall had a number of predecessors, some of them virtually indistinguishable from the creations of the 1850s. They fall into two groups. On the one hand there were the Judge and Jury shows, the song and supper rooms, the pleasure gardens, the saloon theatres, and the tavern concert-rooms which go into the making of music-hall in London, and it is on these that music-hall history almost exclusively concentrates. And on the other hand there are pre-1850 developments in the provinces, some of them bearing the name of music-hall.

So far as the London music-hall is concerned, the Judge and Jury shows, presided over by 'Baron' Nicholson, and the song and supper rooms have received more than their fair share of attention. They catered for an upper-class and bohemian man-about-town clientele, and had no pretensions to being mass entertainment. Their importance for music-hall lay in the fact that some of the performers in them, for example Sam Cowell and Mackney at Evans's, were able to transfer their talents to the halls. The pleasure gardens handed down a more relevant tradition for the history of popular entertainment. Although their heyday was unquestionably in the second half of the eighteenth century, many of them survived into the nineteenth century and there were new creations – the Royal Surrey Gardens at Walworth (1831-77) and Cremorne Gardens (1843-77) being the chief examples. The pleasure gardens survived by becoming popular, and lowering their prices; for example at Vauxhall the admission price was lowered from 2s 6d to 1s in 1833. Moreover the entertainment became less formal and more spectacular and participant; at Cremorne there was an American bowling saloon. Indeed the pleasure garden of the first half of the nineteenth century was one of the homes of variety.

Another was the saloon theatre which had an even closer link with music-hall. The names of most of them are much less familiar than those of the early music-halls. The Eagle or Grecian Saloon in the City Road was the most famous, but there were also the Union Saloon, Shoreditch, the Britannia Saloon, Hoxton, the Apollo Saloon, Marylebone, the Bower Saloon, Stangate Street, Lower Marsh, the Albert Saloon, Shepherdess Walk, and the Effingham Saloon, Whitechapel Road. Their locations suggest the working- and lower-middle-class audience they attracted. The programmes normally consisted of a mixture of opera, drama, farce, singing, music and dancing. The 1843 Theatres Regulation Act was in part aimed at them, for under it the saloons had to become either theatres without refreshment in the auditorium or regular music-halls with drinks licences, but without the right of producing stage plays. Some, most notably the Britannia at Hoxton, chose to become theatres. The development of the others led straight to the music-hall, and in terms of programme there was nothing to distinguish what was being offered at the Grecian Saloon in the 1830s from the music-hall fare of the 1850s and 1860s.[40]

The connection between the drink trade and the saloons was of course a close one, but not as intimate and immediate as that linking the sale of alcohol and the development of the music-hall. For the Canterbury Hall developed directly from the tavern-concert tradition, one in which a regular salary for the performer only gradually supplanted direct reward in the form of alcohol. The tavern-concert was in many ways simply a smaller version of the saloons and minor theatres. What happened in the 1840s was that some of them began to expand quite dramatically. In that decade, for example, The Grapes Inn, Southwark Road was an imposing building with an auditorium to seat about 1,000. It was little more than a change of name when it opened in November 1848 as the Surrey Music Hall. Morton when he took over the Canterbury Arms in the late 1840s found his parlour concerts successful, and this induced him to build the Canterbury Hall, to hold some 700 people, on the land occupied by the four skittle alleys that belonged to the pub. 'Morton's scheme was a revolutionary one only in respect of its geographical position', wrote Harold Scott. Even that must be doubted for the South Bank was the chief location for popular entertainment. What was unusual about Morton was his ability to gain favourable publicity for his venture among the respectable by playing Gounod's Faust, and by providing an art gallery.[41]

There is one further and much neglected forerunner of the London music-hall — the penny gaff. Too much emphasis in the history of music-hall has been put on what was passed downwards from above, too little on what came upwards. James Grant described the gaffs in horrific terms in 1838 as 'no better than so many nurseries for juvenile thieves'. What alarmed him was the youth of the audiences — mainly boys between eight and sixteen — and the size and number of the gaffs. He estimated that there were between 80 and 100 in London, with an average attendance of 150 at each performance, and with sometimes as many as nine houses each night. The largest of the gaffs held up to 2,000 people. Mayhew, later, was equally critical of the gaffs — 'a platform to teach the crudest debauchery' — but no less impressed by their size. The Christmas pantomime, a penny gaff clown told him,

> played to upwards of twelve hundred persons a night, according to the size of the house, for few penny ones hold more than four hundred, and that's three times a-night. The Rotunda in the Blackfriars'-road, and the Olympic Circus in the Lower Marsh, Lambeth, do an immense business, for they hold near a thousand each, and that's three thousand spectators the night.

The pantomime season aside, the performances at penny gaffs consisted of melodrama, singing and dancing, and were not dissimilar to the music-hall.[42]

If Morton's initiative was hardly revolutionary when considered in the context of London entertainment as a whole, it appears even less so when developments in the provinces are taken into account. As in London there were before mid-century 'Saloons' or 'Casinos' on the one hand and tavern-concerts or free and easies on the other which presage the music-hall of the second half of the century. The former sometimes bore the name, music-hall, as with the Star Music Hall, Bolton, opened in 1840, and eventually offering not only music, but a picture gallery, a museum and a menagerie. Probably similar both in the variety of the entertainment which they offered and the respectability for which they strove were The Temple of the Muses, described by Disraeli in *Sybil*, the Rodney in Birmingham, and the various enterprises run by Thomas Youdan in Sheffield. Youdan, originally a labourer, became proprietor of the Spink Nest public house, and later ran 'Youdan's Royal Casino' putting on nightly musical entertainments and 'Sacred Music on Sunday Evenings, with an Efficient Band' (admission free). This developed into the Surrey Music Hall, by which time Youdan was offering opera.[43] By mid-century most of the Northern and Midlands industrial towns must have been offering something similar. In Manchester, in the early 1850s, J.W.Hudson described how some 25,000 working mill hands attended each week one of the three large music saloons which were attached to licensed beer-houses, and offered 'singing in character, dancing of various kinds, clog and grotesque dancing, juggling and tumbling by performers specially engaged'. Entrance to these three, the Casino in Lower-Moseley Street, the Victoria Saloon, and the Polytechnic in Salford, each of which held about 1,000 people, was by 2d refreshment ticket. In a smaller town like Hartlepool similar entertainment was being offered at the Royal Casino, Dock Hotel in 1850 and at Smith's Royal Music Saloon in 1851.[44]

Our current knowledge of these provincial developments is at best patchy, though there is at least here the probability that research in local archives and newspapers will tell us more, for these saloons, or music-halls, or casinos were large, and they advertised. It is much more difficult to assess the importance of the free and easies, and probably wrong to draw a hard and fast line between them and the larger enterprises. Their development is peculiarly hard to trace because until 1851, and in many places until long after that, magisterial control could be asserted only through the normal liquor licences; hence numbers are

hard to come by. Thus in evidence given before the 1866 Select Committee on Theatrical Licences and Regulations it was stated that in
Manchester there were three or four specially-built music-halls, and
smaller halls 'in every street, almost' with a spirit licence, but no
licence for music or dancing. In Liverpool, said the Head Constable,
there were no music-halls in the London sense at all, but some 33 pubs
with music and dancing, each holding up to 100 people; at one-third
of these, performers were specially engaged. There simply was no clear
differentiation between a music-hall and a pub offering entertainment.
In Dudley, claimed a disenchanted manager of a travelling theatre, 'go
into one of the great places there, which are all like glass; you cannot
here a word; there is the music, and there is a collier and his wife
fighting, and a child crying, and that they call a concert-room; it is all
in front of the bar.' This kind of tradition, wherein pub-based and relatively small-scale entertainment did not require special licensing, clearly
pre-dated the music-hall and lived on in the provinces long after there
were larger and more formal music-halls. There is a good account of
such a free and easy in Arnold Bennett's *Clayhanger*. In the provinces,
we may conclude, a deep-rooted tradition of popular pub-based entertainment continued with little change into the second half of the century, while from the 1840s onwards there emerged out of and alongside
this tradition much larger prototype music-halls with considerable
pretensions to respectability.[45]

In London, in contrast, the development of the halls was affected
by the law. Their pretensions to respectability were hampered by the
theatrical interest's opposition to their aspirations to play straight
drama, while their development in the 1860s may have been aided by
the magistrates' refusal to license pubs for music and dancing.

The first of these effects received most attention. It is difficult to
be certain of the exact forces at work. On the one hand there is the
well-attested love of drama among popular audiences, and it was not
surprising that music-hall proprietors should try to cater for it. Music-
hall is too often thought of simply in terms of songs whereas in fact it
embraced much more — acrobats, jugglers, dancing and, if the law permitted, drama. It was natural, and quite in line with the saloon tradition, that drama should be part of the programme. On the other hand,
however, is Morton's drive for respectability, in this instance curiously
enough to be attained by breaking the law. Morton was able to pose as
a man anxious to provide the public with uplifting fare, and hampered
only by the jealousy of the licensed theatre with its unjustified monopoly of legitimate drama. He won much sympathy and in 1866 a Select

Committee of the House of Commons, summoned to resolve the dispute, decided in favour of the music-halls. No action on the part of the legislature resulted, however, and drama was thus excluded from the music-hall. It is intriguing to speculate whether a popular love of drama might have continued within the music-hall had the law been different.

The effect of the licensing laws as operated by the magistrates is equally uncertain, not least because of ambiguity in the wording of the relevant Act of 1752. The magistrates wanted to control the growing pub-based entertainment by issuing licences for music, but the only licences which could be granted under the 1752 Act, it appeared, were for 'public dancing, music, or other public entertainment of the like kind'. This was far too wide in scope to meet the magistrates' needs, and not surprisingly they were chary about issuing them. The Middlesex magistrates licensed only seven such places in the first 40 years of the Act's operation. Thereafter they issued more: in 1845 67 places were licensed for music and dancing. In 1851 the lawyers at last agreed that music-only licences could be issued under the Act, and in Middlesex, in Birmingham, and gradually elsewhere, the magistrates made use of this long-wanted opportunity to assert control; previously one must assume, in London as much as in the provinces, pubs where singing and music were performed were controlled only by the liquor licences.

The impact of the new ruling can be shown clearly in Middlesex. In contrast to 1845, in 1855 there were issued 255 licences for music only, and 50 for music and dancing, and in 1865 291 for music only, and 60 for music and dancing. These figures are consonant with the *Era*'s estimate that there were 200 to 300 smaller halls in London in 1856. It has been suggested that these smaller halls were hit by a harsh licensing policy and declined from the early 1860s. Perhaps growth was halted, but right at the end of the century there remained in the new County of London 328 places licensed for music, and Charles Booth was to stress that 'especially in poor neighbourhoods, the old-fashioned style of sing-song still continues in force'. As in the provinces it was not so much that the larger music-halls swallowed up the smaller as that they grew alongside them.[46]

The larger halls entered into their first major period of growth in the later 1850s. Morton, as we saw, did little that was new in building the Canterbury. By the end of the decade, however, there were a number of important developments which suggest that the larger music-hall was becoming an institution. Dates of foundations of halls point to the late 1850s and early 1860s as the period of take-off for the metropolitan halls. Little happened immediately after the opening of the Canterbury, then came Wilton's (1856), Weston's Music Hall, Holborn (1857), the South London Palace (1860), the London Pavilion, the Oxford, the Bedford, Camden Town, and Deacon's, Clerkenwell (all in 1861), and Collins', Islington (1862). Of these the most significant foundations were Weston's, the London Pavilion, and the Oxford, for they mark the spread of music-hall to the West End.[47] Music-hall was becoming not simply an enlarged type of neighbourhood tavern-concert, but a universal and (at least in embryo) mass form of entertainment.

The growth in the number of music-halls is paralleled by the beginnings of professional organisation. The first music-hall agency started in London in 1858, and the agency system then developed very rapidly in the early 1860s. Music-hall newspapers came into existence: *Era, Magnet* and *London Entr'acte. Era* was first a general paper, representing the licensed victuallers, but it gradually became more theatrical in tone. *Magnet* from 1866 onwards was the pioneer of the professional music-hall press, circulating mainly in the provinces. By 1865 a further sign of professional organisation was the foundation of the Music Hall Provident Society.

Overshadowing all these developments, however, was the increasing organisation of the owners. In 1860 the London Music Hall Proprietors' Protection Association was founded, organised to defend the halls in their battle with the legitimate theatre. Its formation was a recognition that music-hall was a major investment. Morton's reconstruction of the Canterbury in 1854 is estimated to have cost at least £40,000. Morton and Stanley, the first chairman of the Association, spent £35,000 on the Oxford before it opened in 1861. In 1864 the first music-hall limited liability company was formed for the Alhambra. By 1866 there were 33 large music-halls in London with an average capitalisation of £10,000 and an average seating capacity of 1,500.[48] The owners of these halls had grown far beyond the small tavern-concert room proprietors. The source of their money is uncertain, and there must be at least speculation that they borrowed from the brewers, for drink sales remained an important source of revenue. Whatever the case there can be no doubt that music-hall had become big business by the mid-1860s.

The next major phase of development started in 1878 with the Metropolis Management and Building Act Amendments Act which introduced stricter fire regulations and led to the closure of many smaller halls. It was soon after this that there began a new injection of capital, the rebuilding of the West End halls on much grander lines – the new London Pavilion opened in 1885 is typical – and the concentration into chains of ownership. And that these developments were by no means solely metropolitan is indicated by the fact that many of the new entrepreneurs were northerners, bringing to London experience in the management of halls which had been gained in the provinces.

Authority smiled on these developments. By the mid-1860s magistrates and police officers had become convinced that the larger music-halls were an aid to peace. In evidence before the 1866 Select Committee on Theatrical Licences and Regulations Sir Thomas Henry, Chief Magistrate at Bow Street Police Court, declared the halls to be well-conducted, and found 'there is scarcely ever a case of drunkenness from any of the music-halls'. The Hon. G.C. Norton, Magistrate at the Lambeth Police Court, believed that the halls reduced drunkenness, and generally improved the conduct and habits of the people; one reason they did so was because music-hall entertainment was family entertainment. From the police point of view Sir Richard Mayne, Chief Commissioner of the Metropolitan Police, confirmed that music-halls were generally well-conducted: 'There are a great number in some parts of the town, especially in the eastern parts, where the audiences are a very low class of people, and many of them are very young, but they are well-behaved.' Prostitutes, admittedly, frequented the halls, but even they behaved with decorum, and neither magistrates nor police knew of any private rooms attached to halls; such, according to Mayne, were more likely to be found 'in the low class of beer-houses'. The realistic police attitudes were explained to Bracebridge Hemyng, an investigator for Mayhew, by a sergeant:

> The *British Queen*, a concert-room in the Commercial Road, is a respectable, well-conducted house, frequented by low prostitutes, as may be expected, but orderly in the extreme, and what more can be wished for? The sergeant remarked to me, if these places of harmless amusement were not licensed and kept open, much evil would be sown and disseminated throughout the neighbourhood, for it may be depended something worse and ten times lower would be substituted. People of all classes must have recreation. Sailors who come on shore after a long cruise *will* have it; and [added the sergeant] we give it them in a way that does no harm to themselves or anybody else.

Music-hall proprietors co-operated with the authorities in the maintenance of order. They paid for police to be present at the halls, and they anticipated the theatre managers by some 20 years in exiling the rowdy elements to the gallery. Wilton's, for example, was rebuilt with the gallery set apart for the sailors and their women, while tradesmen and keepers of tally-shops filled the body of the hall.[49]

Music-hall, then, as it developed in the 1860s was a commercial initiative positively welcomed by authority, and we need to bear this in mind when we come to consider the type and significance of the entertainment which was offered to the public.

Music-hall has been interpreted in two quite different ways: on the one hand as an authentic expression of working- and lower-middle-class values, with composers, singers and audiences all coming from the people; and on the other hand as a commercially-exploited debasement of folk song. The latter view was not without contemporary support. James Greenwood, touring *The Wilds of London*, visited the Grampian, and was horrified at the 'trash . . . tolerated by the pleasure-seeking Englishman'. He suggested 'an Anti-Idiotic Entertainment Company as a means of freeing you – us – from the tyranny of ignorant men who monopolise the control of your chief place of amusement . . .'[50] But it would be naive to view the music-hall as a simple case of capitalist exploitation of the leisure time and money of the working class. Rather the music-hall embodied a tension between the demand released by the growth in opportunity for leisure at mid-century and a particular form and structure of entertainment which was both profitable and respectable; respectable in the sense that it attained a level of order and decorum which was the most that middle-class common sense could expect. It was better than the alternatives, but it was hardly rational, even if it might advertise itself as such. At that level, in rejecting the rational, demand was dominant.

But to what extent, we may ask, did demand affect the content and tone of what was offered? The traditional answer is in terms of an increasing alienation between audience and performer as the layout of the halls became more formal. Martha Vicinus writes:

> Beginning as an entertainment by and for the working-class, with a sprinkling of bohemians, by the end of the nineteenth century the music hall had a mass appeal, and was produced entirely by professionals who realized immense profits. The major snift was away from a form of entertainment that spoke directly to the working class out of a shared experience to one that was provided for 'the masses' by those familiar with their experiences but apart from it.

There is much truth in this, but in order to damn the later music-hall it may imply too rosy a view of the early music-hall. The evidence of the songs themselves suggests that the singers were closer to the every-day life of their audiences in the 1890s than they were in the heyday of the *lion comique* and the female serio-comic in the 1860s and 1870s. The latter, it is true, sang of everyday experiences, but the former played to a need for escapism. This does not imply that the Great Vance more than Gus Ellen was foisted on an unwilling if captive audience by capitalists, but it does point to the complexity of determining how far demand shaped the early history of the halls. The truth is probably that the level of demand encouraged investment, and the amount of investment suggested the erection of a respectable façade. The songs themselves were only one part of the performance which bore much more the character of variety than one might suppose. There was a wish for escapism and for pleasure, and the music-halls catered for it.[51]

They were not alone in so doing, however. Popular theatre continued vibrant and alive, as the history of the Britannia Theatre, Hoxton, is testimony. Thomas Wright in 1867 described the theatre as 'the most popular resort of pleasure-seeking workmen', and the music-hall as second only to that.[52] And besides the theatre, there were other large-scale enterprises, rivalling the music-hall in the extent of capital investment, and in the evolution from earlier origins. The most important of these was the circus which, as we have seen, was already big business in the first half of the century. The increase in size and capital investment continued. More and more permanent amphitheatres were opened. It was around mid-century that Newsome opened his own circus with permanent buildings in large towns in the north of England. Charles Hengler was to adopt the same plan, discontinuing tenting in the summer, locating his circus in permanent buildings and staying several months in each. Sanger too emerged from the ranks of small-time entertainers to build up a circus with locations in Manchester, Birmingham, Liverpool, Glasgow, Dundee, Aberdeen, Bath, Bristol, Exeter and Plymouth. He also rented the Agricultural Hall, Islington, and in 1871 bought his own London base, Astley's, for £11,000. Sanger, although influenced by the trend towards permanent sites, also continued to travel, but on a scale far surpassing anything known previously. When in the early 1870s Sanger dissolved his partnership with his brother there was £100,000 of property to split up, and on his first continental tour in the 1870s he took with him 46 carriages, 160 horses, 11 elephants, 12 camels and 230 people. The circus was now big business. There were of course smaller concerns, but many of them, like Wild's, collapsed under the strain of competition.[53]

Circus had always been international in the sense that performers could travel abroad. Now whole vast companies like that of Sanger transported themselves across the seas. Moreover there was an invasion of American companies, the greatest among them that of Barnum. Barnum had established a familiarity with Europe with his 1840s tours with Tom Thumb and Jenny Lind. In the 1870s his huge circus was to put intense competitive pressure on Sanger and other British rivals.[54]

As with the music-halls, authority favoured size. It was the patronage of the Marquis of Westminster and the support of the clergy which enabled Hengler to open in Liverpool. Sanger was often aided by the police. Barnum noted how the early opposition of the clergy turned to support; and with good reason, for as he himself said in 1873, 'For many years it has been my pleasure to provide a class of instructive and amusing entertainments to which a refined Christian mother can take her children with satisfaction.' In Bristol in the 1880s the circus moved to a richer area of the city and increased its appeal to families.[55] For authority there could be no sorrow in seeing the large swallow the small when the outcome was apparently so favourable to morality.

Fairs underwent much the same process. Viewed as relics of a barbarous age in the 1830s, they revived in the 1850s on the basis of new technology and new investment. In this instance the initiative came from East Anglian agricultural machinery makers who saw possibilities in elaborating the roundabout. They made participant movement rather than the theatre or dance the focus of the fair; and the new machinery was much more expensive than the old portable booths. Inevitably there was a desire to get a proper return on investment, and to travel only to the larger fairs which attracted people from a wide surrounding area; and here, as we have seen, the excursion train worked towards the survival and enlargement of fairs. The big concerns now no longer found a one-night stop at the smaller fairs worth their while. Authority too had no more time for the smaller fairs and many of them were eliminated under a permissive Act of Parliament of 1871. The larger fairs, however, were now winning the support of the police and the Home Office.[56]

In music-hall, circus and fairs, it was in the third quarter of the century that there occurred a new level of investment and a new scale of organisation. Although they are separable genres the connections between the three were strong. Buildings were multipurpose. Consider the Alhambra in Leicester Square. Opening in 1854 as the Royal Panopticon offering performances intended 'to assist by moral and intellectual agencies the best interests of society', it became a waxworks, a circus, a music-hall and a restaurant, then offered ballet, but had its licence

removed when it introduced the can-can in the 1860s. It turned then to
opera and promenade concerts before emerging in 1884 as the Alhambra Theatre of Varieties. Performers too passed from one kind of entertainment to another. There was, it is true, a special breed of circus performers, but acrobats were as likely to be found in the music-hall as in
the circus, especially in the 1860s. Equestrians who had learned their
skills in the circus were in demand at the theatres. 'The amusing
classes', as Thomas Frost described them, 'whether connected with
circuses, theatres, public gardens, or music halls — actors, singers, dancers, equestrians, clowns, gymnasts, acrobats, jugglers, posturers' were
mostly to be found in daytime in a small area on the South Bank where
the agencies were concentrated. They were a new footloose often unemployed proletariat in an increasingly capitalised entertainment industry. There were also many more of them. Between 1851 and 1881 the
number of actors increased from 1,398 to 2,197, the number of actres-
ses from 778 to 2,368.[57]

The novelty of this situation can be gauged by looking at the fate of
those who obstinately clung on to the ownership of the means of
production without the capital to expand to meet the new conditions.
The Punch and Judy men and the *fantoccini* described by Mayhew at
mid-century depended on two kinds of performance — in the parlours
or beneath the windows of the rich, and in the streets of the poor. Both
were under threat. The rich ceased to patronise; as Mayhew's *fantoccini*
man said, 'I think it's the people that gave the half-crowns are tired of
it, but those with the ha'pence are as fond of it as ever.' The latter,
however, were in fact being wooed by more exotic entertainment. The
Punch and Judy man who 20 years previously had been able to earn £5
a week throughout the year was now struggling for a livelihood. The
future for such men and their successors lay in catering for the juvenile
market, a situation to which they seem to have adapted by the 1870s;
but it was a sad decline from the vigorous puppet tradition of the late
eighteenth century. The only successful street showmen were those
with some modern technology — a telescope or a camera; the others
were being obliterated by competition. David Prince Miller records the
same processes at work. After a 15-year interval he travelled England
with the 'Bosjemans', but

found that people were not so prone to listen to the oft-repeated
jokes of Mr. Merryman, or watch with wonder and amazement the
proceedings of the fire-eater outside. An old showman whom I had
known in years gone by, addressed me with a sorrowful countenance,

'. . . people in my opinion, haven't got half the sense they used to have; there was a time when they would stand and listen to the clown, and tumble up in hundreds, and be satisfied above a penn'orth, with ever so *quisby a slang*; (bad a show) but now when they do come they arn't half satisfied, and then look at 'em, they're all rail-road mad, going their cheap trips as they calls 'em and wandering about the green lanes and fields — what have they got to look at there, I wonder? Ah, things are coming to a pretty pass!'[58]

If the small-scale popular entertainer was under threat, so also was the small-scale producer of literature for the poor. The connection between the two was strong. For popular literature — the broadside or broadsheet — was sold by the patterers and ballad-singers who sang or acted them out, and by mid-century ballad-singing was a dying profession. In the earlier nineteenth century, in contrast, it had been alive and vigorous, and so had been the literature on which it was based. In London alone there were 75 printers in the early nineteenth century selling broadsides and chapbooks. With their emphasis on crime, sex, patriotism and the celebration of public occasions they achieved colossal sales — over one million in some cases — and they sold to the poor. Their producers — James Catnach and John Pitts of the Seven Dials being the best known — might make money, but they did so by unremitting attention to pennies and halfpennies. If they were the forerunners of the popular press, they were distinguished from it by their close connection with the sellers and readers of their product and by the smallness of their capital investment. The broadsides were short and ephemeral and produced on cheap paper, and although it was a form of literature which survived into the 1870s, it was manifestly in decline by mid-century if not before.[59]

Musically the broadside ballad tradition was carried over into the very different conditions and environment of the music-hall. In terms of reading matter it was transmuted into the popular press. A vital aspect of the emergence of leisure as a separate category in the lives of men and women was the explosion in the sales of literature. In the early nineteenth century newspapers sold about 24 million copies a year. The rate of expansion of sales thereafter — 33 per cent between 1816 and 1838, 70 per cent between 1836 and 1856, and about 600 per cent between 1856 and 1882 — confirm the importance of the third quarter of the century in the history of leisure. Sunday newspapers were the most popular. In them and in other newspapers there was continuity with the past, in content and appeal, but a vast increase in the scale of production.[60]

The publishers of these newspapers were not necessarily reaching a wider market than the publishers of the broadsides, but their sales were more regular — weekly — their papers were longer, and the successful management of the business required some capital investment, and more modern methods of sale and distribution. The removal of duties in the 1850s gave a colossal boost to new methods of newspaper management, most of all in the provinces. Selling cheaply, and exploiting the railway and the telegraph, newspapers and magazines catered to and filled a huge demand for literature. Their influence and spread became much greater than the tracts distributed in such large numbers by voluntary societies. Once again it was in the third quarter of the century that there occurred an intensification in the capitalisation of leisure, which was a response to and an exploitation of a new level of demand for reading material.

The history of horse-racing may serve as a last example of the processes we are considering here, that is of both an increase in scale and in capital investment, and of a curtailment of the small in favour of the large. Here the breakthrough came at the end rather than the beginning of the third quarter of the nineteenth century. In 1874 there were 130 courses in the country, in 1884 only 65. Some of these had been abolished by law. The Racecourses (Metropolis) Act of 1879 gave magistrates the power to licence, and of course not to licence, races within ten miles of the metropolis. The Act was aimed at what were regarded as rough and rowdy meetings particularly at Enfield, Bromley and Streatham. The Act coincided in time with the beginnings of new enclosed park courses, of which the first was Sandown Park (1875), followed by Kempton Park (1878). Good railway communications and fee-paying spectators encouraged a massive wave of investment, some £1½ million being invested in courses and grandstands between the mid-1870s and the mid-1890s.In the history of this development betting was, as Vamplew has argued, 'the keystone'. And betting itself, the demand for tips and news, played a large part in the development of the popular press. Not only were there special sporting journals — *Sporting Life* in 1863, *Sporting Chronicle* in Manchester in 1871, two sporting papers in Birmingham by 1880 — but also no less than half the evening papers started in the 1870s and 1880s had a close association with sport and gambling.[61]

It has been the argument of this section that in the third quarter of the century the facilities for leisure, whether provided by the government, philanthropy or commerce, expanded at a rate and in directions which justify us in seeing this period as a turning-point in the history of leisure. Clearly some qualifications are necessary. It is one of the aims of this book to stress the continuity in the history of leisure, to make the point that what historians tend to regard as 'traditional' often survived the turmoil of the Industrial Revolution. And we have noted that in excursions, in resort development, in music-hall, in circus, in popular literature there were important and substantial precursors of mid-Victorian developments; there was a base to build on, and there was continuity with the past. And at the other end of the period, it is obvious that the processes we have outlined speeded up and became more significant in the last quarter of the century when demand was further boosted by the decrease in working hours achieved in the 1870s and by the rising working-class standard of living that came with the Great Depression, and when on the supply side capital showed strong signs of integration and combination.

Despite these qualifications the evidence is strong enough to support the argument that the mid-century marks a turning-point in the history of leisure. Of course not all aspects of leisure were transformed at exactly the same time and in the same way — large-scale capitalisation of music-hall, for example, precedes that of horse-racing — but more striking than the differences is the interconnectedness and the similarity of development of the different leisure facilities we have examined, and indeed of others, like football. Granted the increase in working-class time and money which we have argued in the first section, that is to say an increase in potential demand, it is the railway which stands out in this period as the great technical breakthrough in the history of leisure, and the force which makes possible one, rather than many disparate histories of leisure. Morally neutral as we have seen, it left no aspect of leisure untouched and imposed a similarity of development which otherwise would not have occurred.

Voluntary Organisations and Leisure

There is one further line of argument which points to the third quarter of the nineteenth century as a crucial one in the history of leisure. It was in this period that voluntary organisations founded to promote religion, or education, or military preparedness, found that in order to survive and grow they had to offer leisure to their members. It is true of course that religious observance or education had always taken place in leisure time, but in the early nineteenth century to see it as such is to impose a later notion on those to whom the term would have been almost meaningless. Methodists, for example, met to worship God, to save people from sin, not to offer them a relatively harmless way of amusing themselves. And if they mounted counter-attractions, this was a missionary gambit, a proclamation of a different way of life, not of an alternative way of amusing oneself. The delimitation of leisure at mid-century and the power of the demand for leisure which was implicit in the delimitation, forced voluntary organisations, and not only religious ones, into a more ambiguous and eventually defensive relationship with the secular world. Partly this was caused by developments internal to themselves. Initial growth and enthusiasm was replaced by bureaucrat-isation and institutionalisation. There was an increasing concern with levels of membership and with finance; and as a result there was a willingness to compromise to the end of recruiting and holding mem-bers. But the fact that they did this reflected the much greater competi-tion that was being posed by leisure facilities which claimed only to amuse. From about mid-century voluntary organisations, whatever their ostensible aims, were operating in a competitive leisure market. Their adjustment to that situation was necessarily painful.

It was among the churches that the debate was most deep-searching. The Nonconformists in particular found it difficult to adapt to a world in which religion itself was not regarded as a sufficient amusement. In the late eighteenth and early nineteenth centuries the Methodists especially were fully aware of the entertainment value of religion; in the 1800s Reverend William Myles described the love-feast as 'a religious entertainment'. The Baptist churches of East Kent, concerned about low attendance in 1786 recommended 'That our Ministers endeavour to diversify the service to excite their attendance.' The aim was that the strictly religious life of the church, with its music, song and the sense of community it generated, should satisfy any craving for entertainment among the members. In this situation it was almost a reflex action to denounce the leisure life of the secular world. In 1850 the *Bible Christian Magazine*'s catalogue of sins consisted of 'the ballroom, the card-table, the village wake, the race-course, the bowling-green, the cricket-ground, the gin-palace, or the ale-house'. These were but the worst. Other things too were condemned — novel-reading, concert-going and the theatre. There was a sense of shock in Evangelical circles when the biography of Wilberforce published in 1838 revealed that he had read Shakespeare, Scott and Bulwer. The correct attitude at that time was to eschew all contact with the secular world.[62]

In two stages the churches began to come to terms with the secular world and its entertainments. The first was to start offering counter-attractions, events which might remove as many people as possible from the scenes of temptation. To be effective the counter-attractions had to be good entertainment, something which would actually lure people away from race-course or wake. The counter-attraction which came to seem to the churches to be most effective was the excursion, and however well-controlled it might be, however many prayers might be offered in the course of the excursion, it was difficult to disguise the fact that the churches were now competing for the leisure time of the people by offering not the excitement of the religious service but something which was essentially secular.

The counter-attraction could be defended as a missionary gambit, an attempt to pull in the unfaithful. The second stage was internal to the life of the churches, a seemingly innocent provision of amusements for the congregation itself. In Mark Rutherford's Cowfold this took the form of a 'religious picnic' confined to the principal members of the congregation who

with their wives and children, had an early dinner, and went in gigs and four-wheel chaises to Shott Woods, taking hampers of bread, cake, jam, butter, ham, and other eatables with them. At Shott Woods, in a small green space under an immense oak, a fire was lighted and tea was prepared. Mr. Broad [the minister] and his family always joined the party. These were the days when Dissenters had no set amusements, and the entertainment at Shott mainly consisted in getting sticks for the fire, fetching the water, and waiting on one another; the waiting being particularly pleasant to the younger people. Dancing, of course, was not thought of. In 1840 it may safely be said that there were not twenty Independent families in Great Britain in which it would have been tolerated, and, moreover, none but the rich learned to dance. No dancing-master ever came into Cowfold; there was no music-master there; no concert was ever given; and Cowfold, in fact, never 'saw nor heard anything', to use a modern phrase, save a travelling menagerie with a brass band. What an existence! How *did* they live? It is certain, however, that they did live, and, on the whole, enjoyed their life.

In this ironic passage, Rutherford, writing in 1887, was aware of the changes that had occurred in the previous half-century. As the secular world came to offer more in the way of entertainment, so religious picnics ceased to satisfy, and the churches, in a bid to recruit and hold members, began to tolerate what they had previously condemned. The young in particular, it was recognised, expected secular amusement, and

'If the Church will not provide it, the Devil will'. At varying points in the second half of the century most Methodists came to accept outdoor games, the religious novel was being serialised in the journals by the late 1870s, and even dancing began to be admitted by the 1890s. Nonconformists tried to persuade themselves that all this was to the good, but it was not easy to do so. As R.W. Dale described the situation in the 1860s,

What amusements are lawful to persons who wish to live a religious life, is one of the questions by which many good people are sorely perplexed. The stricter habits of our fathers are being everywhere relaxed, and there are very many who wish to do right, but know not what to think of the change; they yield to the current of the times, but yield with hesitation, discomfort, and apprehension.

Dale's solution, and it was one followed by many churchmen, was to admit the necessity for recreation and at the same time to elevate its objectives. 'The object of all recreation', he wrote, 'is to increase our capacity for work, to keep the blood pure, and the brain bright, and the temper kindly, and sweet' — objectives it may be said from which an earnest atheist would not have dissented. Nor would he have disagreed with the *Bible Christian Magazine*'s claim in 1881 that 'Occasional leisure and relaxation was an element in the robuster manhood of the time'.[63]

The truth was that the terms of trade as it were between the churches and society had changed. By the end of the third quarter of the century the churches were accommodating to society, rather than changing it, and this meant that they had come to accept secular leisure as a good. There is no hint of irony or doubt in Joseph Lawson's reflections, in the 1880s, on the changes in chapel life in Pudsey:

Chapels now are more inviting — have better music, — service of song, — which cannot help being attractive to the young as well as beneficial to all. They have sewing classes, bazaars, concerts, and the drama; cricket and football clubs, and harriers; societies for mutual improvement, and excursions to the seaside.

Churches and chapels now knew that if they did not offer some leisure they would lose members. Moreover, those distinguished in some form of secular leisure were now welcomed by the churches and exploited for evangelistic purposes. In the early part of the century cricketers gave up the game on conversion, whereas from about the 1860s sporting ability was seen as an advantage to the work of conversion. Secular leisure had become recognised as a separate and necessary part of life, and one in which prowess could confer both distinction and respectability. Leisure called the tune, and the churches danced to it.[64]

For the churches the changing balance of forces within society as a whole which made leisure such a powerful force gave rise to a long and anguished debate. Other voluntary organisations, with less ideological commitment, accommodated themselves to the new situation with less show of resistance.

The Volunteer Force provides a good example. Founded in 1859 as a middle-class military organisation to cope with the threat of French invasion, the Force had been joined by members of the working class who quickly came to form a majority within it. Many of the middle-class officers were delighted at this as the Force seemed to be acting as a successful counter-attraction to less respectable ways of spending leisure time as well as being a forum where the classes could meet in leisure in acceptable ways. But before the end of the Force's first decade there were signs that not only the military purpose but also the recreational counter-attraction of rifle-shooting were becoming subordinate to the more powerful pressures of leisure. That is to say that in order to recruit and hold members, Volunteer corps were beginning to offer other entirely non-military recreations. In 1872 in East Surrey the officers were keeping the men together 'by social gatherings, cricket clubs and quadrille parties'. In East Kent there was a choral society in connection with the Ramsgate corps, a Volunteer theatrical show in Margate in 1871, and in Ashford a club room with chess, skittles, dominoes, cards and a pea rifle range. By 1870, and increasingly thereafter, a voluntary organisation with a specifically military aim found itself operating in a competitive leisure market. Growth, even survival, depended on offering something attractive, and the numerical dominance of the working class within the Force is to be explained by the fact that the recreational attraction of the Force was greater to it than to the middle class, for the former had fewer alternatives.[65]

No voluntary organisation could escape this sense that it was competing in an increasingly crowded market. The competition came from two sources, from the supply side in the form of profit-oriented and commercially-organised entertainment, and from the demand side in a vast increase in its strength. The latter was perhaps the more powerful. Even before mid-century it was this which had forced the mechanics' institutes to temper their ambitions, and to cater more and more for the working man's desire for entertainment.

It was a sense of the power of this demand which had led to the establishment of the working men's clubs. The approach was that of James Hole when he wrote in 1854, 'To raise the working man we must take hold of him where he is, not where he is not. Attract him, get possession of him and you may lead him by degrees to something better.' Henry Solly was another who after 20 years of trying to reach the working classes through education came to believe that 'What working men wanted was a place of amusement, a place of intercourse and fellowship.' Recreation would be the bottom of the 'inclined plane' up which 'many of the working men and youths should be rolled into the lecture and class room'. Leisure at this stage then was simply a bait to entice the working man into an environment where the next natural step was education. And by offering the bait the Working Men's Club and Institute Union was unquestionably successful; founded in 1862 it had 23 clubs affiliated to it within a year, 245 by 1873, 550 by 1883, over 1,000 by 1904. But equally there was not much ascent up the 'inclined plane'. Working men remained hooked on the bait of leisure. The strength of the demand for it led first to the introduction of beer to the clubs and later to close links with the world of professional entertainment.[66]

It was in the third quarter of the century that voluntary organisations first faced the challenge from the increase in both the supply of and the demand for leisure. That the challenge became stiffer in the last quarter of the century and in the twentieth century is not in dispute. What is being asserted here is that the kinds of condition under which all voluntary organisations now have to operate — competitors for the leisure time of their members — first became apparent in the third quarter of the century, and that this is testimony to the new mid-century delimitation of leisure, and to its new status and power.

Conclusion

Part of the argument in this chapter has been that there was a turning-point in the history of leisure at about mid-century, and that in the third quarter of the century there emerged a role and status for leisure which is recognisable a century later. In itself I think this argument is unlikely to raise much dissent. I do not wish to imply that nothing of significance happened after some more or less arbitrarily chosen date like 1880. As we have seen there were severe limitations both as to time and money which prevented the full emergence of working-class demand for leisure in this period, a demand which *was* released towards the end of the century. This has rightly led many commentators to focus on the 1880s and 1890s as key decades in the emergence of recognisably modern forms of leisure.[67] The contention here is simply that the conditions for that emergence and the elements that went into its making came into being in the third quarter of the century.

If that is accepted, then the interesting problem is to isolate the elements that went into this making, and see how they interacted. For if the role and status of leisure have remained relatively unchanged for a century, so also have the elements that go into its making. From the first half-century of the Industrial Revolution was inherited on the one hand a vigorous and on-going popular culture and on the other the remnants of the class-based attack on all forms of leisure for the people. These had provided the reference points for reformers, both middle and working class, who had posited against them their particular remedies: Methodism, or secular radicalism, or rational recreation, whether philanthropic or governmental. The growing concentration of people into towns, and the release of more time and money for leisure at mid-century, provided new opportunities for the petty-capitalist entrepreneurs of the popular culture to increase the scale of their operations. This coincided in time with an awareness on the part of authority that there was going to be leisure for the mass of the people and an acceptance that, provided it was open to public supervision, then not too much should be expected of it. Thus Matthew Browne in 1866 argued in favour of 'the removal of all restraint but police restraint, such as is exercised in the next street, from places of public entertainment in which the common standards of decency are maintained'.[68] Hence the new big circuses, music-halls, sports venues and fairs were acceptable to authority. Of course many continued to condemn them as immoral, but they were now in a minority. Leisure for the mass of the people was now judged to be legitimate.

It was legitimate not simply because it was reasonably orderly. Since it was visible it had other useful functions. One of these was political. In *Hansard*'s paraphrase Robert Slaney in 1833 had declared that 'it was well known that healthy happy men were not disposed to enter into conspiracies. Want of recreation generated incipient disease, and disease, discontent; which, in its turn, led to attacks upon the Government.' This old argument – older by far than Slaney – seemed to be confirmed in the second half of the century, and spokesmen for the working class lamented the displacement of political energy into apolitical and hence conservative leisure.[69]

Leisure also had uses so far as work was concerned. The spread and sophistication of the machine led to more rather than less intensive work. Both employers and employees could find some compensation for this in promoting the notion that the challenges and satisfactions of life were to be found in leisure. In some ways this amounted to a transference of the Puritan ethic from the world of work, where routine now ruled, to leisure, where free choice could be exercised. Work provided its own disciplines and controls. Leisure was now the problem. 'Is it possible', asked Walter Besant in 1884, 'that, by any persuasion, attraction, or teaching, the working men of this country can be induced to aim at those organized, highly skilled, and disciplined forms of recreation which make up the better pleasure of life?' Besant put his hopes in the People's Palace. At the beginning of the twentieth century Lady Bell was equally insistent on the importance of leisure: 'The resources provided for a man's leisure matter incomparably. It is during these that he may be ruined and dragged down, and not in the hours of his work.'[70] Work, it is implied, is by nature fixed and immutable. Leisure posed the problem. But important though the problem was perceived to be for all classes, it was essentially a limited problem. The level of civilisation of a society might be judged by its leisure, but whatever that level was, work would continue. In the minds of those with power and influence work and leisure were now separated. This sense of separation, it is important to emphasise, was not some inevitable and determined consequence of industrialisation and urbanisation. Rather it was bound up with the ideological needs of the mid-Victorians. If capitalism and its work structure were permanent then leisure, in increasing quantities, and more and more generously provided for both by government and private enterprise, was both justification and compensation. As an ideology this persists. And it neither bore nor bears much relation to reality. Leisure, and the way it is spent, remain locked in the closest possible relationship with work.

To the mid-Victorian middle class, leisure was too important to be left to the entrepreneurs and the free play of market forces. By their leisure they would be judged. Hence leisure's emergence as a favourite subject of charity, hence the growing insistence on government provision, hence the hope that entrepreneurs might prove susceptible to moral arguments — as they did. Hence too the necessity for the historian to pay as close attention to what people said about leisure as to what they actually did. In the making of leisure, words were as important as deeds.

In all the flurry of argument about leisure it is easy to portray the working class as passive consumers. From one kind of left-wing stance they are seen as being tricked, fobbed off with a diet of commercial entertainment which anaesthetised their political instincts. And from a right-wing stance they are incapable of standing on their own two feet when tempted by the trivialities of that commercial entertainment. Neither of these stances does justice to the role of the working class in the making of leisure.

In the first place the growing working-class demand for leisure affected not simply the amount but also the form of what was offered. The diffusion of leisure up as well as down the social scale continued into the second half of the century – and indeed continues. The forms set by the popular culture of the early Industrial Revolution have proved to have a remarkable vitality and staying power. Technology may change, but melodrama, for example, is as popular in cinema or on television screen as it was in the theatres of the nineteenth century. Circus, too, invented in the early Industrial Revolution, and originating in the popular culture, has remained true to its early forms while diffusing itself upwards.

Secondly, the direction of working-class demand put an end to many of the wilder hopes invested in leisure, and led to a resigned acceptance on the part of the middle class of the ways the working class chose to enjoy itself.

And thirdly, while parts of the popular culture expanded to flourish in the world of mass entertainment of the late nineteenth century, other parts remained immune from outside influences. Although the campaign to make working-class leisure public had much success it was not completely successful. Much of working-class leisure remained privatised in the sense of being class-bound and invisible to those outside the culture. Drinking was the prime example, and it is worth remembering that it is right at the end of our period that per capita consumption of alcohol reached its peak. Drinking remained the most pervasive leisure-time occupation, and it was essentially class-bound. Gambling was increasingly associated with it, illegal but widely prevalent, again one of those pastimes impenetrable from outside. If working-class people sought in leisure some compensation for the hardship of work they increasingly did so within their own impenetrable world. The compensations were of their own making, imbued with their own meanings.[71]

The making of leisure then was complex, and the outcome one which it is exceedingly difficult to evaluate as one can see from the divergent judgements which historians have passed on football or music-hall. On the one hand they seem to be expressions of a class, on the other hand forms of social control. The truth is that they were both. The working class had come to accept small gains within capitalism, and leisure was the chief of them. As such, pressure from working-class demand pushed leisure in directions which many in authority deplored. Yet eventually authority came to tolerate the new forms of leisure because it saw them as fundamentally safe. In the process leisure had acquired a new definition and role, and developed forms which have proved to be remarkably durable.[72] In the capitalist bureaucratic state which had emerged in England by the late nineteenth century leisure was a consolation for the working class, an anxiety to reformers both middle and working class, and tolerated by a government which could be thankful that leisure was now safely neutered.

Notes

1. G. Best, *Mid-Victorian Britain*, pp. 199 and 5-13 for the growth in the size of towns; G. Chapman, *Culture and Survival* (London, 1940).

2. W. Besant, *As We Are*, p. 282.

3. M. Hodgson, 'The Working Day and the Working Week in Victorian Britain 1840-1900', p. 222; E.J. Hobsbawm, *Industry and Empire*, p. 71; C. Reid, 'Temperance, Teetotalism and Local Culture: the Early Temperance Movement in Sheffield', *Northern History*, vol. XIII (1977), p. 253; P. Bailey, *Leisure and Class*, p. 26.

4. Quoted in J.A.R. Pimlott, *The Englishman's Holiday* (London, 1947), p. 94.

5. R.C. on Factory & Workshop Acts, PP 1876 (C1443-I), vol. XXX, qq. 2450-2, 5140, 6542, 6773, 6857, 12040; R.C. on Employment of Children & Young Persons in Trades & Manufactures, PP 1864 (3414), vol. XXII, p. liii.

6. M. Hodgson, 'The Working Day', pp. 244-5; J.K. Walton, 'The Windermere Tourist Trade in the Age of the Railway, 1847-1912' in O.M. Westall (ed.), *Windermere in the Nineteenth Century*, p. 24; J.A.R. Pimlott, *Englishman's Holiday*, pp. 144-9; R.C. on Factory & Workshop Acts, PP 1876, vol. XXX, q. 1147.

7. S.C. on Public Houses, PP 1854, vol. XIV, q. 261; W.B. Whitaker, *Victorian and Edwardian Shopworkers* (Newton Abbot, 1973), pp. 36-78.

8. R.C. on Employment of Children & Young Persons in Trades & Manufactures, PP 1864, vol. XXII, p. 57; D. Reid, 'The Decline of Saint Monday', *Past & Present*, no. 71 (1976), pp. 84-90; R.C. on Factory & Workshop Acts 1876, PP 1876, vol. XXX, q. 6858.

9. J. Brand, *Observations on Popular Antiquities* (Newcastle-upon-Tyne, 1777), pp. 148, 154; M.A. Bienefeld, *Working Hours in British Industry*, pp. 16, 61, 71, 86; Hodgson, 'The Working Day', pp. 150-1.

10. Bienefeld, ibid., pp. 88-116; Hodgson, ibid., pp. 157-70; Reid, 'The Decline of Saint Monday', p. 86.

11. E.P. Thompson, 'Time, Work-Discipline, and Industrial Capitalism', *Past & Present*, no. 38 (1967), pp. 73-6; E. Young, *Labor in Europe and America* (Philadelphia, 1875), p. 409; Wharncliffe Muniments, Wh.M.459, Sheffield City Library.

12. S.C. on Public Houses, PP 1854, vol. XIV, q. 4701; C.P. Darcy, *The Encouragement of the Fine Arts in Lancashire 1760-1860*, p. 86; T. Wright, *Some*

Habits and Customs of the Working Classes, pp. 108-30; R. Wood, *Victorian Delights*, p. 168; Reid 'The Decline of Saint Monday', pp. 82-4.

13. E.J. Hobsbawm, *Labouring Men* (London, 1964), pp. 344-70; Marx, *Capital*, vol. I, pp. 435-45; K. Burgess, *The Origins of British Industrial Relations* (London, 1975), pp. 25-6, 159-60; J. Burnett (ed.), *Useful Toil* (London, 1974), p. 269.

14. Hodgson, 'The Working Day', pp. 6-33; Bienefeld, *Working Hours*, pp. 88-107.

15. e.g. by both Bienefeld and Hodgson.

16. Bienefeld, *Working Hours*, p. 104; N. Smelser, *Social Change in the Industrial Revolution* (London, 1959), pp. 305-12; Reports of Inspectors of Factories, PP 1849 (1017), vol. XXII, pp. 13-17; cf. D.T. Rodgers, *The Work Ethic in Industrial America 1850-1920* (Chicago & London, 1978), pp. 155-9.

17. J. Myerscough, 'The Recent History of the Use of Leisure Time' in I. Appleton (ed.), *Leisure Research and Policy* (Edinburgh, 1974), pp. 3-16; J.A.R. Pimlott, *Englishman's Holiday*, p. 143.

18. R.A. Church, *The Great Victorian Boom 1850-1873* (London, 1975), pp. 71-5.

19. G.F. Chadwick, *The Park and the Town*, pp. 100-10; J.G. Branston, 'The Development of Public Open Spaces in Leeds during the Nineteenth Century', pp. 23-39, 66-7.

20. Lord Eversley, *Commons, Forests and Footpaths* (London, 1910).

21. Chadwick, *Park and the Town*, p. 52.

22. T. Kelly, *A History of Public Libraries in Great Britain 1845-1965*, pp. 16-85; W.S. Jevons, 'The Rationale of Free Public Libraries' in Jevons (ed.), *Methods of Social Reform* (London, 1883), p. 48.

23. S.C. on Health of Towns, PP 1840 (384), vol. XI, qq. 3056-315; H. Shimmin, *Liverpool Life*, pp. 51-9; C.M. Davies, *Mystic London*, pp. 157-63.

24. T. Kelly, *History of Public Libraries*, p. 122; H.E. Meller, *Leisure and the Changing City, 1870-1914* (London, 1976), p. 97 and passim; cf. J. Minihan, *The Nationalization of Culture*.

25. A.R. Warwick, *The Phoenix Suburb* (Richmond, 1972), pp. 102-72; G. Gissing, *The Nether World*, p. 109; W.S. Jevons, 'Amusements of the People', *Methods of Social Reform*, pp. 7-8.

26. C. Aspin, *Lancashire, the First Industrial Society* (Helmshore Local History Society, 1969), pp. 149-57; R.C. into the State of Large Towns and Populous Districts, PP 1845 (602), vol. XVIII, p. 133; W. Fraser Rae, *The Business of Travel* (London, 1891), pp. 20-39; P.E. Razzell and R.W. Wainwright, *The Victorian Working Class*, p. 320.

27. T.C. Barker and M. Robbins, *A History of London Transport*, vol. I (London, 1963), pp. 55-8; S.C. on Public Houses, PP 1852-3, vol. XXXVII, qq. 9453, 9462.

28. W. Fraser Rae, *Business of Travel*, pp. 44-7; R.J. Morris, 'Leeds and the Crystal Palace', *Victorian Studies*, vol. XIII (1970), pp. 283-300; Razzell and Wainwright, *Victorian Working Class*, p. 302; A. Howkins, *Whitsun in 19th Century Oxfordshire*, p. 45; J.A.R. Pimlott, *Englishman's Holiday*, pp. 161-4; J. Lowerson and J. Myerscough, *Time to Spare in Victorian England* (Hassocks, 1977), p. 31.

29. C. Knight, *Excursion Companion* (London, 1851), p. iv; J.M. Ludlow and Lloyd Jones, *Progress of the Working Class*, p. 194.

30. A. Lloyd, *The Great Prize Fight*, pp. 61-6; 'Copy of all Correspondence between the H.O. and the Directors of the South-Eastern Railway Company . . .', PP 1860 (317), vol. LXI, pp. 261-3; A. Delgado, *The Annual Outing and Other Excursions* (London, 1977), p. 132; T. Frost, *The Old Showmen and the Old London Fairs*, p. 246; M. Jones, 'The Social Control of Barnet Fair in the Nine-

teenth Century' (Unpublished Univ. of Kent BA Dissertation, 1973); S. Alexander, *St Giles's Fair, 1830-1914*, p. 38.

31. D. Brooke, 'The Opposition to Sunday Rail Services in North-Eastern England, 1834-1914', *Journal of Transport History*, vol. VI (1963-4), p. 101; W. Vamplew, *The Turf*, pp. 32-40; J.F. Russell and J.H. Elliot, *The Brass Band Movement* (London, 1936), pp. 96-7, 165.

32. J. Whyman, 'Water Communications to Margate and Gravesend as Coastal Resorts before 1840', *Southern History*, vol. II (1980); and 'Kentish Seaside Resorts before 1900' (Cyclostyled, Univ. of Kent, 1970), pp. 8-12.

33. R. Manning-Sanders, *Seaside England* (London, 1951), p. 127; C. Dickens, 'The Tuggs's at Ramsgate', in *Sketches by Boz*, Tales, ch. IV; A.B. Granville, *The Spas of England*, 3 vols. (London, 1841), vol. II, pp. 10-15.

34. Granville, ibid., vol. III, pp. 512-36.

35. Census 1851 and 1871; J.K. Walton, 'Residential Amenity, Respectable Morality and the Rise of the Entertainment Industry: the Case of Blackpool 1860-1914', *Literature & History*, no. 1 (1975), p. 77, n. 39.

36. C. Gould, 'The Coming of the Railway to Brighton' (Unpublished Univ. of Kent BA Dissertation, 1973).

37. H. Perkin, *The Age of the Railway* (London, 1970), pp. 201-37.

38. H. Perkin, 'The "Social Tone" of Victorian Seaside Resorts in the North West', *Northern History*, vol. XI (1975), pp. 180-94; J.K. Walton, 'Residential Amenity' and *The Blackpool Landlady* (Manchester, 1978); J. Lowerson and J. Myerscough, *Time to Spare*, p. 41; R. Gurnham, 'The Creation of Skegness as a Resort Town by the 9th Earl of Scarbrough', *Lincolnshire History*, vol. VII (1972), pp. 63-76.

39. H. Perkin, 'The "Social Tone" of Victorian Seaside Resorts', pp. 184-5; S.H. Adamson, *Seaside Piers* (London, 1977), pp. 16-46.

40. For these developments see C.D. Stuart and A.J. Park, *The Variety Stage* (London, n.d. [1895]); H. Scott, *The Early Doors* (London, 1946); D.F. Cheshire, *Music Hall in Britain* (Newton Abbot, 1974), pp. 11-20; G. Speaight, *Bawdy Songs of the Early Music Hall* (London, 1975).

41. Scott, *The Early Doors*, pp. 55-6, 133-41; R. Mander and J. Mitchenson, *British Music Hall* (London, 1965), pp. 13-14.

42. J. Grant, *Sketches in London*, pp. 161-92; H. Mayhew, *London Labour*, vol. I, pp. 42-4, 532, vol. III, p. 136; see also G. Godwin, *Town Swamps and Social Bridges*, pp. 94-5; M. Browne, *Views and Opinions*, pp. 275-8; G. Doré and B. Jerrold, *London, a Pilgrimage*, pp. 164-7; S.C. on Theatrical Licences and Regulations, PP 1866 (373), vol. XI, qq. 7829-66.

43. P. Bailey, *Leisure and Class*, pp. 29-34; G.J. Mellor, *The Northern Music Hall* (Newcastle-on-Tyne, 1970), pp. 17, 21; B. Disraeli, *Sybil* (London, 1845), Book II, ch. X; E.D. Mackerness, *Somewhere Further North*, pp. 83-4.

44. S.C. on Public Houses, PP 1852-3, vol. XXXVII, qq. 3818-3840; R. Wood, *Victorian Delights*, pp. 35, 39.

45. S.C. on Theatrical Licences, PP 1866, vol. XI, qq. 6171-6181, 6375, 7112-7116, 7176, 5522-5532; A. Bennett, *Clayhanger* (London, 1910), Book I, ch. 10.

46. S.C. on Theatrical Licences, PP 1866, vol. XI, qq. 397-493, 521-770, 1008, App. 2; P. Summerfield, 'The Effingham Arms and the Empire: Working-Class Culture and the Evolution of Music Hall' (Paper to Society for the Study of Labour History Conference, Brighton, 1975), p. 12; Bailey, *Leisure and Class*, pp. 149-50; S.C. on Theatres and Places of Entertainment, PP 1892 (240), vol. XVIII App. 16; C. Booth, *Life and Labour of the People in London*, final volume (London, 1902), p. 53.

47. Mander and Mitchenson, *British Music Hall*, p. 16.

48. Stuart and Park, *The Variety Stage*, pp. 116-57; Bailey, *Leisure and Class*,

pp. 148-50; S.C. on Theatrical Licences, PP 1866, vol. XI, App. 3.

49. S.C. on Theatrical Licences 1866, qq. 956, 1230, 1297-9, 969-1132; H. Mayhew, *London Labour*, vol. IV, pp. 227-8.

50. J. Greenwood, *The Wilds of London* (London, 1874), pp. 90-7, 304-9.

51. M. Vicinus, *The Industrial Muse* (London, 1974), p. 239; See also G. Stedman Jones, 'Working-class Culture and Working-class Politics in London, 1870-1900; Notes on the Remaking of a Working Class', *Journal of Social History*, vol. VII (1974), pp. 490-6; J.S. Bratton, *The Victorian Popular Ballad* (London, 1975); Bailey, *Leisure and Class*, ch. 7; C. MacInnes, *Sweet Saturday Night* (London, 1967).

52. A.L. Crauford, *Sam and Sallie* (London, 1933); T. Wright, *Some Habits and Customs of the Working Classes*, pp. 196-8; F. Rogers, *Labour, Life and Literature* (Brighton, 1973), pp. 7-10.

53. T. Frost, *Circus Life and Circus Celebrities*, pp. 128, 192-213; 'Lord' George Sanger, *Seventy Years a Showman* pp. 233-45.

54. *Struggles and Triumphs: or, The Life of P.T. Barnum, written by himself*, 2 vols. (London, 1927).

55. T. Frost, *Circus Life*, pp. 198-201; H. Cunningham, 'The Metropolitan Fairs in the Nineteenth Century' in A.P. Donajgrodzki, *Social Control in Nineteenth Century Britain*, p. 180; Barnum, *Struggles and Triumphs*, vol. II, pp. 688, 793-8; K. Barker, *Bristol at Play*, pp. 34, 39.

56. Cunningham, 'The Metropolitan Fairs', pp. 163-84.

57. MacInnes, *Sweet Saturday Night*, pp. 141-2; Frost, *Circus Life*, pp. 184-5, 314-5; census 1851, 1881.

58. Mayhew, *London Labour*, vol. II, pp. 51-230; G. Speaight, *The History of the English Puppet Theatre* (London, 1955), pp. 206-15; D.P. Miller, *The Life of a Showman*, p. 148.

59. E.D. Mackerness, *A Social History of English Music*, pp. 133-47; Bratton, *Victorian Popular Ballad*, p. 24; Mayhew, *London Labour*, vol. II, pp. 205-6; Vicinus, *Industrial Muse*, pp. 13-21; V. Neuburg, *Popular Literature: A History and Guide* (Harmondsworth, 1977), pp. 123-43; D. Jerrold, 'The Ballad-Singer', in *Heads of the People*, 2 vols. (London, 1864), vol. II, pp. 289-97.

60. R. Williams, *Communications* (London, 1962), p. 15.

61. W. Vamplew, *The Turf*, pp. 38-46, 197-231; G. Chapman, *Culture and Survival*, pp. 113-15; A.J. Lee, *The Origins of the Popular Press in England 1855-1914* (London, 1976), pp. 127-8.

62. R. Currie, *Methodism Divided* (London, 1968), pp. 131-3; W.B. Whitaker, *The Eighteenth-Century English Sunday* (London, 1940), p. 181; R. Colls, *The Collier's Rant*, pp. 138-41; M. Hennell, 'Evangelicalism and Worldliness, 1770-1870' in G.J. Cuming and D. Baker (eds.), *Popular Belief and Practice*, Studies in Church History, vol. 8 (London 1972), p. 233.

63. M. Rutherford, *The Revolution in Tanner's Lane*, pp. 262-3; Currie, *Methodism Divided*, pp. 133-8; R.W. Dale, *Week-day Sermons* (London, 1867), pp. 218-59.

64. J. Lawson, *Progress in Pudsey*, p. 73; P. Scott, 'Cricket and the Religious World'; cf. S. Yeo, *Religion and Voluntary Organisations in Crisis* (London, 1976), pp. 185-210.

65. Cunningham, *The Volunteer Force*, pp. 117-19.

66. R. Price, 'The Working Men's Club Movement and Victorian Social Reform Ideology', pp. 117-47; J. Taylor, *Self-Help to Glamour*.

67. See esp. A. Briggs, *Mass Entertainment: The Origins of a Modern Industry* (Adelaide, 1960).

68. M. Browne, *Views and Opinions*, p. 279.

69. *Hansard*, 3rd ser., vol. XV, p. 1054; T. Cooper, *Autobiography*, pp. 392-3; W.E. Adams, *Memoirs*, pp. 599-600.

70. Besant, *As We Are And As We May Be*, p. 287; Lady Bell, *At the Works* (London & Edinburgh, 1911 edn), p. 192.

71. A.E. Dingle, 'Drink and Working Class Living Standards in Britain 1870-1914', *Economic History Review*, 2nd ser., vol. XXV (1972), pp. 608-22; R. McKibbin, 'Working-class Gambling in Britain 1880-1939', *Past & Present*, no. 82 (1979), pp. 147-78; G. Stedman Jones, 'Working-class Culture and Working-class Politics', *Journal of Social History* (1974), pp. 460-508.

72. e.g. Christmas: see J.A.R. Pimlott, *The Englishman's Christmas* (Hassocks, 1978), esp. p. 148.

6 CONCLUSION

It is usual for an author to state any theoretical perspectives at the beginning rather than at the end of a book. But what follows is the product rather than the starting-point of my work, and it seems appropriate to place it at the end. Like many historians I am most comfortable when my feet are firmly planted on empirical ground, but I cannot help asking myself why the assumptions with which I started, representing as they did the prevalent state of opinion, proved to be so misleading. The answer lies in the particular way English history of the Industrial Revolution period has been perceived and written about in the last two decades; and this is something I find it easiest to write about in the probably inexcusable form of intellectual autobiography.

In company with so many other historians of my generation the most profound single influence on my intellectual development has been E.P. Thompson's *The Making of the English Working Class*. My first reading of the book, in 1964, had a particularly sharp impact because I was then living in West Africa. Thompson, like other historians of the British Industrial Revolution, addressed himself in part to the citizens of the Third World. All except Thompson seemed to believe that if one could discover from the British experience the recipe for success – the perfect blend of capital accumulation, population growth, provision of overheads, supply and demand, and so on – one could export this more or less unchanged to an expectant Third World. Living in that Third World the absurdity and the disastrous consequences of such thinking were only too apparent all around me, and I was therefore particularly receptive to Thompson's argument. As I saw it then, and still do now, what Thompson was saying, amongst other things, was this: first, within limits which we must strive to understand, people can make their own history, and no one people's history will ever be the same as that of another's; second, individual lives and whole societies will be shaped to a discernible degree by the lived experience of the past; and third, one cannot separate out any particular aspect of a people's life and treat it in isolation from other aspects – it is one of the merits of Thompson's book that it cannot easily be described as 'social' or 'economic' or 'political' or 'intellectual' or 'cultural' for it is all of these things.

When I returned to England in the mid-1960s it was for a number of reasons difficult to hold fast to these central issues. As a graduate student I had a choice of doing an MA in Pre-revolutionary or in Post-revolutionary History. The Revolution was the dual one of the Industrial and French Revolutions. And herein lay a danger which has proved to have a damaging impact on our study of the Industrial Revolution period. Taught as we were that the Industrial Revolution was not simply *a* but *the* most important turning-point in the history of the world, we quickly forgot any pre-industrial revolution history that we had studied, and came to think of that history as belonging to a 'traditional', 'rural' and static world all aspects of which were changed in revolutionary fashion during and by the Industrial Revolution. It was thus peculiarly difficult to remember, from Thompson, that the lived experience of the past was one necessary way in which people understand and live the present, even in times of rapid social change.

The second difficulty lay in the way the English academic profession responded to the massive challenge to orthodox thinking implicit in Thompson's work. To be blunt there was evasion and trivialisation. The central question – the one about which students have been asked to write ever since – became some variant of this: 'Do you agree that whereas there were working classes in 1793 there was a working class by 1832?' A question expecting the answer no. An important question admittedly, but one which enabled a student and his teacher to avoid the key issues of Thompson's book, and in particular that of the extent to which people can make their own history. Students wrote essentially static accounts of the structure of society at the two dates, and concluded, as they must, that at the latter date there were still 'tailors here and weavers there' together making up 'the working classes'.

Just how far this assumption that people do not make their own history had gone was apparent in Harold Perkin's *The Origins of Modern English Society*, published in 1969. No one has had a more profound influence on our thinking about British social history in the last decade than Perkin. It was he who argued for the centrality of social history as 'nothing more and nothing less than the history of society', he who occupied the first chair of social history in Britain, he who with his emphasis on the social origins of the Industrial Revolution helped emancipate us from the thrall of economic growth historians and theorists, he who as the editor of a series of studies in social history and as the founding chairman of the Social History Society has helped in the emergence of social history as a self-conscious discipline with appropriate institutions. All of this has seemed, at the very least, mildly progressive. And in contradistinction to other non-Marxist historians, Perkin made clear his belief that class existed, and indeed he placed class at the centre of his analysis: class as fact not simply as explanatory tool.

In face of all this it was easy to avoid noticing that Perkin's account of 'the birth of class' was an implicit and in places explicit attack on the work of Thompson. Whereas Thompson's emphasis was on human activity and creativity, Perkin saw class as an embryo conceived it seems (the parentage is never made explicit) by the yoking together of industrialism and urbanisation. With religion as midwife, the child emerges, appropriately bawling, after a complicated and highly traumatic birth in which, passively, it is first held in check by the womb of patriotism, then buffeted by aristocratic reaction and post-war depression, and finally pushed forth into a hostile world when patriotism fails to hold. It is a complicated metaphor which in the end leaves one wondering whether Perkin is not more ignorant of the process of child-birth than he is of the formation of class. But the message is clear. People do not 'make' a class, class is 'born' because of the conjunction of various impersonal forces, chief amongst them industrialisation and urbanisation.[1]

Now Perkin, of course, was not alone in thinking in this way. When it became apparent that economic theory on its own was not going to haul the Third World into 'take-off into self-sustained growth', social scientists of all kinds began to examine the relationship between economy and structure of society. Out of this emerged 'modernisation' theory, a theory which historians in their belated way have begun to adopt precisely at the time when its theoretical foundations are beginning to look shaky. Let me try to show the inability of the theory to explain social change by attacking it in one of its strongest manifestations: Eugen Weber's *Peasants into Frenchmen. The Modernization of Rural France 1870-1914*.[2] In this richly human book there lies a weakness which stems directly from the adoption of the modernisation model. Weber divides the book into three parts: 'The Way Things Were', 'The Agencies of Change' and 'Change and Assimilation'. The agencies of change are external forces such as better communications, contact with towns, a new 'national' politics, military service and schools. The impact of these, Weber argues, is such that old customs die out and the peasants are assimilated into French society. What the theory does not allow for — and herein lies its weakness — is any continuing influence of peasant norms on French society. Peasant culture simply dies out, it leaves nothing, it contributes nothing, it is ultimately something that survives much longer than one might have expected, but is powerless before external agencies of change. People are passive not active in the making of their own history. I doubt whether such a theory fits the facts of French history, and it is certainly inadequate for a study of cultural change in the British Industrial Revolution. For as we have seen, the past, including the past of people of low social status, had a marked influence on the cultural forms of new urban ways of living.

The same kind of passivity underlies another theory which for a time beguiled me: that used by Herbert Gutman in his study of 'Work, Culture and Industrializing America 1815-1919'.[3] Faced with the problem of explaining the reason for the survival of 'traditional' practices in industrialising America, Gutman has recourse to a distinction which some anthropologists make between culture as a kind of resource and society as a kind of arena. Thus for Gutman 'An analytic model that distinguishes between culture and society reveals that even in periods of radical economic and social change powerful cultural continuities and adaptations continued to shape the historical behavior of diverse working-class populations.' This is valuable so far as it goes: it allows for survivals. But the point about survivals is that ultimately they cease to exist. For Gutman 'similarities in the work habits and expectations of men and women who experienced quite different premodern cultures are indicated.' In the end, in modern society, we are all the same, and our 'premodern culture' has played no part in the making of our modern selves.

As with Weber, I believe it is the analytic model rather than empirical fact which has led Gutman to his conclusion. The problem with the model is two-fold. In the first place culture becomes as it were something one has in the bank, stored up, but earning no interest, never replaced, and subject to the ravages of inflation. Ultimately it is used up. But in fact, as I have argued in the body of this book, culture is something constantly changing, and active and influencing, as much as something that is used. Secondly, the model embodies a highly abstract and disabling distinction between two parts of people's lives, a distinction which in cruder hands than those of Gutman leads once again to passivity.

The kinds of thinking I have described here have, whether explicitly or implicitly, shaped our understanding of change in the Industrial Revolution. There was, it seemed, an old traditional, rural, pre-industrial society which yet had enough dynamism in it to generate the Industrial Revolution, and that in turn transformed every aspect of people's lives, and necessarily their leisure; hence 'the vacuum'. By the 1830s, this line of argument continued, despite some survivals, this older culture was effectively dead, wiped out by the pressures of industrialism, urbanisation, evangelicalism and a reactionary government.

Then came new initiatives from above, whether in the form of rational recreation or in the provision of modern commercial entertainment. And in the context of a vacuum, rational recreation had sufficient attraction to appeal to members of the working class; hence that linking of the respectable of all classes against the rough, and the theory that the key divisions were within rather than between classes.

This hypothetical structure, I have argued, was misleading. The modes of thinking about cultural change were vitiated in two fundamental ways. First, because culture was seen as something passive, reflecting, but for odd survivals, an economic base; this is a kind of thinking, without the Marxist language, to be found very frequently in anti-Marxist writers. Indeed in recent years the crudest economic determinism has been voiced by those on the right. And secondly, and following from this, because human society was split up into various separate sections − 'culture', 'economic activity', 'politics', 'thought', and so on.

This brings us back to Thompson, for it was precisely these errors which he avoided. Yet these very emphases in Thompson's work were, one may suspect, directed as much against orthodox Marxists as against conservatives. For Marxism is of course very precisely concerned to establish the degree to which history is determined; and Thompson, it could be argued, seemed to want, in a romantic way, to escape that determination. In 1963 it was easier to show in empirical fact how people could be active in the shaping of their history than it was to explain this in theoretical terms. Since then Marxist theory has become a subject of hot and productive debate, and there is now, based on the work of Gramsci, a theory through which we can better understand the process of cultural change. For the purpose of what follows, Gramsci's theory and other Marxist approaches, including his own, have been most cogently argued by Raymond Williams in *Marxism and Literature*.[4]

The basic problem may be put in this way. Many, whether or not they call themselves Marxists, write or think in fundamental agreement with Marx's famous formulation of the relationship of base or infrastructure to superstructure in the 1859 Preface to *A Contribution to the Critique of Political Economy*:

In the social production of their life, men enter into definite relations that are indispensable and independent of their will, relations of production which correspond to a definite stage of development of their material productive forces. The sum total of these relations of production constitutes the economic structure of society, the real foundation, on which rises a legal and political superstructure and to which correspond definite forms of social consciousness. The mode of production of material life conditions the social, political and intellectual life process in general. It is not the consciousness of men that determines their being, but, on the contrary, their social being that determines their consciousness . . . With the change of the economic foundation the entire immense superstructure is more or less rapidly transformed . . .

This kind of thinking, crudely interpreted, lies behind much of our interpretation of cultural change in the Industrial Revolution. The economic foundation changed, goes the argument, hence so did 'the entire immense superstructure' which is taken, without question, to include leisure. Now if we accept this crude interpretation of what Marx was saying, then, if the argument of this book has any validity, Marx was clearly wrong; the relationship of leisure to the economic structure was exceedingly complex, and not a simple one-way process of influence; leisure cannot be reduced to or explained in terms of something else. The problem we are left with, however, is to gain more understanding of the relationship between leisure and the economic structure, and to see in what ways leisure was 'determined'.

In the passage quoted above I deliberately omitted parts which modify the crude force of Marx's formulation. Marx in the remainder of the passage, and both he and Engels in their later lives, qualified the 1859 statement. It may be, as Williams suggests, that no amount of qualification will remove the difficulties of the formulation, and that we should abandon the language of base and superstructure, but that is more easily said than done. Whether or not we retain it we must be clear of two things. First, with regard to determination. Many Marxists, uncomfortable with the notion of strict economic determinism, have argued that the base does not strictly determine but merely sets limits to the form of the superstructure. This, Williams argues, is not enough: we must look not only for 'the negative determinations that are ex- perienced as limits' but also for positive determinations which may be pressures either to maintain or otherwise 'a given social mode'. In any real social process, writes Williams, there is 'an active and conscious as well as, by default, a passive and objectified historical experience'. Secondly, we must think of 'productive forces' as more than particular kinds of agricultural or industrial production. Marx himself wrote that a maker of a piano was a productive worker whereas a pianist was not. Clearly though, as Williams argues, the production of music as well as of its instruments is an important branch of capitalist production. Music, and by extension culture generally, and in some of its meanings, leisure, must be seen as themselves productive and material practices, not as something abstracted and divorced from economic life. Leisure, therefore, if we retain the language, can function as part of the infrastructure during our period as more and more leisure was 'produced': not simply as commercialised leisure, but also in the non-profit-making but nevertheless very material form of parks, museums, libraries and so on.

Once we begin to think of leisure as a form of production with specific social relations of production (and for Marx, remember, it was the relations of production which constituted the economic structure), then our understanding of it is transformed. We can see not only the fact that it is something active and changing, not simply a resource, but also why that should be so.

But, and this is where Gramsci's thought becomes important, it is active and changing within a complex interlocking of economic, political, social and cultural forces in a total situation of dominance and subordination. In the nineteenth century, in the complicated and ongoing process whereby hegemony was established and maintained, leisure was important. At the outset it was perceived to pose a real threat. It was an economic problem, for its quantity and irregularity for the mass of the people were counterposed to the work ideals of the industrialists. And it was a political, social and moral problem for its practice, and the ideology bound up with that practice, could be threatening, disorderly and immoral. Its legitimacy for the people was denied: only 'the leisured' had leisure. By the end of our period, however, its legitimacy for all could be accepted; hegemony had been maintained, but not without meeting a series of challenges the outcome of which was the modern leisure we have described. Those challenges, alternative or counter-hegemonies, took the form both of an amoral and therefore uncivilising commercialism, and also, in Owenism and Primitive Methodism for example, of an outwardly respectable (but actually threatening, because consciously working-class) form of rational recreation. Both these threats were headed off, though not totally defeated.

The same could be said for what might be called the idealist expression of hegemony, the notion that leisure might be the instrument of class conciliation. The outcome was in one sense a compromise, but it was a compromise in which the hegemony was unthreatened. Leisure became legitimate for the mass of the people precisely because it was shorn of other associations, and in particular of economic and political (or rather radical political) associations. A part of people's lives – that not spent working – and areas of public space became isolated as 'leisure'. Over that leisure the dominant culture had acquired a degree of control which was sufficient to enable it to legitimise that leisure. What people did in their spare time was not always or often uplifting, it might be irritating or annoying, as at Bank Holidays, but it was no longer a threat to hegemony. The outcome of a century of battles over the problem of leisure was that for the dominant culture leisure was safely residual, unconnected with and possibly a counterweight to new and socialist challenges to hegemony. Publicists continued and continue to talk about a problem of leisure, but it occupies only a very minor part of the dominant culture's concern. For since the later nineteenth century both the provision and the control of leisure have, from the point of view of hegemony, been adequately dealt with by increasingly powerful leisure industries, and by a new but minor branch of bureaucracy, the leisure services. It has become too the subject of an equally minor branch of academic life in which scholars spend much time debating both the importance and the nature of what they are studying. That situation is very precisely the outcome of the ambiguous victory for hegemony whereby leisure in the century we have studied became both tamed and legitimate because separated from the other concerns of people's lives.

Notes

1. H. Perkin, 'Social History' in H.P.R. Finberg (ed.), *Approaches to History* (London, 1962), pp. 51-82; *Origins of Modern English Society*, ch. VI, esp. p. 209.

2. Stanford, 1976.

3. *American Historical Review*, vol. 78 (1973), pp. 531-88.

4. London, 1977, esp. Part II.

FURTHER READING

This is not a comprehensive bibliography of the history of leisure, nor is it simply a list of the works which appear in the footnotes. It is a guide to further reading, divided into two sections: 1. Contemporary works. Many of these books contain only relatively brief, but in my view significant, passages which are specifically on leisure. Dates of publication are of the first edition unless otherwise indicated. With the exception of books that are easily available (e.g. the novels of Dickens), I have added dates of recent reprints. 2. Secondary works, subdivided into (a) books; and (b) articles and essays. The place of publication is London unless otherwise indicated.

The difficulty with a guide of this kind is to keep it manageably short while at the same time doing justice to the literature. The danger is that, however select, such a guide may give the impression that there is nothing more to be said. That is far from the truth. Despite the output of work in the last decade there remain large gaps not just in the history of this or that leisure activity, but also in three more serious respects. First, nearly all the literature, and nearly all this book, has been about male leisure. Secondly, there has been remarkably little detailed work on the relationship between work and leisure. And thirdly, we know virtually nothing about leisure patterns through the life-cycle.

There are, however, some positive aspects to this relatively neglected state of the subject. Almost anyone who has access to the Parliamentary Papers, or to local newspapers, or to a local record office, can make some contribution to the history of leisure. My hope is that this book and the guide to further reading may stimulate such endeavours.

1. Contemporary Works

Acton, W., *Prostitution*, 1857, 2nd edn 1870, repr. 1972.
Adams, W.E., *Memoirs of a Social Atom*, 1903, repr. New York, 1968.
Alken, H., *National Sports of Great Britain*, 1821.
Bamford, S., *Autobiography* (ed. W.H. Chaloner, 1967), vol. I (1st edn 1848-9).
Barnum, P.T., *Struggles and Triumphs*, 2 vols. (ed. G.S. Bryan, 1927), compiled from earlier edns, 1855, 1869, 1889.
Besant, W., *As We Are And As We May Be*, 1903.

Blaine, D.P., *An Encyclopaedia of Rural Sports*, 1840.

Brand, J., *Observations on Popular Antiquities*, Newcastle-upon-Tyne, 1777.

Browne, M., *Views and Opinions*, 1866.

Chambers, R., *The Book of Days*, 2 vols. 1863-4.

Dale, R.W., *Week-Day Sermons*, 1867.

Davies, C.M., *Mystic London*, 1875.

Dickens, C., *Hard Times*, 1854.

Dickens, C., *Sketches by Boz*, 1836.

Dickens, C., *Sunday under Three Heads*, 1836.

Dickens, C., *The Old Curiosity Shop*, 1841.

Disraeli, B., *Sybil*, 1845.

Doré, G. and Jerrold, B., *London, a Pilgrimage*, 1872, repr. New York, 1970.

Egan, P., *Book of Sports*, 1836.

Egan, P., *Boxiana*, vol. I, 1812, repr. Leicester, 1971.

Egan, P., *Life of an Actor*, 1825, repr. 1904.

Escott, T.H.S., *England: Its People, Polity, and Pursuits*, revised edn, 1885.

Eversley, Lord, *Commons, Forests and Footpaths*, revised edn, 1910.

Faucher, L., *Manchester in 1844*, 1844, repr. 1969.

Frost, T., *Circus Life and Circus Celebrities*, 1875.

Frost, T., *The Lives of the Conjurors*, 1876.

Frost, T., *The Old Showmen and the Old London Fairs*, 1874.

Gissing, G., *The Nether World*, 1889, repr. Brighton, 1974.

Godwin, G., *Town Swamps and Social Bridges*, 1859, repr. Leicester, 1972.

Grant, J., *Sketches in London*, 1838.

Granville, A.B., *The Spas of England and Principal Sea-Bathing Places*, 3 vols. 1841, repr., 2 vols., Bath, 1971.

Greenwood, J., *Low-Life Deeps*, 1875.

Greenwood, J., *The Seven Curses of London*, 1869.

Greenwood, J., *The Wilds of London*, 1874.

Grimaldi, J., *Memoirs*, 1838, repr. (ed. Findlater, R.), 1968.

Guest, R., *A Compendious History of the Cotton Manufacture*, 1823, repr. 1968.

Hindley, C. (ed.), *The Life and Adventures of a Cheap Jack*, 1881.

Hone, W., *The Every-Day Book*, 2 vols., 1826-7.

Hone, W., *Table Book*, 1827.

Hone, W., *Year Book*, 1832.

Howitt, W., *The Rural Life of England*, 2 vols., 1838, repr., 1 vol.,

Shannon, 1971.

Hudson, D. (ed.), *Munby, Man of Two Worlds*, 1972.

Hudson, J.W., *The History of Adult Education*, 1851, repr. 1969.

Hughes, T., *Tom Brown's School-Days*, 1857.

Jevons, W.S., *Methods of Social Reform*, 1883.

Lawson, J., *Letters to the Young on Progress in Pudsey During the Last Sixty Years*, Stanninglen, 1887, repr. Caliban Books, Firle, 1979.

Ludlow, J.M. and Lloyd Jones, *Progress of the Working Class 1832-1867*, 1867, repr. Clifton, N.J., 1973.

Marx, K., *Capital*, vol. I, 1867.

Mayhew, H., *London Labour and the London Poor*, 4 vols., 1861-2.

Miles, H.D., *Pugilistica*, 3 vols., 1880-1.

Miller, D.P., *The Life of a Showman*, 1849.

Mitford, M.R., *Our Village*, 5 vols., 1824-32.

Morley, H., *Memoirs of Bartholomew Fair*, 1857.

Nimrod, *Memoirs of the Life of the Late John Mytton, Esq.*, 1835, repr. 1903.

Osbaldeston, Squire, *His Autobiography* (ed. E.D. Cuming), 1926.

Place, F., *Autobiography* (ed. M. Thale), 1972.

Procter, R.W., *Manchester in Holiday Dress*, 1866.

Rae, W. Fraser, *The Business of Travel*, 1891.

Razzell, P.E. and Wainwright, R.W. (eds.), *The Victorian Working Class: Selections from Letters to the Morning Chronicle*, 1973.

Ritchie, J.E., *The Night Side of London*, 1857.

Sanger, G., *Seventy Years a Showman*, 1910.

Shaw, C., *When I was a Child*, 1903, repr. Caliban Books, Firle, 1977.

Shimmin, H., *Liverpool Life*, Liverpool, 1856.

Shimmin, H., *Town Life*, 1858.

Solly, H., *Working Men's Social Clubs and Educational Institutes*, 2nd edn, 1904.

Southey, R., *Letters from England*, 1807, repr. 1951.

Strutt, J., *The Sports and Pastimes of the People of England*, 1801, new edn, 1830.

Stuart, C.D. and Park, A.J., *The Variety Stage – A History of the Music Halls from the earliest period to the present time* [1895].

Surtees, R., *Jorrocks' Jaunts and Jollities*, 1838, repr. 1968.

Taylor, W. Cooke, *Notes of a Tour in the Manufacturing Districts of Lancashire*, 1841, 2nd edn, 1842, repr. 1968.

Thackeray, W., *The Newcomes*, 1854-5.

Torr, C., *Small Talk at Wreyland*, 1918.

Trollope, A. (ed.), *British Sports and Pastimes*, 1868.

Veblen, T., *The Theory of the Leisure Class*, 1899, repr. 1970.

Wild, S., *The Original, Complete and only Authentic Story of 'Old Wild's'*, 1888.

Wood, R., *Victorian Delights*, 1967.

Wright, T., *Some Habits and Customs of the Working Classes*, 1867, repr. New York, 1967.

2. Secondary Works

a. Books

Alexander, S., *St Giles's Fair, 1830-1914*, Ruskin College, Oxford, 1970.

Altham, H.S., *A History of Cricket*, vol. I, 1962.

Altick, R.D., *The English Common Reader 1800-1900*, 1957.

Altick, R.D., *The Shows of London*, 1978.

Ashby, M.K., *Joseph Ashby of Tysoe 1859-1919*, 1961.

Aspin, C., *Lancashire, the First Industrial Society*, Helmshore, 1969.

Bahlman, D.W.R., *The Moral Revolution of 1688*, New Haven, 1957.

Bailey, P., *Leisure and Class in Victorian England: Rational Recreation and the Contest for Control, 1830-1885*, 1978.

Banks, J.A. and O., *Feminism and Family Planning in Victorian England*, Liverpool, 1964.

Barker, K., *Bristol at Play: Five Centuries of Live Entertainment*, Bradford-on-Avon, 1976.

Barker, K., *Entertainment in the Nineties*, Bristol, 1973.

Barker, K., *The Theatre Royal, Bristol, 1766-1966*, 1974.

Best, G., *Mid-Victorian Britain 1851-1875*, 1971.

Bienefeld, M.A., *Working Hours in British Industry*, 1972.

Bovill, E.W., *The England of Nimrod and Surtees 1815-1854*, 1959.

Bowen, R., *Cricket: A History of its Growth and Development Throughout the World*, 1970.

Brailsford, D., *Sport and Society: Elizabeth to Anne*, 1969.

Bratton, J.S., *The Victorian Popular Ballad*, 1975.

Briggs, A., *Mass Entertainment: The Origins of a Modern Industry*, Adelaide, 1960.

Bristow, E.J., *Vice and Vigilance: Purity Movements in Britain since 1700*, Dublin, 1977.

Brown, F.K., *Fathers of the Victorians: The Age of Wilberforce*, 1961.

Burke, P., *Popular Culture in Early Modern Europe*, 1978.

Cardwell, D.S.L. (ed.), *Artisan to Graduate*, Manchester, 1974.

Carr, R., *English Fox Hunting: A History*, 1976.

Chadwick, G.F., *The Park and the Town: Public Landscape in the 19th and 20th centuries*, 1966.

Chapman, G., *Culture and Survival*, 1940.

Cheshire, D.F., *Music Hall in Britain*, Newton Abbot, 1974.

Clayre, A., *Work and Play*, New York, 1974.

Colls, R., *The Collier's Rant: Song and Culture in the Industrial Village*, 1977.

Cousins, G., *Golf in Britain: A Social History from the Beginnings to the Present Day*, 1975.

Cunningham, H., *The Volunteer Force: A Social and Political History 1859-1908*, 1975.

Cunnington, P. and Mansfield, A., *English Costume for Sports and Outdoor Recreation from the Sixteenth to the Nineteenth Centuries*, 1969.

Currie, R., *Methodism Divided*, 1968.

Darcy, C.P., *The Encouragement of the Fine Arts in Lancashire 1760-1860*, Manchester, 1976.

Davidoff, L., *The Best Circles: Women and Society in Victorian England*, 1973.

De Grazia, S., *Of Time, Work, and Leisure*, New York, 1962.

Delgado, A., *The Annual Outing and Other Excursions*, 1977.

Donohue, J., *Theatre in the Age of Kean*, Oxford, 1975.

Dorson, R.M., *The British Folklorists: A History*, Chicago, 1968.

Dunning, E. (ed.), *The Sociology of Sport: A Selection of Readings*, 1971.

Dunning, E. and Sheard, K., *Barbarians, Gentlemen and Players: A Sociological Study of the Development of Rugby Football*, 1979.

Ehrlich, C., *The Piano: A History*, 1976.

Eliot, E., *Portrait of a Sport: The Story of Steeplechasing*, 1957.

Fawcett, T., *The Rise of English Provincial Art: Artists, Patrons, and Institutions outside London, 1800-1850*, Oxford, 1974.

Ford, J., *Cricket: A Social History 1700-1835*, Newton Abbot, 1972.

Ford, J., *Prizefighting: The Age of Regency Boximania*, Newton Abbot, 1971.

Fuller, Margaret D., *West Country Friendly Societies*, Reading, 1964.

Furniss, E.S., *The Position of the Laborer in a System of Nationalism*, Boston & New York, 1920.

Girourard, M., *Victorian Pubs*, 1975.

Gray, R.Q., *The Labour Aristocracy in Victorian Edinburgh*, Oxford, 1976.

Guest, I., *The Romantic Ballet in England: Its Development, Fulfilment and Decline*, 1954.

Haley, B., *The Healthy Body and Victorian Culture*, 1978.

Hammond, J.L. and B., *The Age of the Chartists 1832-1854*, 1930.

Harris, N., *Humbug: The Art of P.T. Barnum*, Boston, 1973.

Harrison, B., *Drink and the Victorians: The Temperance Question in England 1815-1872*, 1971.

Harrison, J.F.C., *Learning and Living, 1790-1960: A Study in the History of the English Adult Education Movement*, 1961.

Hart, G., *A History of Cheltenham*, 1965.

Hill, C., *Society and Puritanism in Pre-Revolutionary England*, 1964.

Hogan, C.B., *The London Stage*, Part V (1776-1800), 3 vols., Carbondale, Illinois, 1968.

Houghton, W.E., *The Victorian Frame of Mind 1830-1870*, 1957.

Howard, D., *London Theatres and Music Halls 1850-1950*, 1970.

Howkins, A., *Whitsun in 19th Century Oxfordshire*, Ruskin College, Oxford, 1973.

Huizinga, J., *Homo Ludens: A Study of the Play Element in Culture*, 1949.

Hunt, C.J., *The Lead Miners of the Northern Pennines in the Eighteenth and Nineteenth Centuries*, Manchester, 1970.

Itzkowitz, D.C., *Peculiar Privilege: A Social History of English Foxhunting 1753-1885*, Hassocks, 1977.

James, C.L.R., *Beyond a Boundary*, 1963.

James, L., *Print and the People 1819-1851*, 1976.

Kelly, T., *A History of Public Libraries in Great Britain 1845-1965*, 1973.

Lanfant, M.-F., *Les Théories du Loisir*, Paris, 1972.

Laqueur, T.W., *Religion and Respectability: Sunday Schools and Working Class Culture 1780-1850*, 1976.

Lee, A.J., *The Origins of the Popular Press in England 1855-1914*, 1976.

Lennard, R. (ed.), *Englishmen at Rest and Play: Some Phases of English Leisure 1558-1714*, Oxford, 1931.

Lloyd, A., *The Great Prize Fight*, 1977.

Lloyd, A.L., *Folk Song in England*, 1967.

Longrigg, R., *The Turf*, 1975.

Lowerson, J. and Myerscough, J., *Time to Spare in Victorian England*, Hassocks, 1977.

MacInnes, C., *Sweet Saturday Night*, 1967.

McIntosh, P.C., *Physical Education in England since 1800*, 1968.

McIntosh, P.C., *Sport in Society*, 1963.

McKechnie, S., *Popular Entertainment Through the Ages*, 1931.

Mackerness, E.D., *A Social History of English Music*, 1964.

Mackerness, E.D., *Somewhere Further North: A History of Music in Sheffield*, Sheffield, 1974.

Malcolmson, R.W., *Popular Recreations in English Society, 1700-1850*, 1973.

Mander, R. and Mitchenson, J., *British Music Hall*, 1965.

Marples, M., *A History of Football*, 1954.

Marrus, M.R. (ed.), *The Emergence of Leisure*, New York, 1974.

Mason, T., *Association Football and English Society, 1863-1915*, Hassocks, 1980.

Mayer, D., *Harlequin in his Element: The English Pantomime, 1806-1836*, Cambridge, Mass., 1969.

Meller, H.E., *Leisure and the Changing City, 1870-1914*, 1976.

Minihan, J., *The Nationalization of Culture: The Development of State Subsidies to the Arts in Great Britain*, New York, 1977.

Money, J., *Experience and Identity: Birmingham and the West Midlands 1760-1800*, Manchester, 1977.

Mortimer, R., *The Jockey Club*, 1958.

Neuburg, V.E., *Popular Literature: A History and Guide*, Harmondsworth, 1977.

Newsome, D., *Godliness and Good Learning: Four Studies on a Victorian Ideal*, 1961.

Nicholson, W., *The Struggle for a Free Stage in London*, Boston & New York, 1906.

Obelkevich, J., *Religion and Rural Society: South Lindsey 1825-1875*, Oxford, 1976.

Palmer, R., *A Touch on the Times: Songs of Social Change 1770-1914*, Harmondsworth, 1974.

Palmer, R. and Raven, J., *The Rigs of the Fair: Popular Sports and Pastimes in the Nineteenth Century through Songs, Ballads and Contemporary accounts*, 1976.

Parker, S.R., *The Sociology of Leisure*, 1976.

Pearsall, R., *Victorian Popular Music*, Newton Abbot, 1973.

Pimlott, J.A.R., *Recreations*, 1968.

Pimlott, J.A.R., *The Englishman's Christmas: A Social History*, Hassocks, 1978.

Pimlott, J.A.R. *The Englishman's Holiday: A Social History*, 1947.

Plumb, J.H., *The Commercialisation of Leisure in Eighteenth-century England*, Reading, 1973.

Poulsen, C., *Victoria Park: A Study in the History of East London*, Stepney, 1976.

Quinlan, M.J., *Victorian Prelude: A History of English Manners 1700-1830*, New York, 1941.

Radzinowicz, L., *A History of English Criminal Law and its Administration from 1750*, vol. III, 1956.

Reid, J.C., *Bucks and Bruisers: Pierce Egan and Regency England*, 1971.

Renevey, M.J., *Le grand livre du Cirque*, 2 vols., Paris, 1977.

Revels History of Drama in English, vol. VI, 1750-1880, 1975.

Richards, K. and Thomson, P. (eds.), *Nineteenth-century British Theatre*, 1971.

Roberts, K., *Leisure*, 1970.

Rodgers, D.T., *The Work Ethic in Industrial America 1850-1920*, 1978.

Rosenfeld, S., *Strolling Players and Drama in the Provinces, 1660-1765*, 1939.

Rosenfeld, S., *The Theatre of the London Fairs in the 18th Century*, 1960.

Rowell, G., *The Victorian Theatre: A Survey*, 1956.

Russell, J.F. and Elliot, J.H., *The Brass Band Movement*, 1936.

Saxon, A.H., *Enter Foot and Horse: A History of Hippodrama in England and France*, 1968.

Saxon, A.H., *The Life and Art of Andrew Ducrow and the Romantic Age of the English Circus*, Hamden, Conn., 1978.

Scott, H., *The Early Doors: Origins of the Music Hall*, 1946.

Sheppard, L., *The Broadside Ballad*, 1962.

Simon, B. and Bradley, I. (eds.), *The Victorian Public School: Studies in the Development of an Educational Institution*, Dublin, 1975.

Smith, B.S., *A History of Malvern*, Leicester, 1964.

Taylor, J., *From Self-Help to Glamour: The Working Man's Club, 1860-1972*, Ruskin College, Oxford, 1972.

Thompson, E.P., *The Making of the English Working Class*, 1963.

Thompson, F.M.L., *English Landed Society in the Nineteenth Century*, 1963.

Trinder, B., *The Industrial Revolution in Shropshire*, 1973.

Trudgill, E., *Madonnas and Magdalens: The Origins and Development of Victorian Sexual Attitudes*, 1976.

Turner, E.S., *All Heaven in a Rage*, 1964.

Tylecote, M., *The Mechanics' Institutes of Lancashire and Yorkshire Before 1851*, Manchester, 1957.

Vamplew, W., *The Turf: A Social and Economic History of Horse Racing*, 1976.

Vicinus, M., *The Industrial Muse: A Study of Nineteenth Century British Working-Class Literature*, 1974.

Walker, S.A., *Sporting Art: England 1700-1900*, 1972.

Walton, J.K., *The Blackpool Landlady: A Social History*, Manchester, 1978.

Walvin, J., *Beside the Seaside: A Social History of the Popular Seaside Holiday*, 1978.

Walvin, J., *Leisure and Society 1830-1950*, 1978.

Walvin, J., *The People's Game: A Social History of British Football*, 1975.

Ward, J.T., *The Factory Movement 1830-1855*, 1962.

Webb, S. and B., *The History of Liquor Licensing in England, principally from 1700 to 1830*, 1903.

Webb, S. and B., *The Parish and the County*, 1906.

Weber, W., *Music and the Middle Class: The Social Structure of Concert Life in London, Paris and Vienna*, 1975.

Westall, O.M. (ed.), *Windermere in the Nineteenth Century*, Lancaster, 1976.

Whitaker, W.B., *The Eighteenth-Century English Sunday: A Study of Sunday Observance from 1677 to 1837*, 1940.

Whitaker, W.B., *Victorian and Edwardian Shopworkers: The Struggles to Obtain Better Conditions and a Half-holiday*, Newton Abbot, 1973.

Winter, M.H., *The Theatre of Marvels*, New York, 1964.

Wroth, W., *Cremorne and the Later London Gardens*, 1907.

Yeo, S., *Religion and Voluntary Organisations in Crisis*, 1976.

Young, P.M., *A History of British Football*, 1968.

b. Articles and Essays

Ambler, R.W., 'The Transformation of Harvest Celebrations in Nineteenth-century Lincolnshire', *Midland History*, vol. 3 (1976), pp. 298-306.

Bailey, P., ' "A Mingled Mass of Perfectly Legitimate Pleasures": The Victorian Middle Class and the Problem of Leisure', *Victorian Studies*, vol. XXI (1977), pp. 7-28.

Bailey, P., ' "Will The Real Bill Banks Please Stand Up?" Towards A Role Analysis of Mid-Victorian Working-class Respectability', *Journal of Social History*, vol. 12 (1979), pp. 336-53.

Barker, C., 'The Chartists, Theatre, Reform and Research', *Theatre Quarterly*, vol. I (1971), pp. 3-10.

Borsay, P., 'The English Urban Renaissance: the Development of Provincial Urban Culture *c*. 1680-*c*. 1760', *Social History*, no. 5 (1977), pp. 581-602.

Briggs, A., 'The View from Badminton' in Briggs, A., (ed.), *Essays in the History of Publishing* (1974), pp. 187-218.

Brooke, D., 'The Opposition to Sunday Rail Services in North-Eastern England, 1834-1914', *Journal of Transport History*, vol. VI (1963-4), pp. 95-109.

Coats, A.W., 'Changing Attitudes to Labour in the Mid-Eighteenth Century', *Economic History Review*, 2nd ser., vol. XI (1958), pp. 35-51.

Collins, P., 'Dickens and Popular Amusements', *Dickensian* (1965), pp. 7-19.

Crossick, G., 'The Labour Aristocracy and its Values: a Study of mid-Victorian Kentish London', *Victorian Studies*, vol. XIX (1976), pp. 301-28.

Cunningham, H., 'The Metropolitan Fairs: a Case Study in the Social Control of Leisure', in A.P. Donajgrodzki (ed.), *Social Control in Nineteenth Century Britain* (1977), pp. 163-84.

Dingle, A.E., 'Drink and Working-class Living Standards in Britain 1870-1914', *Economic History Review*, 2nd ser., vol. XXV (1972), pp. 608-22.

Everitt, A., 'The English Urban Inn 1560-1760' in Everitt, A. (ed.), *Perspectives in English Urban History* (1973), pp. 91-137.

Harrison, B., 'Animals and the State in Nineteenth-century England', *English Historical Review*, vol. LXXXVIII (1973), pp. 786-820.

Harrison, B., 'Pubs' in Dyos, H.J. and Wolff, M. (eds.), *The Victorian City*, 2 vols. (1973), vol. I, pp. 161-90.

Harrison, B., 'Religion and Recreation in Nineteenth-century England', *Past & Present*, no. 38 (1967), pp. 98-125.

Harrison, B., 'Teetotal Chartism', *History*, vol. 58 (1973), pp. 193-217.

Harrison, B., 'Two Roads to Social Reform: Francis Place and the "Drunken Committee" of 1834', *Historical Journal*, vol. XI (1968), pp. 272-300.

Harrison, B. and Trinder, B., 'Drink and Sobriety in an Early Victorian Country Town: Banbury 1830-1860', *English Historical Review Supplement*, no. 4 (1969).

Hemming, J.P., 'The Mechanics' Institutes in the Lancashire and Yorkshire Textile Districts from 1850', *Journal of Educational Administration and History*, vol. 9 (1977), pp. 18-31.

Jones, G.S., 'Class Expression versus Social Control? A Critique of Recent Trends in the Social History of "Leisure" ', *History Workshop*, no. 4 (autumn 1977), pp. 163-70.

Jones, G.S., 'Working-class Culture and Working-class Politics in London,

1870-1900: Notes on the Remaking of a Working Class', *Journal of Social History*, vol. VII (1974), pp. 460-508.

Kent, J.H.S., 'The Role of Religion in the Cultural Structure of the later Victorian City', *Transactions of the Royal Historical Society*, 5th ser., vol. 23 (1973), pp. 153-73.

Kirby, C., 'English Game Law Reform' in *Essays in Modern English History in honor of Wilbur Cortez Abbott* (1971), pp. 345-80.

McKibbin, R., 'Working-class Gambling in Britain 1880-1939', *Past & Present*, no. 82 (1979), pp. 147-78.

Mandle, W.F., 'Games People Played: Cricket and Football in England and Victoria in the Late Nineteenth Century', *Historical Studies*, vol. 15 (1973), pp. 511-35.

Mandle, W.F., 'The Professional Cricketer in England in the Nineteenth Century', *Labour History*, no. 23 (1972), pp. 1-16.

Mayer, D., 'Billy Purvis: Travelling Showman', *Theatre Quarterly*, vol. I (1971), pp. 27-34.

Morris, R.J., 'Leeds and the Crystal Palace', *Victorian Studies*, vol. XIII (1970), pp. 283-300.

Mott, J., 'Miners, Weavers and Pigeon Racing', in Smith, M.A., Parker, S. and Smith, C.S. (eds.), *Leisure and Society in Britain* (1973), pp. 86-96.

Myerscough, J., 'The Recent History of the Use of Leisure Time' in Appleton, I. (ed.), *Leisure Research and Policy* (Edinburgh, 1974), pp. 3-16.

Perkin, H.J., 'The "Social Tone" of Victorian Seaside Resorts in the North-West', *Northern History*, vol. XI (1975-6), pp. 180-94.

Pollard, S., 'Factory Discipline in the Industrial Revolution', *Economic History Review*, 2nd ser., vol. XVI (1963-4), pp. 254-71.

Price, R.N., 'The Working Men's Club Movement and Victorian Social Reform Ideology', *Victorian Studies*, vol. XV (1971), pp. 117-47.

Reid, C., 'Temperance, Teetotalism and Local Culture: the Early Temperance Movement in Sheffield', *Northern History*, vol. XIII (1977), pp. 248-64.

Reid, D., 'The Decline of Saint Monday, 1766-1876', *Past & Present*, no. 71 (1976), pp. 76-101.

Rubinstein, D., 'Cycling in the 1890s', *Victorian Studies*, vol. XXI (1977), pp. 47-71.

Scott, P., 'Cricket and the Religious World in the Victorian Period', *Church Quarterly*, vol. III (1970), pp. 134-44.

Senelick, L., 'Politics as Entertainment: Victorian Music-Hall Songs', *Victorian Studies*, vol. XIX (1975), pp. 149-80.

Shiman, L.L., 'The Band of Hope Movement: Respectable Recreation for Working-class Children', *Victorian Studies*, vol. XVIII (1973), pp. 49-74.

Smith, M.B., 'Victorian Entertainment in the Lancashire Cotton Towns' in S.P. Bell (ed.), *Victorian Lancashire* (Newton Abbot, 1974), pp. 169-85.

Storch, R.D., 'Police Control of Street Prostitution in Victorian London: A Study in the Contexts of Police Action' in Bayley, D.H. (ed.), *Police and Society* (1977), pp. 49-72.

Storch, R.D., 'The Plague of the Blue Locusts: Police Reform and Popular Resistance in Northern England, 1840-57', *International Review of Social History*, vol. XX (1975), pp. 61-90.

Storch, R.D., 'The Policeman as Domestic Missionary: Urban Discipline and Popular Culture in Northern England, 1850-1880', *Journal of Social History*, vol. IX (1976), pp. 481-509.

Storch, R.D., 'The Problem of Working-class Leisure: Some Roots of Middle-class Moral Reform in the Industrial North, 1825-50' in Donajgrodzki, A.P. (ed.), *Social Control in Nineteenth Century Britain* (1977), pp. 138-62.

Thomas, K., 'Work and Leisure in Pre-industrial Society', *Past & Present*, no. 29 (1964), pp. 50-66.

Thompson, E.P., 'Eighteenth-century English Society: Class Struggle without Class?', *Social History*, vol. 3 (1978), pp. 133-65.

Thompson, E.P., ' "Rough Music": le charivari anglais', *Annales*, vol. 27 (1972), pp. 285-312.

Thompson, E.P., 'Patrician Society, Plebeian Culture', *Journal of Social History*, vol. VII (1974), pp. 382-405.

Thompson, E.P., 'Time, Work-discipline, and Industrial Capitalism', *Past & Present*, no. 38 (1967), pp. 56-97.

Vernon, S., 'Trouble up at t'mill: The Rise and Decline of the Factory Play in the 1830s and 1840s', *Victorian Studies*, vol. XX (1977), pp. 117-39.

Walton, J., 'Residential Amenity, Respectable Morality and the Rise of the Entertainment Industry: the Case of Blackpool 1860-1914', *Literature and History*, no. 1 (1975), pp. 62-78.

Whyman, J., 'Water Communications to Margate and Gravesend as Coastal Resorts before 1840', *Southern History*, vol. II (1980).

'Work and Leisure in Industrial Society: Conference Report', *Past & Present*, no. 30 (1965), pp. 96-103.

'The Working Class and Leisure: Class Expression and/or Social Control: Conference Report', *Bulletin of the Society for the Study of*

Labour History, no. 32 (spring 1976), pp. 5-18.

Yeo, E., 'Robert Owen and Radical Culture' in Pollard, S. and Salt, J. (eds.), *Robert Owen: Prophet of the Poor* (1971), pp. 84-114.

INDEX